Bob Dylan
His Unreleased Recordings

Paul Cable

SCHIRMER BOOKS
A Division of Macmillan Publishing Co., Inc.
NEW YORK

Many thanks to Ken, Nick, Rob, Mike, Geoff, Mr. Tapes, Bernard, and Jim, for indispensable assistance in gathering information; to Shirley, Bernadette, and Claire, for patient and perfect typing; and to Elly Smith and Pat Feldman of CBS Records, London, for help received.

Schirmer Books
A Division of Macmillan Publishing Co., Inc.
866 Third Avenue, New York, N. Y. 10022

Collier Macmillan Canada, Ltd.

First American Edition 1980

Library of Congress Catalog Card Number: 79-57285

Printed in the United States of America

printing number

1   2   3   4   5   6   7   8   9   10

Library of Congress Cataloging in Publication Data
Cable, Paul.
  Bob Dylan: his unreleased recordings.
  Includes index.
  1. Dylan, Bob, 1941–   —Discography.
ML156.7.D97C3 1980   016.7899′1244924   79-57285
ISBN 0-02-870360-X

Contents

Introduction

The object of this book is to provide a comprehensive, chronological catalogue of that Dylan material which has not been placed before the public by his record company but which has unofficially found its way into circulation, and to appraise that material, albeit on the basis of my own opinion. The main justification for this undertaking is simply that the unreleased recordings include some of the best work Dylan has ever produced.

The degree of interest in the material that Dylan and/or his record company have chosen to withhold from public view is well illustrated by the phenomenal success of the bootleg record industry. Bootlegs were around as early as the nineteen forties but it wasn't until the release of the first Dylan bootleg - "Great White Wonder" - in the late sixties that bootlegging began moving towards the thriving, if risky, business it is today. Since then a staggering number of different Dylan bootleg albums have been released and distributed throughout the world.

During this time there has also developed a huge network of tape collectors, many of them whose interest extends to owning copies of every unreleased tape they can lay their hands on. This need to collect each and every item available, while partially stemming from the collector's instinct, is yet another indication of the sheer power of Dylan's artistry.

It could be argued that, as there are so many significant omissions from Dylan's official albums, it is impossible to look at his musical development without recourse to the unreleased work. Thus this book is intended to be of interest not only to collectors but to anyone acknowledging the massive influence Dylan has asserted over the last fifteen years. At the same time, in order to cater for those readers who are collectors, emphasis has been placed on cross-referencing, completeness and generally leaving as few loose ends as possible.

As far as the legality and ethics of tape trading are concerned, it's a blurred question. Undoubtedly bootlegging involves intrinsic rip-offs both from the point of view of the artists not getting their royalty and from that of the consumer getting a product ungoverned by standards of quality. But I can't really get worked up about losses suffered by official record companies through bootlegging because people who buy bootleg records of a particular artist invariably already own all that artist's official records. In any case with Dylan it could be argued that a record company which omits "I Shall Be Released" and "Mighty Quinn" from "The Basement Tapes" album deserves anything it gets.

With regard to Dylan himself, it's always struck me that his preferences, from the point of view both of what he releases and of what he performs live, often don't seem very directly connected with the relative merit of the material. There is obviously the question of his right to keep private what he wants; but it's a vexed question because all the tapes and bootlegs that are circulating obviously form an integral part of 'the legend'. And 'the legend' is a trip that Dylan possibly doesn't find entirely unpleasant.

I do, however, have some misgivings about this book; not, in all honesty, because I feel it to be ethically dubious or impertinent to appraise material that was never intended for appraisal, but because the project makes me feel like a groupie. Objectively I don't regard Dylan as a messiah - I regard him as a person who, on the whole, is very good at the job of writing and singing songs, and as a personality who is very good at resisting pressure to conform to the string of hypes that people in that sort of job are subject to. But while the major proportion of the material reviewed in this book is of a very high artistic standard some of it is throw-away stuff. The justification for including both is that the book is an attempt at a complete catalogue, and not that I believe Dylan to be incapable of writing a lousy song. Just the same, as the need for completeness necessitates, for instance, the inclusion of a tape of Dylan singing a little rhyme into his Answerphone machine, I have to ask the reader to be prepared to move from the sublime to the ridiculous.

As to the format of the book, the catalogue is primarily based on what is on tape rather than what is on record. This is because there's so much more material on tape, it's usually of better sound quality, and in general the songs are laid out more logically from the point of view of the time period or session from which they come. There's also the point that a lot of bootleg record manufacturers exhibit a similar trait to official companies in that they can't resist putting out albums with just a few new tracks mingled with a whole load of previously released ones. But, having said that, it has to be admitted that there are some excellent bootlegs around; and, again, if this catalolgue is going to be comprehensive it must attempt to cover all the bootlegs, good and bad.

The first section of the book comprises a catalogue of those tapes known to be in circulation plus annotations as to which bootleg records individual tracks appear on, accompanied by critical appraisal of the material and its performance. The latter does not extend to live performances recorded by members of the audience (as opposed to live recordings made direct from the public address system) unless the recordings are of special significance. This is because there are just so many audience recordings around and often the sound quality is too poor to make any sort of judgement on the standard of the performances.

Following the tapes guide there's a Dylan discography that covers all the records, official and bootleg, that are, or ever have been, in existence in the U.K., Europe and U.S.A. as far as I know. It's inevitable that a few will be missed, but then the line's got to be drawn somewhere as to what constitutes a record - you could put a turntable mat in a cardboard cover and call it "The Isle of Wight Rehearsal" and someone would buy it. Though again there have been some bootleg companies whose product was no less dependable than that of official companies. Trade Mark of Quality and Kornyfone, for instance, unlike many official record companies, were conservative enough to make most of their records flat and put the hole in the middle.

But one thing I shouldn't do is turn this into a moan about Dylan's record company. The oddities Columbia have perpetrated over the years will be well-known to Dylan appreciators, and credit should at least be given them for signing up Dylan in the first place. They have, after all, been responsible for putting some of the best and most influential music of all time before the public.

At the time of writing Dylan has just demonstrated that his influence remains as strong as it's ever been. His British and European concerts have been acknowledged by both the music and straight press as total triumphs and his new albums have proven to be as innovative in places as anything he produced in the sixties. Dylan has been around for seventeen years or so now and one thing he's consistently shown is that, while he might appear to be resting on his laurels from time to time, he's incapable of stopping. That's one of the reasons why, even as it's written, this book is becoming out of date. Every new album will produce its crop of out-takes and every concert means another tape and probably another bootleg. I even hear that someone is now the proud producer of his own full length home feature movie of the Earls Court concerts. So the chaos will never be completely sorted out. But then if you like Dylan you accept chaos.

Paul Cable

Dylan, 1974. (Photo by Chuck Pulin)

The Tapes

THE EAST ORANGE TAPE

It is hard to make a judgement on the merit of these performances because I have never heard a tape of decent quality. All the versions around seem to have that dull sound texture from recording on very cheap equipment or from the tape being an umpteenth generation copy.

But it is fairly obvious that this is not exactly classic Dylan - not that there is any reason why it should be. The tape was apparently made informally in 1961 at the house of some people called the Gleasons. Reputedly Dylan was attempting to sing their seven year old daughter to sleep. The songs do not sound much like lullaby material but perhaps even in those days Dylan was not prepared to allow himself to be compromised by his audience's expectations. Possibly Ms Gleason, who must now be in her twenties, could shed some light on this.

The songs he does best are "San Francisco Bay Blues" and "Remember Me". The latter is a very pleasant melody with attractive cadence in the first line while "San Francisco Bay Blues" gives the impression of being more gutsy than the rest of the tape both guitar and vocal-wise. Possibly it was recorded at a different time.

Dylan also does quite a reasonable job on "Pastures Of Plenty" and "Trail Of The Buffalo", while "Jesse James" would probably have been quite good if it had not stopped before it got off the ground. "Jesus Met The Woman At The Well" and "Gypsy Davy" are both pretty dire.

There is generally reckoned to be a lot of Guthrie and not much Dylan on this tape. Certainly, the majority of the songs are Guthrie's and certainly in some places Dylan's accent sounds ultra-American. Just the same the Dylan shows through from time to time and one gets the impression that the process of establishing his own style is just starting to get under way. At one point, having doodled around on his guitar and then given up on two songs after a couple of lines of each, Dylan says 'No, I can't think of anything to ...'. The way he says this it sounds as though he is aware of a feeling of inertia and lacks satisfaction with the stuff he is doing and is about to precipitate himself into a new period. Or perhaps he just means he can't think of anything to ... I don't know. Anyway, regardless of the influences at work here, the harmonica could not be any-one else's but Dylan's.

THE MINNESOTA PARTY TAPE

Although this tape was reckoned to be recorded about six months before the Minnesota Hotel Tape there are some things about it which give the impression that it could have been done later. For one thing there are more

THE EAST ORANGE TAPE   Mono   Date Recorded: Feb-March 1961
(Also known as the Gleason Tape and mistakenly as the Gibson Tape)

Song Titles	Records on which appearing			
San Francisco Bay Blues	Let Me Die In My Footsteps			Walking Down The Line
Jesus Met The Woman At The Well	"	The Villager		
Gypsy Davey	"	"		
Pastures Of Plenty	"	"		
Trail Of The Buffalo	"		The Demo Tapes	Skid Row *
Jesse James (fragment)		"	"	Seventy Dollar Robbery
Remember Me	"	"	"	"

*Existence of this album very dubious

of the vocal idiosyncrasies here that, although familiar today, did not originally emerge until "Freewheelin'". In "Wild Mountain Thyme", for instance, it is really nice to hear Dylan sing 'I will surely find aNURther'. In "Why'd You Cut My Hair" also he does a perfect prototype of the 'oh ho' in "Bob Dylan's Blues", and in "Talkin' Fisherman" he alludes to a shark who is a 'man-EATer.

Regardless of the precise date of the tape, it is obvious that by this stage the Dylan we know and love was well on the way to emergence. In places it even sounds like "The Times They Are A-Changin' ".

Again, it is hard to judge the standard of the performances because I am unaware of a tape of decent sound quality. But there is some interesting material here, some of it not appearing on other available tapes, and some of it apparently written by Dylan.. "Talkin' Fisherman" is one of these. It is the standard sequence used for "World War III Blues" and "John Birch Society Blues" (see the original "Freewheelin' ") and has practically a whole verse from "Talkin' Bear Mountain" (see "Bob Dylan" Out-takes tape). It has the typical ironic ending too - something about giving the fish back to the finance company.

One of the most effective songs on the tape is "Times Ain't What They Used To Be", also known as "James Allen Blues". What is particularly good is the way the guitar provides a recurring counter-theme to the vocal. Certainly the old Dylan vitriol is well in evidence with the suggestion in one verse that the lady he is addressing ought to be buried alive. "Man Of Constant Sorrow" is interesting in that it is completely different from all Dylan's other versions. It is very cheerful and he rips through it in a manner similar to his despatch of "She Belongs To Me" at the Isle of Wight. "Pretty Polly" is also of note in that it is the tune of "Hollis Brown". In a way it illustrates why Dylan's stealing of tunes was not a bad thing simply in that "Hollis Brown" wound up as the far superior song.

"Long Time A-Growin' " is rather good; the tune is unusual for the time, sounding more like something from the mid-sixties. The melody is stretched too far by the length of the song but if the Byrds had done a "Mr. Tambourine Man" on it it might have been a big hit.

"I Want My Milk", although not a classic, may be of interest to people into Dylan's personal life in that, in conjunction with the version of "Cocaine" on the Minnesota Hotel Tape, it positively confirms, with its reference to various sizes of nipples, that Dylan is a tit man.

"Don't Push Me Down" is one of those simplistic things which is hard to evaluate. Sometimes it seems to work - sometimes not. This part of the tape may have provided the reason for its being called the Minnesota *Party* Tape in that "Don't Push Me Down" stops, another song is started and then cuts off with a girl giggling.

It is a pity that on "Howja Do?" the quality of the tape I heard suddenly goes from bad to worse. Nevertheless, it still comes across that the performance has that sort of cheeky "I Shall Be Free No. 10" type atmosphere. Dylan did not write it but he makes it sound as though he did.

"Two Trains A-Runnin' " is not characteristic of the rest of the tape or really of Dylan at all. The guitar is very bluesy and both it and the harmonica are played in a very precise way. The vocal is certainly Dylan but it is possible that someone else was playing one or even both of the instruments.

"Death Don't Have No Mercy", on the other hand, is very characteristic

THE MINNESOTA PARTY TAPE   Mono

Date Recorded: May 1961

Song Titles	Records on which appearing
Railroad Bill	Help *
Will The Circle Be Unbroken	"
Man Of Constant Sorrow	"
Pretty Polly	
Railroad Boy	"
Times Ain't What They Used To Be (James Allen Blues)	"
Why'd You Cut My Hair	"
This Land Is Your Land	"
Two Trains A-Runnin'	"
Wild Mountain Thyme	
Howja Do?	
Car Car	
Don't Push Me Down (incomplete)	
Come See	
I Want My Milk	
San Francisco Bay Blues	
Long Time A-Growin'	
Devilish Mary	
Ramblin' Round	
Death Don't Have No Mercy (incomplete)	
It's Hard To Be Blind	
This Train (incomplete)	
Harp Blues	
Talkin' Fisherman (Talkin' Fish Blues)	
Pastures Of Plenty	

* Supposedly completely different from the other single album of the same title, it is in fact very dubious whether this album exists at all

stuff - especially of the time around the first album. There is a lot of that throaty emphasis and the atmosphere is much like that on "See That My Grave Is Kept Clean". It is a good performance - and a pity it breaks off.

Of the rest of the material on the tape "Devilish Mary" is not very good at all, "Come See" is a vehicle for drunken folk singers to make animal noises, while "Car Car" provides likewise for engine noises - the latter is pleasant but not as good as "Beatnik Fly", the other rip-off of the original tune. There are quite a few Guthrie songs - "Pastures Of Plenty" does not get off the ground but "Ramblin' Round", on the other hand, is superior to the version on the Minnesota Hotel Tape in that, although scrappy, it is more subtle tune-wise. "This Land Is Your Land" also comes over as less of a cheer-leader song than usual. More meaning seems to come out of it this way although it is still somewhat boring.

"Railroad Bill", which has a very similar tune to "Cocaine", moves pleasantly with nice positive guitar but "Railroad Boy", which Dylan also did sixteen years later on the Rolling Thunder T.V. Special, does not offer much more than folk hype. "Will The Circle Be Unbroken" is quite reasonable but I think there have been better versions of the song, while there is no doubt at all that there have been better versions of "Wild Mountain Thyme".

"It's Hard To Be Blind" is very similar to the version on the Minnesota Hotel Tape. The words are good but the tune is a little lacking in interest. "San Fransisco Bay Blues" is not as good as the East Orange Tape version while "Harp Blues" is train imitations again. Not as bad as "Long John" (see Minnesota Hotel Tape) but still pretty awful.

So, not as good as the Minnesota Hotel Tape from the point of view of sound quality or overall material and performance quality, but plenty of high spots plus some points of historical and academic interest.

INDIAN NECK FOLK FESTIVAL

This event took place at the Montewese Hotel, Branford, Connecticut. The tape in circulation is probably from a P.A. recording but the voice is so drowned by the guitar, presumably because of bad microphone adjustment, that you cannot tell much more about the songs, apart from the fact that they are all Guthrie compositions, than you could from a mediocre audience tape. On "Talkin' Columbia" hardly a single word can be made out, and a talking blues with inaudible lyrics is inevitably a bit futile. Possibly the audience could hear better as evidenced by their fairly enthusiastic applause, but from the tape it is not possible to make any comment other than to report that Dylan's guitar is in tune.

"Slipknot" is a shade more audible and you can just get enough of the lyrics to understand that the title refers to the knot in a hangman's noose; the tune is familiar, though not particularly strong. "Talkin' Fisherman" appears on the Minnesota Party Tape where the lyrics are a shade clearer, so, again, comment here is pointless, except to bemoan the presence of intermittent thumping noises that could have been caused by anything from Dylan knocking against the microphone with his guitar to people in the front row falling over as a result of leaning too far forward trying to hear.

Song Titles
Talkin' Columbia
Slipknot
Talkin' Fisherman (Talkin' Fish Blues)

RIVERSIDE CHURCH NEW YORK

This is a live concert and Dylan seems to be rather nervous at first. There are false starts and a large amount of time spent tuning up. Considering he was probably not very well known at the time it is either a remarkably patient audience or the Dylan charisma was already a binding force.

When he finally does get going he does a nice job on "Handsome Molly", especially the guitar work. The song has a pleasant tune anyway and, with the melodic accompaniment Dylan gives it, the whole thing works well in spite of the nervy edge in his voice. Following that "Omie Wise" is efficient but just not that good a song. "Poor Lazarus", on the other hand, comes over well and has a lot more body than the Minnesota Hotel Tape version.

On "Mean Old Southern Train", a duet with Danny Kalb, although Dylan plays harmonica quite skilfully and does some background singing, the limelight is basically Kalb's. It is not a particularly good song but Kalb's rendering is very tight and acts as a foil to Dylan's rather more casual approach to performing.

Dylan is called back at the end of the concert to do a duet with Jack Elliot. The song - "Acne" - is a makeshift send-up of the pop trends of the time. It's the C-Am-F-G sequence with constant 'doowahs' from Jack Elliot and Dylan improvising (apparently) a lyric about misunderstood teenagehhod, acne, junior proms etc. The interesting thing about it is that it seems to mark one of the few occasions when Dylan was upstaged by someone else in that at one point Jack Elliot begins screeching his 'doowahs' at such a pitch that he completely drowns Dylan's lyric. Dylan seems to take it in very good part as well. It is dubious whether Jack Elliot could have got away with it on the Rolling Thunder Revue.

CARNEGIE RECITAL HALL

This concert, of which the tape seems to be a portion only, has been reported in some quarters as being a flop, with an audience of fifty in a hall of two hundred capacity. I do not think this can be right, the applause sounds as though it would be very hard work for fifty people to produce. From the tape it sounds as though the whole thing was all very jolly and successful.

What is surprising, in the light of the fact that Dylan was not very widely known at the time, is that a tape of the performance should have been made at all - a good quality P.A. tape at that. It transpires that there was someone working at the hall who purely for his own interest made

Song Titles	Records on which appearing	
RIVERSIDE CHURCH, NEW YORK (broadcast on W.R.V.R. FM radio) Mono Date Recorded: July 29th, 1961		
Handsome Molly (also known as "I Wish I Was In London")	Early '60s Revisited	Help
Omie Wise (also known as "Naomi Wise")	"	
Poor Lazarus	"	
Mean Ol' Southern Train *1	"	
Acne (also known as "Doo-wah") *2	"	"

*1 Danny Kalb - vocal, Bob Dylan - harmonica
*2 With Jack Elliott

recordings of absolutely everyone who appeared there. This simple twist of fate has given the world three unique items - "Where Did You Sleep Last Night?", "1913 Massacre" and "It Rained 5 Days" - plus the only good quality recording of "Long Time A-Growin' ". In qualification I should say that "1913 Massacre" is unique in this form but it is in fact the tune, note for note, of - would you believe it - "Song To Woody". It does seem impertinent to steal the tune from the very person you are dedicating the song to and put it on an album without even a mention of his name under the composing credits.

"It Rained 5 Days" is typical of the sort of material and performances on the first album. It is a Leadbelly song which Dylan does with a lot of throat plus relatively complex, if occasionally haphazard, guitar. It is definitely one of the most successful songs of the set; the quieter ones tend to suffer more from Dylan's nervousness. Thus "Gospel Plow", "Fixin' To Die" and "Pretty Peggy-O" tend to work better, unfortunately, than the unique items.

"Where Did You Sleep Last Night?" is a rather weak working of a song of which other people have done very good versions. In fact Dylan's rendering seems to bear very little relation to the more familiar version, usually known as 'Black Girl' and sometimes as 'In The Pines'. If I remember rightly the chord sequence of "Black Girl" is very similar to that of "House Of The Rising Sun". I do not know which is the original, but Dylan uses a sequence that is totally different and, by comparison, rather unremarkable. Still, it was the first song of the concert and if it is true that there were only fifty people there it must have been hard to get up and sing at all.

"1913 Massacre" is succesful simply because it has a good tune. But, good quality though the tape is, it is hard to distinguish a lot of the words.

This is a pity because the song tells a story and the inaudible words are often very salient ones. It concerns a fire that takes place at a miners' Christmas party. A group of people referred to as 'the scabs and the thugs' are somehow involved in the situation escalating into tragedy but neither the precise events nor the apparent political nuances are possible to grasp specifically.

"Long Time A-Growin' " is a great disappointment compared to the Minnesota Party Tape version. Dylan's singing is very tentative and at times he seems to choke on his diffidence before getting to the end of the lines. It may be that he is not too familiar with the song - he does warn the audience at the start of the concert that he has copied a list of songs down off other performers and he does not know all of them that well. As he seems to be trying quite hard to be funny at this stage one tends to assume that he is effecting a bit of bravado in saying this. On the other hand, perhaps appearing at your first Carnegie Hall concert - albeit Carnegie Recital Hall - without having rehearsed your material is precisely the sort of thing that defines Dylan's personality.

One interesting academic point that "Long Time A-Growin' " proves is that Dylan's Nashville Skyline voice of eight years later was not produced, as some claimed, by a clever combination of echo chambers, singing lessons and giving up smoking. In the most quiet and tentative bits during the song his voice is exactly "Nashville Skyline". I wonder how music history would read now if in 1961 he had opted to stay with that voice.

CARNEGIE RECITAL HALL   Mono   PA tape (not on disc) Date Recorded: Nov 1961
Song Titles
In The Pines (also known as "Where Did You Sleep Last Night" and "Black Girl")
Pretty Peggy-O
Gospel Plow
1913 Massacre
It Rained 5 Days
Long Time A-Growin'
Fixin' To Die

THE MINNESOTA HOTEL TAPE

Scaduto, in his informative book "Bob Dylan", actually spoke to Dylan himself and reckons that this tape was recorded not in a Minnesota hotel but in the home of some people called the Whittakers.

Given that there is some disagreement as to the source, this is one of the best-known early tapes and is mostly, with some notable exceptions, now freely available on the "Bob Dylan Volumes 1, 2 and 3" albums imported from Italy in 1975, much to C.B.S.'s chagrin, in vast quantities. I am given to understand, in fact, that the reason C.B.S. did not manage to sue the importers was that they could not work out which sessions the songs came from. This does not say much for communication within the company because the Italian albums actually contained some out-takes recorded in Columbia's studios.

To get back to the tape, it does contain some rather good performances by Dylan, and a few of the songs would have perhaps made preferable material to some of the stuff on the first official album. I do not want to comment on each individual number but there are a few I feel inclined to single out. Greil Marcus, in his Rolling Stone article, praised the guitar work on "Baby Please Don't Go", and I have to agree. It is very strident, very precise and generally a bit more efficient than a lot of Dylan's playing. The vocal is good too and strikes a nice feel half way between self-pity and humour.

"Dink's Song" is one of the rarer tracks from the tape in that it appears only on the "Great White Wonder" album. I have never heard it done by anyone else so it is hard to gauge how near Dylan comes to the original. But the way he does do it, it comes over as a superb song done justice. The aggressive guitar rhythm, which at first seems incongrous with the sad feeling of the lyrics, combines after a while into unity with the voice and sense of the song. The pathos he gets into the number is magnificent and the result is one of his best performances.

"Hard Times In New York" was presumably written by Dylan and is easily good enough to have gone on the first album. At least I say written by Dylan, but there is another rather odd, piano-accompanied version on a rare tape which sounds like Dylan speeded up slightly and has a title something like "Down On Keddie's Farm". The general consensus seems to be that it is not in fact Dylan - though if it is not, it raises the interesting question as to whether it is someone imitating Dylan or if it is the original and it is Dylan's version that is the rip-off. Whichever came first, "Hard Times In New York" is certainly the superior version. It has a plunky guitar accompaniment, is basically a complaint about what a cut-throat place New York is and is one of the most Dylanish things on the tape.

"V.D. City" is a simple, pleasant melody with highly evocative, if slightly over-romantic lyrics about people lying around in gutters and doorways rotting to death. This, the song tells us, is what you get for 'an hour of passion and vice'. Not particularly enlightened philosophy, but it is only a song.

Although it was apparently the first song on the tape it sounds as though Dylan was fairly well-oiled at the time he did "Candy Man". I do not know what the words are supposed to be but I do not think the original can have contained the line 'run and get the buggy, get the baby some beer'. A portent of things to come perhaps - if you imagine an electric backing the line would not be amiss in "Memphis Blues Again".

"Man of Constant Sorrow" would warrant considerable praise if it was not for the superior version on the first official album which contains rather less strained notes and coughing - albeit that coughing makes up a considerable portion of any decent Dylan collection. Dylan's version of "Cocaine" is very pleasant and so also is "Stealin'" which contains some nice little observations about the nature of male-female relationships.

Dylan's renowned talent for understatement comes out very well on "Hezekiah Jones", the story of a black farmer lynched for not believing in God or the Church. The story is spoken, not sung, to a simple strummed accompaniment and in quoting comments of Hezekiah's neighbours Dylan

THE MINNESOTA HOTEL TAPE   Mono   Date Recorded: December 1961

Records on which appearing

Song Titles					Bob Dylan Volume 1 *1	Bob Dylan Volume 2 *1		Bob Dylan Volume 3	
Candy Man	Great White Wonder (double & single)				Bob Dylan Volume 1 *1				
Baby Please Don't Go	"				"				
Hard Times In New York	Great White Wonder Part 2	Stealin' *2	Blind Boy Grunt	And Now Your Mouth Cries Whoops		Bob Dylan Volume 2 *1			At Home
Stealin'	"	"	"	"		"			"
Poor Lazarus	Great White Wonder (double only)			Daddy Rolling Stone		"			
I Ain't Got No Home	"				"	"		Hear Me Holler *3	
It's Hard To Be Blind		" *4	" *4						
Dink's Song (Dink's Blues)	Great White Wonder (double and single)								
Man Of Constant Sorrow	"				"				
East Orange N.J. (monologue)									
Omie Wise (Naomi Wise)	Talkin' Bear Mountain Massacre Picnic Blues	70 Dollar Robbery	"	"			Walking Down The Line *5	Bob Dylan Volume 3	
Wade In The Water	Great White Wonder Part 2	Stealin'	"	"		"	Dylan - (Don't) Look Back (triple)		"
I Was Young When I Left Home	"	John Birch Society Blues		"					Help (double)
In The Evening	"	"		"					"

*1 N.B. "Bob Dylan Volumes 1 & 2" – There is a similar pair of albums in circulation on the Joker label titled "A Rare Batch Of Little White Wonder Volumes 1 & 2" with the same tracks but some of poorer quality. There is also "A Rare Batch Of Little White Wonder Volume 3" but that is totally different from "Bob Dylan Volume 3"
*2 The album "Stealin'" was also available as two EPs which ironically omitted the track "Stealin'"
*3 Existence of this album is very dubious
*4 Appears under the title "There Was A Time When I Was Blind"
*5 Appears under the title "Cool Water"
Continued...

THE MINNESOTA HOTEL TAPE (Continued)   Mono   Date Recorded: December 1961

Records on which appearing

Song Titles		Blind Boy Grunt					Bob Dylan Volume 2	Bob Dylan Volume 3	
Baby Let Me Follow You Down									
Sally Gal		"						Bob Dylan Volume 3	
Gospel Plow		"							
Long John	Great White Wonder Part 2		John Birch Society Blues						Help (double)
Cocaine (Cocaine Blues)	" (incomplete)	"	Stealin' "	And Now Your Mouth Cries Whoops	Daddy Rolling Stone (incomplete)	Dylan – (Don't) Look Back (triple) (incomplete)	"	70 Dollar Robbery	At Home (incomplete)
See That My Grave Is Kept Clean	Great White Wonder (double only)							Bob Dylan Volume 3	
Ramblin' Round	Great White Wonder (double & single) *1				Daddy Rolling Stone				
V.D. Blues	V.D. Waltz	"	V.D. Waltz				"		Skid Row *2
V.D. Waltz (fragment)		"	"						"
V.D. City		"	"						"
V.D. Gunner's Blues (V.D. Woman)			"					"	
Hezekiah Jones (Black Cross)		"	"						

*1 The single "Great White Wonder" album was also pressed under the title "Robert Zimmerman – Just As Well" with a slightly different track arrangement
*2 Existence of this album is very dubious

manages to get into his voice an indolent, simple-minded tone that works perfectly.

A lot of people seem to like "I Was Young When I Left Home", which is "500 Miles" with some of the lyrics changed. It lasts a little too long and is a trifle gushy but it is still good. The only awful number, in fact, is "Long John. Greil Marcus could find nothing kind to say abour this. He called it 'one of those super-ethic Dave Ray train hollers and pretty dismal'. Quite right. I think the reason it comes over so badly is that it is pure hype and what Dylan has always been about is the opposite of hype.

There is another track which is basically awful but it is so bad that it practically comes off - it is the East Orange Monologue where Dylan is talking about the dream he has had which is inspired by everybody in East Orange being chess-mad. The punch line is that in the dream, having bought a beer with some chess pieces he has been given instead of wages, he gets four pawns, two bishops and a rook for change. What is funny is certainly not the story itself but the way he lets you know he has just done the punch line by self-consciously adding 'That's a little story about East Orange, New Jersey'.

Most of the other songs on the tape have their good points - it might have made quite a fair double album.

THE McKENZIE TAPE

The McKenzie Tape in circulation lacks a lot of what is on the original McKenzie Tape. This is reputedly because Anthony Scaduto took a copy of the original surreptitiously when visiting the McKenzies to gather information for his book. Apparently he was left alone to listen to the tape but he had to get his own tape recorder out of sight every time someone came into the room. Hence it cuts off from time to time.

How much is missed is impossible to tell. But what is left is extensive enough to indicate that what is missing is not worth getting too distraught about. For a start the sound quality, on the tape I heard at least, is terrible, although McKenzies' tape may be much better. Even if you discount the hiss it still sounds as though Dylan and the microphone were in different rooms. From what you can hear of them some of the performances are O.K. but there is little that comes across as particularly remarkable. The items I found most interesting are the snatch of "See That My Grave Is Kept Clean" which has a very unusual and attractive guitar accompaniment and a version of "House Of The Rising Sun" that uses totally different chords from the familiar version. In fact, although it retains a vaguely similar tune, it is nearly all on one minor chord. This, I assume, must be the traditional version, while the one that wound up as the Animals' single must be the Dave Von Ronk working.

It would have been better if "Bells Of Rhymney" extended to more than a snatch, especially as Dylan seems to have temporarily got nearer the microphone. It might have been pleasant also if what sounds like a banjo and a mandolin entering the scene briefly had been made more use of. Whoever is playing them sounds fairly proficient. But this is not really any sort of session as such - it is just a collection of recordings made over the period, presumably, when the McKenzies were putting Dylan up. From the amount of time Dylan spends tuning up and doodling one hopes that even if he did not pay for his board and lodging he at least paid for the tape.

One piece of Dylan assassination I can perhaps allow myself is to tell you that at one point on the tape where there is a pause in the proceedings a girl starts singing solo and unaccompanied. Before she has finished a couple of bars Dylan's guitar cuts over the top of her with a totally unrelated song. She does not raise any objection at the time, but, assuming it is the same girl you can hear from time to time calling him 'Barby', there is a bit towards the end of the tape where it sounds as though she is having a little go at him. Good for her, even if Dylan does studiously fail to notice her annoyance.

THE McKENZIE TAPE   Mono   (not on disc)
Date Recorded: 1961-63

Song Titles

Hard Times In New York Town (fragment)
? (fragment)
? (fragment)
Lonesome Whistle Blues
Worried Blues (fragment)
? (fragment)
Baby Let Me Follow You Down
You're No Good (fragment)
San Francisco Bay Blues
House Of The Rising Sun
? (fragment)
? (fragment)
Bells Of Rhymney (fragment)
? (fragment)
Highway 51
This Land Is Your Land (fragment)
See That My Grave Is Kept Clean (fragment)
Ballad Of Donald White
A Hard Rain's A-Gonna Fall
? (fragment)
Times Ain't What They Used To Be (fragment)
? (fragment)
? (instrumental fragment)
Long Time Gone
Only A Hobo
House Of The Rising Sun
? (instrumental fragment)

THE LEEDS MUSIC DEMOS

This is almost certainly a studio recorded tape as indicated by its availability in excellent quality. All the performances except "Ramblin', Gamblin' Willie" appear on the record "Early 60s Revisited" again in very good quality, apart from the addition of some hiss, and all are on "Poems In Naked Wonder" without even the hiss.

There are some good songs here too, several of them unique to this tape (i.e. unique in the context of what is in circulation,). There is also material that appears elsewhere, some of it superior, some of it inferior to the other versions. The version of "Talkin' Bear Mountain" on this tape, for instance, from the point of view of both timing and general delivery, is not nearly as good as the best known version (see "Bob Dylan" Out-takes). On the other hand, "Ramblin', Gamblin' Willie" has the edge on the version on the original "Freewheelin' " album. Again "Hard Times In New York" does not come over nearly as well as on the Minnesota Hotel Tape largely because the hurried way Dylan dashes it off gives the impression he is bored with it - one reason perhaps why it never got on an album.

"He Was A Friend Of Mine" has been done by the Byrds with lyrics changed to refer to John F. Kennedy. Dylan's version is pleasant but not nearly as good as another song on the tape which expresses much the same sentiment - "Ballad For A Friend". Both songs mourn the death of a friend but while "He Was A Friend Of Mine" has an aura of hyped sentimentality, "Ballad For A Friend" simply draws a gentle and evocative sketch of the relationship between the singer and the dead friend in terms of their shared background. It has a much better tune as well. Definitely the best song on the tape.

One gets the impression that "Poor Boy Blues" is one of those prototypes that might have developed into something good if Dylan had pursued it. As it stands it is not much more than a solo jam. "Standing On The Highway", on the other hand, is a well worked-out blues that makes good use of a cascading guitar riff and comes off very successfully. Another song that could have gone on an official album.

Definitely not up to official album standard are either of the takes of "Man On The Street". The lyrical content is very similar to "Only A Hobo" (see Witmark Demos and "The Times They Are A-Changin' " Out-takes), but it does not come off nearly as well as the latter because it has no melody to speak of and Dylan sounds as if he has sung it hundreds of times before and he has had enough. Admittedly this impression does not actually tie in with the fact that the reason he does two takes is that he forgets the words the first time round. But perhaps one should bear in mind that he forgot the words of "Like A Rolling Stone" at the Isle Wight and he had sung that a good few times before.

THE GASLIGHT TAPE (1)

There are two Gaslight Tapes - a 'private' one and a 'live' one. This is the private one, though it is confusing in that an audience is in evident on a number of the tracks. Anyway, of the two tapes this is definitely the better one, sound quality and performance-wise. And some of the things on it are really superb.

There are a few Dylan standards like "Don't Think Twice", "Blowin' In The Wind", "Hard Rain" and "Hollis Brown", a few lesser known

LEEDS MUSIC DEMOS   Mono   Date Recorded: Early 1962

Song Titles	Records on which appearing	
	Early '60s Revisited	Poems In Naked Wonder
He Was A Friend Of Mine		"
Man On The Street (take 1)	"	"
Hard Times In New York	"	"
Man On The Street (take 2)	"	"
Talking Bear Mountain Picnic Massacre Disaster Blues	"	"
Standing On The Highway	"	"
Poor Boy Blues	"	"
Ballad For A Friend	"	"
Ramblin' Gamblin' Willie		"

songs that nevertheless turn up on other tapes, and then one or two items that are unique.

One of the latter is "Barbara Allen" with Dylan sounding in places again very much like he did on "Nashville Skyline". It is very pleasantly done but, unlike some of the other standard folk numbers he was performing at this time, he does not manage to make it his own. I think it is just too Joan Baez-ish for him.

"No More Auction Block", on the other hand, is perfect. It is very beautifully sung and played and the whole effect is very emotive. Dylan's guitar accompaniment seems to have been produced with a mandolin-like plucking technique and in places the chords achieve a sort of waterfall quality that is hard to describe.

"Moonshine Blues" is good too - one could even call it brilliant if it was not for the outstandingly superior version on the Witmark Demo Tape. But that is a reoccurring facet of Dylan - he seems to put everything he has into a song on one occasion, then you hear another version on a different tape and by comparison he chucks the whole thing away.

This does not strictly apply in the case of "Moonshine Blues" because both versions are good and anyway the best one was recorded much later when Dylan had evolved and personalised it. But "Rocks And Gravel" is a classic example. There are several other versions of this which I had happened to have heard before I heard the Gaslight version, and after hearing them I thought "Rocks And Gravel" was a pretty boring song. Then when I heard the Gaslight (1) version I thought it was really good. It is not *that* much different from the others - the rhythm of the guitar is spot-on whereas on some of the versions it is irritatingly draggy, and the vocal, especially where it goes falsetto, is just more at one with the sense of the lyrics and the feeling of the guitar. The result is a song that comes across as having guts, atmosphere and a subtly distinctive tune as opposed to the other versions which condemn themselves as tuneless non-starters.

If there was another Dylan version of "Ain't No More Cane On The Brazo" this might also appear here. In places, admittedly, the vocal is very good, but the guitar is somewhat similar to, though not quite as dead-on-its-feet as, Leonard Cohen's accompaniment for "The Butcher" - and that could kill any song.

Unreservedly excellent is "Two Trains A-Runnin' ". It is good funky blues guitar, even the muffed notes adding rather than detracting, and a vocal that gets more and more vehement as it goes along. This version is spot-on - none of your Dylan throwaway stuff here.

For sheer abortive monotony you cannot beat "John Brown", probably the worst song Dylan ever sang. It is about a woman proudly waving her son off to war and him coming back blinded, hands blown off and his body held together with a metal brace. The audience evidently thought it was wonderful.

There are one of two other awful things on the tape - viz "Emmett Till" (this is on so many bootlegs I can no longer be objective about it), "Muleskinner Blues" which Dylan tries in about four different keys, and then, thankfully, gives up, and "West Texas" which is O.K. really but has a guitar introduction of interminable length. Of academic interest is "Quit Your Low Down Ways" in which Dylan inserts a verse from "Milk Cow Blues", and "Kind Hearted Woman" which contains that verse from "Times Ain't What 'They Used To Be" about burying someone alive (see

Minnesota Party Tape).

Dylan's version of "Cocaine" on this tape is equally as pleasant, if not quite as lascivious, as the Minnesota Hotel version, though you have to be aware of the bit near the end where he gets too near the microphone and sounds eerily as though he is suddenly in the room with you. "Handsome Molly" he does beautifully and sensitively; it is a lovely song and this performance is far superior to the Riverside Church version - in the right mood it can bring tears to your eyes.

His introduction to "Let Me Die In My Footsteps" goes: 'I'm going to sing a couple of dirty songs now.' (c.f. his introduction to "It's Alright Ma - I'm Only Bleeding" in his 1965 B.B.C. concert). This is one of the songs from the original "Freewheelin' " and I am at a loss to understand why it was withdrawn. The version here is well performed, though not quite as polished as the studio versions.

I cannot make up my mind about "Hiram Hubbard". It took a long time to grow on me, I liked it for half a play and then started getting bored with it; with a little more working out it could have been a singalong classic. "Kind Hearted Woman" could be good too. It has a splendid repeated guitar phrase very reminiscent of the Rolling Stones' "King Bee" but the song itself needs more development. More work on "Motherless Children" and "The Cuckoo Is A Pretty Bird" would also have possibly tipped the balance. As they stand they are O.K. but do not quite make it.

All things considered, I think this tape is one of my favourites. The sound quality is quite good throughout and there is some essential stuff on it. If you are collecting Dylan selectively this is a good one to choose.

Note. A point of controversy that has come up since writing the above is that it is claimed in some quarters that the eleven tracks listed below were not recorded at the Gaslight but at the Finjan Club, Montreal in June 1962:

Blowin' in the Wind	Let Me Die in My Footsteps
Quit Your Low Down Ways	Ramblin' on My Mind
Hiram Hubbard	Muleskinner Blues
Two Trains A-Runnin'	Emmett Till
Rocks and Gravel	Stealin'
He Was a Friend of Mine	

This would tie in to a certain extent with the Gaslight Tape being known in some quarters as 'The Canada Party Tape'.

THE GASLIGHT TAPE (2)

This is another case of not being able to judge the quality of the performances because there does not seem to be any good sound quality tapes around. The dullness of the sound texture on this one really makes Dylan sound as if he is about to slump unconsciously from his stool. But again the audience reaction indicates that they were enjoying it, and if you can go with the sound quality, after a while the atmosphere starts to come through.

All the same, most of the songs here have been done better elsewhere with the exception perhaps of "He Was A Friend Of Mine", which comes across less sentimentally than the other versions, and "Car Car". The latter is done as a duet with Dave Van Ronk whom Dylan introduces to the audience as an 'ex-blues singer'. The mateyness between the two of them comes over quite genuinely and you can imagine that the Gaslight Cafe must have been quite a good scene.

Legend has it that these recordings were originally made straight onto an acetate. It would certainly explain the terrible sound quality but it also adds a nice romantic touch to the image of the Gaslight. I suppose it is really the American equivalent of the Cavern.

THE GASLIGHT TAPE (1) Mono Date Recorded: 1962		
Song Titles	Records on which appearing	
Barbara Allen	Ode For Barbara Allen *1	
A Hard Rain's A-Gonna Fall	"	The Gaslight Tapes *2
Don't Think Twice, It's All Right	"	"
Hezekiah Jones	"	"
No More Auction Block	"	"
Moonshine Blues	"	" (incomplete)
Hiram Hubbard		The Gaslight Tapes
Blowin' In The Wind		"
Rocks And Gravel (1)	"	"
Rocks And Gravel (2)		"
John Brown	Dylan '62	
Hollis Brown	"	
See That My Grave Is Kept Clean	"	
The Cuckoo Is A Pretty Bird	"	
Cocaine	"	
Motherless Children	"	
Ain't No More Cane On The Brazo (Go Down Old Hannah)	"	
Kind Hearted Woman		
Handsome Molly (I Wish I Was In London)	"	
Quit Your Low Down Ways		"
He Was A Friend Of Mine	Help (double)	"
Let Me Die In My Footsteps		
Two Trains A-Runnin'		
Ramblin' On My Mind		
Muleskinner Blues		
Emmett Till	"	
Stealin'		
West Texas		
*1 Also released as one half of a double album entitled "Barbed Wire Blues" *2 Also released under the title "Alias" (not to be confused with the EP of that title)		

THE GASLIGHT TAPE (2) Mono Date Recorded: 1962

Song Titles	Records on which appearing		
Man On The Street	The Villager	1000 Miles Behind	
He Was A Friend Of Mine	"	"	
Talkin' Bear Mountain Picnic Massacre Disaster Blues	"		
Song To Woody	"	"	
Pretty Polly	"		
Car Car *	"	"	Dylan - (Don't) Look Back (triple)

* With Dave Van Ronk

W.B.A.I. NEW YORK Mono Date Recorded: May 1962

Song Titles	Records on which appearing			
Ballad Of Donald White	Blind Boy Grunt 1000 Miles Behind	Long Time Gone (EPs) Help (double)	Broadside Reunion Volume 6 *	
Emmett Till	Great White Wonder (double only)	Bob Dylan Volume 1	"	
Blowin' In The Wind				

Also extensive chat including a conversation between Dylan and Pete Seeger, an extract from which appears on "Great White Wonder"
* Official Recording

W.B.A.I. NEW YORK

This tape of a radio show which was not broadcast is chiefly of interest for its inclusion of the only good sound quality performance of "The Ballad Of Old Donald White", a tune written, as Dylan himself tells us in his introduction, by Bonnie Dobson, with new words added by Dylan.

Dylan's words are about a person who asks to be put in an institution because he cannot cope with society and who, when his request is refused, goes out and kills someone. For this of course, instead of being put in an institution, he is hanged. While this is obviously a protest song it is not over clear what Dylan is protesting about - the fact that Donald White is hanged or the fact that his request to be put in an institution is turned down. Either way the lyrics evoke an image of Donald White having a slightly simplistic attitude to the whole business. Maybe a touch of the famous Dylan duality - I don't know.

The ubiquitous "Emmett Till" shows up again on this tape, this time with Dylan admitting that he stole the tune. It has a very similar chord sequence to "House Of The Rising Sun" but seem to have had the zest taken out of it. The words are about a black man who is tortured and killed by some whites who subsequently are found innocent by a bent jury. One of the reasons I do not like listening to the song is that the description of the torturing is too real and very disturbing. On the other hand the exhort-atory patriotism of the last verse is a bit excessive on any level. However, perhaps one should remember that Dylan was possibly no more than eight-een when he wrote the song, and maybe then he was actually capable of a degree of naivety.

This, incidentally, is the tape where Dylan makes his relatively famous comment to Pete Seeger that he does not so much write his songs as takes them out of the air. Not a bad way to make a living.

"BOB DYLAN" OUT-TAKES

This is another tape where there is disagreement as to source. On the cover slip of the album "Talkin' Bear Mountain Massacre Picnic Blues" Trade Mark of Quality suggests that some of the tracks come from a Warner Brothers demo, some from "Freewheelin' " and some from the Witmark Demos. The Warner Brothers demo tape is certainly a possibility but if "Corrina Corrina" and "Rocks And Gravel" come from the "Freewheelin' " sessions that amounts to three versions of "Corrina Corrina" all from the same sessions and two of "Rocks And Gravel". There is no reason why this should not be so - especially in view of the fact that both numbers wound up with a vaguely electric backing. But what does seem unlikely is that "Talkin' Bear Mountain", "Quit Your Low Down Ways", "Emmett Till" and "Baby I'm In The Mood For You" come from the Witmark Demos. The quality is too perfect on the last three, and it would again mean that there were two versions of each on the Witmark tape - unless the versions normally accepted as the Witmark ones in fact got in by mistake. As regards "Talkin Bear Mountain" Dylan had already put that on the Leeds Music demo tape. Though, again, I suppose the idea of selling the same song to two different publishers might have appealed to Dylan.

The other suggestion, made in Scaduto's tapeography, is that all these tracks were "Freewheelin' " out-takes. This could well be true. The only thing which makes me opt for their being from the "Bob Dylan" sessions

BOB DYLAN OUT-TAKES   Mono   Date Recorded: 1962

Song Titles	Records on which appearing		
	Talkin' Bear Mountain Massacre Picnic Blues	Best Of Great White Wonder *1	Aspects Of Bob Dylan On Tour Volume 2 / Walking Down The Line *2
Baby Please Don't Go	Talkin' Bear Mountain Massacre Picnic Blues		
Milk Cow Blues	"		
Talkin' Bear Mountain Picnic Massacre Disaster Blues		Best Of Great White Wonder *1	"
Corrina Corrina		"	" *2
Emmett Till		"	"
Talkin' Hava Nagilah Blues		"	" *3
Babe, I'm In The Mood For You		"	
Quit Your Low Down Ways		"	
Worried Blues		"	" *4
Going To New Orleans		"	
Lonesome Whistle Blues		"	
Wichita Blues		"	" *5
Rocks And Gravel		"	
Let Me Die In My Footsteps	Let Me Die In My Footsteps		" *6

*1 Also released under title of "Great White Wonder Revisited"
*2 Under title "Carena"
*3 Under title "Chanuka"
*4 Under title "Worry Blues"
*5 Under title "Salad Road"
*6 Under title "Die In My Footsteps"

is that there are a lot of early songs here and they just seem to fit in more with the mood of the first album.

Unlike later out-takes it seems fair enough that most of these tracks did not get on an official album - most of them are not that good. "Babe I'm In The Mood For You" and "Quit Your Low Down Ways", for instance, are much more polished than previous versions but they still lack real essence. "Baby Please Don't Go" is good but it is not a patch on the Minnesota

Hotel Tape Version, and "Milk Cow Blues", "Going To New Orleans" and "Wichita Blues" are not much short of drab.

It is interesting to hear a completely acoustic "Corrina Corrina" especially as the actual guitar phrases are virtually the same as those played by the electric guitar on the other two versions. Certainly this early discreet flirtation with electric music improved "Corrina Corrina" no end.

Exceptions to the general rule on this tape are "Talkin' Bear Mountain", "Let Me Die In My Footsteps", "Worried Blues" and "Lonesome Whistle Blues" which are all excellent. "Talkin' Bear Mountain" is really funny in places. But possibly one reason this track was not used on "Bob Dylan" was that "Talkin' New York" was just that bit funnier. "Talkin' Bear Mountain" to my mind though is as good as "World War III Blues", but I assume the latter fitted the "Freewheelin' " image better.

"Lonesome Whistle Blues" is just a good gutsy tune to which Dylan does ample justice. The guitar and the vocal are well balanced and the whole effect is undemandingly pleasing.

"Worried Blues" also has a very attractive tune, so attractive in fact that it allows Dylan to get away with very simplistic and repetitive lyrics. If the words had been more up to his usual standard it could have been a real classic.

"Let Me Die In My Footsteps" *is* a classic. The version contains one less verse than the original "Freewheelin' " track but it makes no difference to its merit. The tune is excellent and the words are a quintessence of uncompromised idealism. It is a very positive sort of protest song which is basically objecting to those who get a kick out of prophesying doom. It is a great shame it did not get on the final version of "Freewheelin' " - it would not have dated at all. I suppose Columbia thought that one album just was not big enough for a "Hard Rain" and a "Let Me Die In My Footsteps". As to why it did not get on the first album, perhaps Dylan was a folk singer, not a protest singer, when he cut that.

CARNEGIE HALL HOOTENANNY Mono Audience tape Date Recorded: Sept 1962	
Song Titles	Record on which appearing
Sally Gal	Friends Of Chile
Highway 51	"
Talkin' John Birch Society Blues	"
Hollis Brown	"

THE OSCAR BRAND SHOW (ACTUAL TITLE: THE WORLD OF FOLK MUSIC)

This is definitely the least embarrassing of the radio show tapes in existence. Oscar Brand does not gush quite as much as most of Dylan's subsequent hosts and the talk between the songs is extremely brief and to the point. Dylan himself is uncharacteristically pithy in his introductions to the songs and it sounds as though he has actually gone over what he is going to say beforehand.

The performances are good and crisp also. "Girl From The North Country" which Dylan calls "North Country Girl" is very close to the "Freewheelin' " version except for harmonica inserts between the lines of the last verse which are quite effective. "Only A Hobo" is not particularly distinguishable merit-wise from the other versions but it is interesting from the point of view of why Dylan chose it. In the intro to the show we are told that the programme is sponsored by, of all people, the Social Security Administration - later on Oscar Brand and Dylan even break off for 'a true story from the Social Security files'. This does not refer to "Only A Hobo" - the 'true story' is omitted from the tape. But obviously "Only A Hobo" is about someone *not* catered for by the Social Security Administration, and it is apparent from the tone of Oscar Brand's voice that he knows Dylan is making a point, though it is still about the most tactful example I have heard of Dylan making a point.

THE BILLY FAIER SHOW

The major item of interest here is "Make Me a Pallet On Your Floor", of which this is the only Dylan performance in circulation. It is a Guthrie song on a subject of sexual infidelity and could be cited by someone in pedantic mood for sexist lyrics. In fact it is a very pleasant, good-natured song with quite a strong tune and a generally good atmosphere. Dylan does a good job on it even though he indicates by what he says in introducing it that he has not performed it before.

One blessing about this tape is that it contains none of the intense chat that characterises most of the early radio broadcasts. The nearest thing to intensity is when Billy Faier mentions that an irate listener has telephoned to say that having done an anti-John Birch song Dylan is now under an obligation to do an anti-communist song. Dylan says that he does not know any and Billy Faier adds, somewhat dubiously, that most of the anti-communist songs have been done by people to the left of the Communist Party.

MADHOUSE ON CASTLE STREET

While a lot of people are at a loss to understand how Dylan managed to get himself into a B.B.C. play, I am also at a loss to understand how a B.B.C. play got to be called "Madhouse *On* Castle Street" instead of "Madhouse *In* Castle Street". I am not just being pedantic - until recently I had wondered if some misinformation had crept in here over the years. In fact a copy of an extract from Radio Times for January 10, 1963, confirms the whole thing as fact. The play was actually called "The Madhouse On Castle Street", and as to how Dylan got into it - 'Appearing as Bobby the hobo is Bob Dylan, brought over from America especially to play the part. At twenty-one he is already a major new figure in folk music, with a reputation as one of the most compelling blues singers ever recorded.'

It is hard to say whether or not 'compelling' is the word to describe the two performances here. "Swan On The River" is drowned in places by voices in the foreground and what you *can* hear is of terrible quality (on the tape I heard at least). It is interesting for its uniqueness and has a perky sort of tune but it is not what you would call an 'important statement'. "Blowin' In The Wind" obviously is but "Madhouse On Castle Street" was possibly not the best of vehicles for it. Still, the exposure cannot have done Dylan any harm. I wonder what he would charge the B.B.C. now if they offered him a part in 'Play For Today'.

OSCAR BRAND SHOW W.Q.X.R. NEW YORK Mono Date Recorded: October 1962	
Song Titles	Record on which appearing
Girl From The North Country	Skid Row *
Only A Hobo	"
* Existence of this album is dubious	

BILLY FAIER SHOW   W.B.A.I. RADIO   Mono (not on disc)   Date Recorded: Oct 1962
Song Titles
Baby Let Me Follow You Down
Talkin' John Birch Society Blues
Emmett Till
Make Me A Pallet On Your Floor

MADHOUSE ON CASTLE STREET (BBC TV PLAY) Mono (not on disc) Date Recorded: January 1963
Song Titles
Blowin' In The Wind
Swan On The River (incomplete)

THE BANJO TAPE

It is not really fair to look at this tape as a set of performances because it is not much more than a piss-up. It was reputedly recorded in the home of Gil Turner, who seems to be joining in, with Dylan apparently playing a twelve string guitar. Happy Traum is also present playing the banjo, frequently in a different key from the twelve string.

Very few of the songs get finished and the ones that do tend to put one in mind of the Bonzo Dog Doo Dah Band's version of "The Sound Of Music". The fact that some of them became tracks on what, in Italy at least, were official albums just shows you how popular Dylan is.

"If I Could Do It All Over, I'd Do It All Over You" is probably the most successful thing on the tape, and in some ways is better than the studio version (see Witmark Demos). Dylan actually plays the twelve string like a twelve string on this, and the banjo and raucous harmonising help make it the nearest thing to a rugby song that has yet come out of America.

"Farewell" is alright if you have not heard any of the other versions. But compare it to either the Witmark Demo or the out-take from "Another Side Of ....." and you will see how it has been murdered here. Certainly a bit of a come-down for people who bought "Bob Dylan Volume 1" expecting to get a Dylan rendering of "Farewell Angelina". I think the nearest anyone is going to get to that will be by playing the Joan Baez single at thirty-three r.p.m.

Going back to the tape, it is a pity that some of the snatches of songs are not sung in full. "Lonesome River's Edge", "You Don't Do Me Like You Used To Do", and "Goin' Back To Rome" sound quite promising. They do not turn up on any other tape either. Unless, of course, Columbia have got them.

THE BROADSIDE SESSIONS

Broadside Magazine was a legitimate enterprise that used to put out albums containing contributions from various different folk singers. The ones that Dylan is on, under the name of Blind Boy Grunt, were still available in the States at the time of writing.

Having said that, I would not particularly recommend them; the sound quality is not always too good and one gets the impression that when he was recording for them Dylan was saving his energy and best material for elsewhere.

Of the performances on this tape Broadside used, as far as I can gather, only five tracks, though they also managed to get away with including on one of the albums two tracks - "The Ballad Of Donald White" and "Emmett Till" - which in fact came from Dylan's performance on a W.B.A.I. Radio tape (see W.B.A.I. New York Tape). None of the five Broadside tracks is particularly stunning. The best one is probably "Only A Hobo", though this is not Dylan's best performance of it. "Train A-Travelling" is pleasant but not outstanding while "Cuban Blockade" I cannot decide about. It uses the tune of "Trail Of The Buffalo" and attempts to depict the trauma of the U.S.A.'s confrontation with Russia over Cuba. In its own way it is quite evocative but it still seems to lack something. "I'd Hate To Be You On That Dreadful Day" is a write-off except for the cadence of the main verse. This cadence survives in the vastly superior "Bob Dylan's Blues" on "Freewheelin' ".

"Talkin' Devil" is just two quick jokey verses in standard talking blues format. As far as I can gather it is either about a politician or an arms manufacturer personified as the devil. Not Dylan satire at its best. The last of the five released tracks is "John Brown" - totally dire.

Why Broadside chose the above tracks to release I do not know - there are two fairly good songs on the tape that I would not have thought would have posed any copyright problems, viz. "Playboys And Playgirls" and "Walking Down The Line". Spruced up a bit the latter would have made a good album track. In fact it has been spruced up by various other singers including Joan Baez, but I still prefer Dylan's own untidy rendering. It is nice to hear "Playboys And Playgirls" without Pete Seeger (see Newport 1963) to whom it is hard to feel charitable after his monopolisation of the

THE BANJO TAPE (WITH HAPPY TRAUM)   Mono   Date Recorded: Jan 1963

Song Titles	Records on which appearing		
Lonesome River's Edge (fragment)	Burn Some More		
Who You Really Are (incomplete)	"	Seems Like A Freeze Out *1	Bob Dylan Volume 1 *2
Bob Dylan's Dream	"		
? (fragment)	"		
Farewell	"	"	
If I Could Do It All Over, I'd Do It All Over You	"	"	Bob Dylan Volume 2
Masters Of War	"		
Keep Your Hands Off Her (fragment)	"		
You Don't Do Me Like You Used To Do (fragment)	"		
Goin' Back To Rome (fragment)	"		
Stealin'	"		

*1 Also released as "Visions Of Johanna"
*2 See *1 on Minnesota Hotel Tape Chart

protest episode of "All You Need Is Love", during which the word 'Dylan' was never spoken. But although on this version of the song Gil Turner does pleasant and discreet harmonies towards the end, I have to admit that the Newport duet with Seeger is the one that gets further off the ground.

Gil Turner also does what could loosely be termed harmonies on "Farewell". This is a great pity because it is a very fine song and Dylan sings it beautifully. It is fine until the chorus and then this hyper-loud, flat voice comes in, achieving a similar effect to that of the newscaster on Simon and Garfunkel's "Silent Night".

Of the remaining songs "Oxford Town" and "Masters Of War" are hardly different from the official versions. "I Shall Be Free", on the other hand, is distinctly less articulate than its "Freewheelin' " counterpart, ending, by no means uniquely, with drunken laughter and Dylan forgetting the words.

Dylan is also in a forgetful mood on "Paths Of Victory", a song with a similar, if less acid, sentiment to "When The Ship Comes In". There are much better versions of this by Dylan and when it is done properly it is quite a pleasant singalong number. But on this version he keeps coming in late and just never really catches up.

In fact it generally seems odd that, considering Broadside must have provided golden opportunities for up and coming folk singers, Dylan's tape for them was so scrappy. Possibly it was just a rehearsal tape which Broadside then used later on as a cash-in, or possibly at the time he recorded it Dylan was already well on the way to stardom.

THE SKIP WESTNER SHOW

Something that has caused a little confusion is that the two verse fragment of "Bob Dylan's Dream" from this radio show has been circulating on a short tape that does not include the other two songs and which goes under the label 'The Lone Ranger Tape'. The complete tape, with the other two songs and the chat, is about thirty minutes long.

"Tomorrow Is A Long Time", which Dylan introduces as "Tomorrow Is A Long Long Time", is also incomplete but, anyway, is not as good as the other two available versions. "Masters Of War", as with most of the other circulating versions of the song, also does not match up to the official rendering. But "Bob Dylan's Blues" - what there is of it - stands up fairly well next to the "Freewheelin' " version. In fact the two verses here are the best two from the song and if there was no other version available you would be left feeling annoyed that Dylan forgets the words at the point he does. The harmonica is rather good as well. Dylan sounds as though he is constantly on the point of getting lost but each time he manages to pull it together at the end of the line. It is definitely more ambitious than a lot of the standard riffs he was using on the early albums and it is one of the few snatches of Dylan harmonica on tape that you would not recognise immediately as none other than the man himself.

THE "FREEWHEELIN' " SESSIONS

The original "Freewheelin' " was withdrawn by Columbia very soon after being issued and four of the songs on it - "Let Me Die In My Footsteps", "Talkin' John Birch Society Blues", "Rocks And Gravel" and "Ramblin', Gamblin' Willie" - were replaced. The replacements were

"Master Of War", "Talkin' World War III Blues", "Girl From The North Country" and "Bob Dylan's Dream".

"Talkin' John Birch" seems to have been the main reason for the withdrawal of the original. Apparently Dylan was to make an appearance on the Ed Sullivan Show but refused to do so after a programme controller vetoed his doing "John Birch" on the grounds, presumably, that anything anti-anti-communist had to be pro-communist. Columbia was the company that handled the Ed Sullivan Show and word about "John

THE BROADSIDE SESSIONS   Mono   Date Recorded: 1963

Song Titles	Records on which appearing		
Oxford Town			
Paths Of Victory			
Masters Of War			
I'd Hate To Be You On That Dreadful Day	Let Me Die In My Footsteps		Broadside Reunion Volume 6 *2
Walking Down The Line	"	Walking Down The Line	"
I Shall Be Free			
Train A-Travellin'	"	Dusty Old Fairgrounds *1	
Cuban Blockade (World War No.3)	"	The Demo Tapes	Hear Me Holler *1
Ye Playboys & Playgirls	Long Time Gone (2 EPs)	Help (double)	"
Farewell			
Only A Hobo	Blind Boy Grunt		Broadside Ballads Volume 1 *2
Talkin' Devil	"		"
John Brown	"		"
Let Me Die In My Footsteps *3			"

*1 Existence of these albums very uncertain
*2 Official recording
*3 Happy Traum - vocal, Bob Dylan - harmonica (under title "I Will Not Go Down Under The Ground")

Song Titles
Tomorrow Is A Long Time (incomplete)
Masters Of War
Bob Dylan's Dream (incomplete)
Plus chat

Birch" got back to the recording division, somewhere along the line becoming a directive to drop the song from the album.

Why the other three songs were withdrawn is unclear. Certainly "Rocks And Gravel" and "Ramblin', Gamblin' Willie" were dispensible but "Let Me Die In My Footsteps" is a great song. Anyway, thankfully good quality tapes of it exist as also with "John Birch" and "Rocks And Gravel". Most of the tapes I have heard of "Ramblin', Gamblin' Willie" are basically good quality too but they all have a clunk running through them. It is interesting actually that until recently all the tapes of "John Birch" had a slight clunk too. Then suddenly one appeared that was virtually perfect. Possibly then someone somewhere has a mint condition copy of the original "Freewheelin' ".

The other two available tracks from the sessions - "Mixed Up Confusion" and "Corrina Corrina" - were released on either side of a single not long after the sessions took place. That too was withdrawn but became available again in Europe in the late sixties. There is not a lot to choose between the single version of "Corrina Corrina" and the one on the album - the album version perhaps just has the edge vocally. "Mixed Up Confusion" is a primitive rock song, interesting academically but not very aesthetic musically. It is Dylan living out his Little Richard fantasy.

THE WITMARK DEMOS

There are some exquisite songs on this tape. Though I must state the reservation that it is possible that not all the material listed is a hundred per cent certain to have come from the Witmark Demos.

"Percy's Song", "Walls Of Redwing" and "Moonshine Blues" could instead have come from the sessions for "The Times They Are A-Changin' ". "Mama, You Been On My Mind" could have come from the latter, or from the Witmark Demos or from the "Another Side Of ....." sessions. There is also some doubt as to which versions of "Seven Curses" and "Paths Of Victory" belong to the Witmark Demos and which belong to the "Times ..." sessions. In areas of doubt like this I have listed the songs as part of the tape that logic indicates they most likely came from. "Mama, You Been On My Mind", for instance, has a click running through one verse, and I have never come across a tape of it that does not have this click. This indicates that it was originally copied from a disc which in turn indicates that it was probably a demo.

I hope the reader will forgive my not commenting on all forty-two tracks here, but there are a lot of standard Dylan things on the tape which, although well-performed, are little different from other versions. There is

THE FREEWHEELIN' SESSIONS   Mono   Date Recorded: Early 1963

Records on which appearing

Song Titles	Great White Wonder Part 2	John Birch Society Blues	Daddy Rolling Stone	Best Of Great White Wonder	Aspects Of Bob Dylan On Tour Volume 2	Dylan - (Don't) Look Back (triple)	At Home
Talkin' John Birch Society Blues *1							
Rocks And Gravel *1	"		"		Dusty Old Fairgrounds *3	40 Red White And Blue Shoestrings	
Let Me Die In My Footsteps *1			" *4		" *4	" *4	
Ramblin' Gamblin' Willie *1	"	"	Help (double)				
Mixed Up Confusion	"	"	Bob Dylan In Concert Volume 2 *2	"		Deleted Single *5	
Corrina Corrina	"	"	"	"		"	"

*1 These tracks appeared on the original pressing of "Freewheelin'" before it was withdrawn and the format changed to its current one
*2 "Bob Dylan In Concert Volumes 1 & 2" was copied and released as "Live Parts 1 & 2"
*3 Existence of this album very dubious
*4 Good quality track marred in places by voices talking in the background
*5 Official Recording

also a number of songs which it seems likely Dylan had already rejected as album material but which he put in here possibly just for somewhere to put them rather than in the specific hope that someone else would record them. Into this grouping would conceivably fall "Walls Of Redwing", "Ain't Gonna Grieve", "I'm In The Mood For You", "Quit Your Low Down Ways", "Bound To Win", "Long Ago, Far Away", "John Brown", "Hero Blues", "Long Time Gone", "Watcha Gonna Do?", "If I Could Do It All Over, I'd Do It All Over You" and maybe a few others.

In "If I Could Do It ....." for instance he starts off by saying to someone 'Let's put this one down just for kicks.' In fact it is a stronger song than many of the others mentioned above. The reason most of these did not get on to an official album is fairly obviously that they were not good enough. In a number of cases what they lack is tune. The lyrics of some of them are also a bit cliché-ridden.

On the subject of melody there is an interesting example on this tape of the process of evolution of a Dylan song. The version here of "I'll Keep It With Mine" has the same melody as the later studio out-take (see "Another Side Of ..." Out-takes) except for the first two lines of each verse. On the Witmark version these two lines are very weak melodically and tend to mar the whole song. But by the time he did the later version Dylan had come up with a melody for these lines which, while only a couple of notes different, was very unusual and stunningly effective. Possibly some of the other weak tunes on this tape also evolved into masterpieces but they never saw the light of day.

Far better than the version which did officially see the light of day is the version here of "Tomorrow Is A Long Time". This song has been recorded by many people but nothing comes close to this magnetically emotive rendering by Dylan. It could have been totally perfect if he had not let the guitar rhythm lag occasionally and had not tried to cram too many syllables into the second line of the first verse. Nevertheless it is still brilliant.

It is interesting that there are two versions of "Paths Of Victory" here - one with guitar and one with a piano (though one of them is very likely to have come from the "Times ..." sessions). It is a pleasant song but not outstanding and one wonders if perhaps Dylan was hoping that someone like Peter Paul and Mary might make a "We Shall Overcome" type of hit out of it.

It is a pity someone, preferably Dylan, did not release an official recording of "Seven Curses". It is a fabulous song and though the version from the "Times ....." sessions has the edge, the one for Witmarks is still excellent. The lyrics are about a judge who demands sex from a girl in payment for preventing her father being hanged. The morning after the judge has had his way the girl wakes up to find that the hanging has already taken place. The story-teller himself then puts seven curses on the judge, the final curse being that 'seven deaths will never kill him'. It is a fine ending in that it could be interpreted as expressing faith in some sort of universal justice. But interpretation aside, it is a beautiful tune which fits perfectly with the mood of the lyrics.

I am not overstruck by "Guess I'm Doin' Fine". The ambivalence of the words I do like; Dylan is saying that while he is not rich and powerful he does have his voice and his health and his memories. But while on the surface it is a very positive, count-your-blessings-type song there is still some intangible bitterness. Perhaps fame was already starting to get to Dylan and he was finding out that when you reach the top you are on the bottom.

A further example of Dylan's contempt for judges is provided by "Percy's Song", a tune borrowed from Paul Clayton. In it Dylan portrays himself appealing to a judge to reconsider his decision to sentence a friend to ninety nine years after a fatal car crash in which he was the driver and only survivor. Eventually in the face of the judge's intransigence Dylan gives up but in attempting to console himself with his guitar finds that its sound only reflects his own melancholy. Dylan's harmonica playing on this track is incredibly good. He sings well too - it is an exquisite tune which tends to distract one from noticing how contrived and self-martyring the lyrics are in places. I would be interested to know whether Percy actually exists. If he does he must be pretty angry that the song never got on an official album - it is much better than "Hurricane".

Other high-spots on this tape are "Farewell", which is "The Leaving Of Liverpool" rearranged, and "Walkin' Down The Line". Each is respectively the best version available though possibly the "Another Side Of ..." out-take of "Farewell" would have beaten the Witmark Demo if it was not so short. Also very pleasant are "Gipsy Lou" and "I Shall Be Free" which contains a verse which the official album version does not have. The version here of "Eternal Circle" would have been easily the best one had Dylan not given it up after a couple of verses. It has a nice jangly guitar and the melody comes across far better than on the comparatively sterile "Times ..." out-take.

"Let Me Die In My Footsteps" also ends abruptly with Dylan commenting that 'it's so long ... it's not that long ... it's just that it's a drag ... I've sung it so many times.' "John Birch Society Blues" is another excellent song - easily the best of Dylan's talking blues numbers. This version lacks the edge and timing of the one on the original "Freewheelin' " but has an interesting addition in the form of a jokey reference to the politics of Albert Grossman, Dylan's manager.

The track that is probably *the* highspot of the tape is "Moonshine Blues", also known by a number of titles including "I've Been A Moonshiner" and "The Bottle Song". This performance is an absolute gem. Dylan has taken a traditional song, added some superb variations to the original tune and come up with a masterpiece of control, expression, melody and pathos that unequivocally *should* have been released officially. No-one could say Dylan cannot sing after hearing this.

On the other hand, "Mama, You Been On My Mind", although a highspot from a collector's point of view, is not the sort of thing you could play to anyone who does not appreciate Dylan and expect to convert them. The words are good, it is true, but the tune is non-existent. And yet Joan Baez's version on her "Farewell Angelina" album has a great tune. Admittedly she has Bruce Langthorne's brilliant guitar accompaniment to enhance it; just the same, either there is another Dylan version in existence or Joan Baez deserves some of the composing royalties.

It is a shame that the songs on this tape have wound up spattered across a whole load of bootlegs. There is a unity about the material and with careful selection you could produce either a very good double album or, if you creamed off only the very best stuff, a single album that would leave "Bob Dylan" and "Freewheelin' " standing.

THE WITMARK DEMOS   Mono   Date Recorded: 1963

Song Titles	Records on which appearing			
Farewell				Poems In Naked Wonder
Bob Dylan's Blues				"
Seven Curses	V.D. Waltz			
Paths Of Victory *1				
If I Could Do It All Over, I'd Do It All Over You	Ceremonies Of The Horsemen			
When The Ship Comes In	"			
The Times They Are A-Changin'	"			
John Brown	70 Dollar Robbery	The Demo Tapes *2	Bob Dylan Volume 1	
I Shall Be Free	"	"	"	Twenty Four
Hero Blues	"	"		
Tomorrow Is A Long Time	Dylan '62			
Walls Of Redwing	V.D. Waltz	"		"
Mama You Been On My Mind	"	"		
Ain't Gonna Grieve	Motorcycle	"		
Long Time Gone	Long Time Gone (2 EPs)	"		Poems In Naked Wonder
Long Ago, Far Away (Nowadays)	"	"		"
Let Me Die In My Footsteps	Dylan '62	"		"
Emmett Till	"	"		
Eternal Circle (fragment)	"			
Moonshine Blues	1000 Miles Behind		The Villager	Twenty Four
Paths Of Victory *1	V.D. Waltz			
John Birch Society Blues				Poems In Naked Wonder
Only A Hobo	Ceremonies Of The Horsemen			

*1 One of the versions of "Paths O: Victory" is reputed to be on an album of very dubious existence titled "Hear Me Holler"
*2 The 9 Witmark Demo tracks on "The Demo Tapes" were originally pressed onto a one sided promotional album by Warner Bros. Seven Arts in the UK
Continued...

THE WITMARK DEMOS (Continued)   Mono   Date Recorded: 1963

Song Titles	Records on which appearing		Bob Dylan Volume 3	Twenty Four	
		Seems Like A Freeze Out			
Whatcha Gonna Do					
Gypsy Lou	Help				
Baby Let Me Follow You Down				Twenty Four	Poems In Naked Wonder
A Hard Rain's A-Gonna Fall			Bob Dylan Volume 2	"	
Oxford Town	Ceremonies Of The Horsemen				
Don't Think Twice, It's All Right	"				"
Masters Of War					
Walking Down The Line					
Girl From The North Country					
Boots Of Spanish Leather					
Bob Dylan's Dream					
Hollis Brown					
Blowin' In The Wind					
Babe I'm In The Mood For You				"	
Guess I'm Doin' Fine				"	
Quit Your Low Down Ways				"	
Bound To Win	Dylan '62				
I'll Keep It With Mine	Help (double)		The Demo Tapes		
I'd Hate To Be You On That Dreadful Day			"		
Percy's Song	"			"	

NEW YORK TOWN HALL   Mono   PA tape   Date Recorded: April 1963

Song Titles	Records on which appearing			Zimmerman - Looking Back (double) *3	Best Of Great White Wonder	More Bob Dylan Greatest Hits *4
	While The Establishment Burns *1	Help (double)	Zimmerman - Live From The Berkeley Community Theater *2			
Ramblin' Down Through The World	While The Establishment Burns *1	Help (double)	Zimmerman - Live From The Berkeley Community Theater *2	Zimmerman - Looking Back (double) *3		
Bob Dylan's Dream	"	"	"	"		
Tomorrow Is A Long Time	"	"	"	"	Best Of Great White Wonder	More Bob Dylan Greatest Hits *4
New Orleans Rag	"	"	"	"	Wonder "	Are You Now Or Have You Ever Been? - (His Gotham Ingress)
Masters Of War						
Walls Of Redwing	"	"	"	"		
Hero Blues	"	"	"	"		
Who Killed Davey Moore?	"	"	"	"		
With God On Our Side	"	"	"	"		

*1 The quality of this album varies from copy to copy; also released as "Live At Town Hall"; there is also a version titled "Black Nite Crash" which was copied from the original album and is inferior quality with the last track on each side fading out
*2 Obviously this title was used in error; some versions are just called "Zimmerman"
*3 Also issued as two single albums
*4 Official Album

NEW YORK TOWN HALL

Apart from "Tomorrow Is A Long Time" Dylan's selection of material for this concert was diabolical. "Ramblin' Down Through The World" is just a big cliché set to the rather non-existent tune of "Born To Win" (see Witmark Demos) and seems about the most unrepresentative thing Dylan could do as an introduction.

"Bob Dylan's Dream" is better but he is nervous and wobbles on the long notes. Then comes "Tomorrow Is A Long Time" which, although is not his best rendering of it, is still a brilliant performance. Then when you think he is really getting going he does "New Orleans Rag" in a way which makes him sound like a repressed schoolboy. It is hard to find tangible vocal differences between this and the "Another Side Of ..." out-take which, with virtually identical lyrics, works perfectly. The stomping piano on the latter does great things for the song and he sounds older admittedly; but I think the essential trouble with this live version is that he sounds as if he is trying too hard to please the audience. In fact their applause indicates that they are pleased - maybe that explains why he is a legend and I am not.

"Masters Of War" is O.K. but it does tend to get just a shade monotonous. "Walls Of Redwing" is extremely monotonous and extremely long but temporary relief is provided by "Hero Blues" which is so terrible it is riveting. It sounds as though it was written very much as a piece of personal therapy after an encounter with a female chauvinist, but I think the subject was dealt with better in "I'm A Lover, Not A Fighter". "Hero Blues" definitely falls into the category of what Joan Baez called 'his crummy stuff'.

But worse is yet to come. We reach a climax of awfulness and monotony with one of the most bootlegged songs of all time, "Who Killed Davey Moore" All on one chord and nearly all on one note, this comes a close second to "John Brown" as Dylan's worst ever.

After this Dylan goes into "With God On Our Side". Rather a *long* song again but at least we are spared "John Brown" which would have been a fitting end.

Of course it is all very well me sitting here in the seventies criticising a one-dimensional picture of a concert that happened fourteen years ago. But what I am not experiencing listening to is the whole thing that must have been going on in 1963. 1963 was right in the middle of the genuine sixties, that brief period between about '61 and '65 that ended when the media seized hold of the expression 'swinging'. During that period a number of rigid pop traditions got eroded, people who were different became objects of interest rather than derision, and girls could not decide whether it was more shameful to be a virgin or not. The audience at this concert was right there with someone who was not just a symbol of it all, but positively one of the main agents of the change. The enthusiasm of the audience is genuine; it is not a hyped response. A lot of the music is weak, and Dylan's comments in between are nervously inane, but he is communicating with his audience on a very basic and friendly level.

Compare that to the '66 Albert Hall concert when the music was brilliant but sixties hype completely scrambled communication between Dylan and the audience.

STUDS TERKEL SHOW (FULL TITLE OF PROGRAMME: STUDS TERKEL'S WAX MUSEUM)

There are some good performances here but in between these the chat is extremely painful. Dylan has not yet acquired his technique for merciless despatch of interviewers and he does his best at first to answer Studs Terkel's embarrassingly intense tirade of questions seriously. As things progress Dylan's voice takes on a very slight send-up tone but it is all extremely polite and discreet.

One interesting point to come out of the interview is that Dylan emphasises that "Hard Rain" is not supposed to represent atomic rain - it is simply supposed to be symbolic of a general crunch that is coming. Dylan actually tries quite hard to avoid singing the song, suggesting that his host plays the record instead. But Mr. Terkel is not that silly and he finally gets the full, live five minutes' worth of "Hard Rain" straight from the horse's mouth.

Dylan also does a fairly brief "Blowin' In The Wind" plus a very nice, normal length version of "Boot Of Spanish Leather". "Farewell", the first song of the set is also neatly done but is spoiled by a contrivance in the middle where Dylan strums while Studs introduces his show.

Unfortunately "John Brown" and "Who Killed Davey Moore?" also rear their heads again here. "John Brown" is as terrible as usual but "Davey Moore" is actually a slight improvement on the other versions. It is now perhaps just a little too good to win the Eurovision Song Contest.

GREENWOOD MISSISSIPPI CIVIL RIGHTS RALLY

A tape of this only exists, as far as I know, as an extract from the "Don't Look Back" soundtrack. Although the latter is basically concerned with the '65 tour a flashback is included showing Dylan at Greenwood.

Some people think that Dylan's taking part in this rally is an indication that his later comments about protest never being anything more to him than a vehicle to success were bullshit, that the situation at the rally was potentially explosive and that Dylan was not only doing his career no good by attending, he was also taking a big personal risk.

I have no idea what the real situation was or whether Dylan's motives were connected with politics, altruism or publicity. From what I remember of the extract in "Don't Look Back", the whole thing appeared a bit sleepy, but perhaps that could have been deceptive.

"Only A Pawn In Their Game" was certainly a very good song to use on such an occasion. To describe white racialists as dim little ciphers being manipulated from above is much more of a put-down than calling them murderers or bigots. It must have taken quite a lot of courage to do the song, and especially to put it permanently on record. There was no guarantee that someone would not put the finger on Dylan as a result.

I should just point out that I could have got it wrong about this tape. The announcer in the "Songs Of Freedom" T.V. programme (see "Songs Of Freedom" - W.N.E.W.T.V. New York) alludes to Dylan at Greenwood as performing on the back of a lorry. There was a lorry in "Don't Look Back" but Dylan was not on the back of it.

SONGS OF FREEDOM -W.N.E.W.T.V. NEW YORK

The fact that this show was recorded in August '63 shows how much more quickly the American media got hold of folk than our own. All we

THE STUDS TERKEL SHOW W.F.M.T. CHICAGO   Mono   Date Recorded: May 1963

Song Titles	Records on which appearing
Farewell	
A Hard Rain's A-Gonna Fall	
Bob Dylan's Dream	Ode For Barbara Allen
Boots Of Spanish Leather	"
John Brown	
Who Killed Davey Moore?	
Blowin' In The Wind	"

Plus extensive chat

GREENWOOD MISSISSIPPI CIVIL RIGHTS RALLY   Mono (not on disc)
Date Recorded: July 1963

Song Title
Only A Pawn In Their Game (fragment)

had in 1963 were folk clubs with people singing songs about jugs of punch and going out one May morning. They were great pick-up places but not many people listened to the music.

This tape seem to have been recorded from a television through a microphone and is consequently fairly poor quality. But as far as one can judge Dylan does good jobs on both songs. Considering the amount of exposure "Blowin' In The Wind" got prior to and around this time it seems strange that Columbia did not release it as a single. Stranger still that when Peter Paul and Mary had a hit with it on another label Columbia did not try to cash in. They even let them get away with them doing "Don't Think Twice" as the follow-up apparently without a murmur of releasing the Dylan version. In fact, apart from the quickly withdrawn "Mixed Up Confusion"/"Corrina Corrina", there does not seem to have been a Dylan single released until 1965. Does one pay them the compliment of assuming this was policy, or was it just oversight?

WASHINGTON CIVIL RIGHTS MARCH

Whatever Dylan's motives for attending this rally were I cannot help but think that he must have been somewhat angry at the way his own performance went. He gets through one verse of "Pawn In Their Game" before a very enthusiastic and loud-voiced gentleman begins orating over the top of him. The oratory sounds less eloquent than the words of the song as well.

WASHINGTON CIVIL RIGHTS MARCH Mono Date Recorded: August 1963		
Song Title	Records on which appearing	
Only A Pawn In Their Game (fragment)	Dylan - (Don't) Look Back (triple) *1	We Shall Overcome *2
*1 Under title of "Ballad Of Edgar Meyers" (should be Medgar Evers) *2 Official Recording		

NEWPORT FOLK FESTIVAL 1963

These tracks are all officially available in the States, so they do not really come within this book's terms of reference. I have included them because the albums they are on are rather obscure and not available in this country except on import, and anyway the two duets are on several bootlegs.

"Playboys And Playgirls" is a catchy tune with words that are a war-cry against various exploitative groups including, apart from the playboys and playgirls, 'you fall-out shelter sellers', 'you red-baiters and red-haters' plus a few others, the American slang for which I cannot quite grasp. It is a good singalong song and Pete Seeger's duetting with Dylan works quite well.

Not so successful is the duet with Joan Baez on "With God On Our

SONGS OF FREEDOM W.N.E.W. TV, NEW YORK   Mono (not on disc)
Date Recorded: August 1963

Song Title
Blowin' In The Wind
Only A Pawn In Their Game

NEWPORT FOLK FESTIVAL 1963   Stereo PA tape   Date Recorded: July 1963

Song Titles	Records on which appearing					
	Bob Dylan In Concert Volume 2 *1	Dylan - (Don't) Look Back (triple)	Help	Newport EP *2	Newport Broadside *2	Evening Concerts At Newport Vol.1 *2
Ye Playboys & Playgirls Concert (with Pete Seeger)						
With God On Our Side (with Joan Baez)	"	"	"	"	"	"
Blowin' In The Wind				"		"

*1 "Bob Dylan In Concert Volumes 1 & 2" was copied & released as "Live Parts 1 & 2"
*2 Official recording

Side". I do not know what actually goes wrong but Joan Baez sounds horrifically off key. It is very out of character for her and I think it may be an audio-illusion created by some freak in the recording. It could even be that she has just been recorded too loud and the harmonies she is singing are simply overpowering the main melody. Anyway, when you add this to a guitar accompaniment that just goes drong drong drong drong without a single upstroke you get the effect of someone who is on page one of his Bert Weedon Guitar Tutor trying to teach his cat to sing. Still, the audience loved it and it is certainly not the worst thing on those Newport L.P.s.

"Blowin' In The Wind" is rather beautiful. It seems to have the entire Newport cast joining in and they are all doing their own thing harmony-wise. There is a couple of strong female voices, one of them I think Joan Baez's, that give the whole thing a real lump in the throat quality.

"THE TIMES THEY ARE A-CHANGIN' " OUT-TAKES

Conceivable additions to the songs listed as coming from the "Times ..." sessions are "Moonshine Blues", "Mama, You Been On My Mind" and the other version of "Percy's Song", which I reckon all come from the Witmark Demos but about which I could be wrong. Of course it is quite feasible that these belong to both tapes; there is no reason why Dylan should not have been able to pass tapes of out-takes to his music publisher.

This cannot apply to the disagreement about "California", "I'll Keep It With Mine" and "Lay Down Your Weary Tune". Some people think these are from the "Times ..." sessions but I am pretty sure they are "Another Side Of ..." out-takes, or were at least done around that time. The piano on the first two has an identical sound to the one on "Black Crow Blues" and the voice too on these sounds much more like his "Another Side Of ..." voice than his "Times ..." voice. "Lay Down Your Weary Tune" is harder to pin down because its sound does not particularly identify it with either session. But its lyrical content is so much more in keeping with the breakaway from protest of "Another Side Of ..." that if it did not actually come from those sessions it must almost certainly have been done after "Times ...",

Further confusion too surrounds "Paths Of Victory". Either there is another version of it which I have never heard or the "Times ..." out-take doubles as one of the Witmark Demos. In which case I really do not know, of the two Witmark versions, which one to plump for. The guitar accompanied one has the right sound but Dylan fluffs the words in one place; I would have thought that if it was from a pukka recording session he would have gone back and started again, but he just carries on. The version with the piano, on the other hand, is performed without a hitch but does not have the right sound. So for now I believe the guitar version as being the "Times ..." out-take on the basis that it could have been an initial run-through after which the song was either dropped or another, as yet undiscovered, take was done.

One other point of disagreement I should mention is that "The Cough Song" is often classified as a Broadside number. This is quite possible especially as it seems unlikely that Dylan would have considered putting what really is not much more than an instrumental doodle on an official album. Equally a mere instrumental doodle would hardly seem to be Broadside's scene either - in fact I should think Broadside would see it as somewhat decadent. Incidentally, I disagree with Greil Marcus and a number of other people that "The Cough Song" *is* "Nashville Skyline Rag". It is true there are similarities - they have a similar structure, comparable rhythms, and both are riffs as opposed to intricate compositions. But on that basis "Outlaw Blues" *is* "From A Buick 6".

Coming on to the tracks about which there is little doubt as to source, the "Times ....." out-take of "Only A Hobo" is probably the best version of the song - the best Dylan version anyway. In the majority of cases, as C.B.S. told us around 1967, 'nobody sings Dylan like Dylan'. "Only A Hobo" is perhaps one of the few exceptions in that being a very simple song it benefited considerably from the relatively complex backing it got on Rod Stewart's version. I quite like this version by Dylan though - in spite of its sounding like Dylan imitating Neil Innes imitating Dylan.

I do not think anyone could beat the version here of "Percy's Song". The Witmark demo version is excellent but this one goes just that bit further. Apart from a more gently played guitar two refinements seem responsible for this. The first is to the melody: in the third line of each verse there is a chord change from C to F on the penultimate word (or in some cases the penultimate two syllables). On the Witmark version the word is sung on just two notes, one for each syllable. But on the "Times ..." out-take the word, while remaining the same length, covers six notes. The four extra ones are simply a very quick melodic squiggle added to the first syllable, but the effect is superb. It is not exactly the same with each verse - sometimes Dylan varies it deliberately and sometimes it just does not work quite as well - but the squiggle and its variations make what was already a good tune into a great one. Of course it is possible that these embellishments were already in the tune when Dylan borrowed it from Paul Clayton. In which case the above is an example of how you can mess up a tune by taking out its squiggles.

The other refinement is one of diction: the final line of each verse ends with the word 'wind'. On the Witmark version Dylan pronounces 'wind' much as anyone else would. But on the "Times ..." version he pronounces it 'whhhind'. It is incredible the way this little contrivance amplifies the pathos.

As to the reasons why "Percy's Song" did not go on the album it may be that the story is half truth and half fiction and could have caused legal problems. Or it could be that, having already taken the tune for "Don't Think Twice" from Paul Clayton, Dylan decided to draw the line at doing it again. Or it could simply be that it was considered too long. It *is* a good seven minutes and, alongside "Hollis Brown", "With God On Our Side" and "Hattie Carroll", which were themselves outrageously lengthy for 1963, it might have made the album too much of a marathon to listen to.

"Eternal Circle" was presumably omitted from the album because it is not very good. At least, this version is not. The snatch Dylan did on the Witmark tape is excellent but the song just seems to have dried up by the time it got to the "Times ....." sessions, unless there is yet another version. Scaduto reckons there is, but so far I have not come across any evidence of it.

A song that should have been included on the album without any qualms is "Seven Curses". It is just *so* good - the words and tune combine to hit something I just cannot define. "Seven Curses" explains *why* people collect unofficial Dylan material.

Chile Benefit, Felt Forum, New York City, 1974. Left to right:
Melanie, Phil Ochs, Dylan, and Jack Elliott. (Photo by Chuck Pulin)

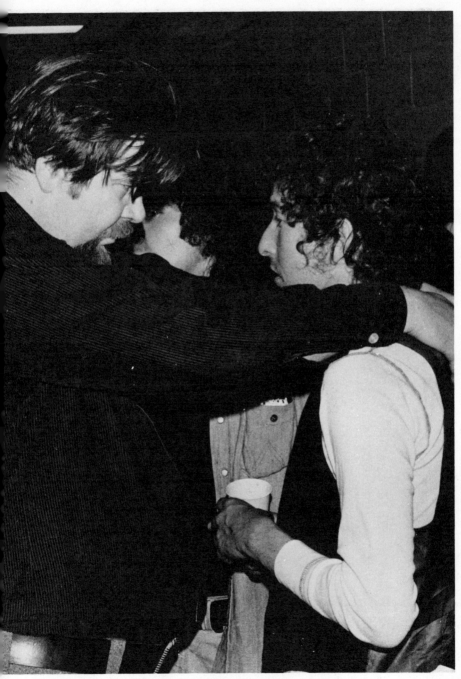

Dave Van Ronk and Dylan backstage at the Felt Forum, 1974.
(Photo by Chuck Pulin)

THE TIMES THEY ARE A-CHANGIN' OUT-TAKES   Mono
Date Recorded: August–October 1963

Song Titles	Records on which appearing						
	Great White Wonder Part 2	Dylan - (Don't) Look Back (triple)	John Birch Society Blues	At Home			
Eternal Circle							
Percy's Song	"	"	"	"			Help (double)
Paths Of Victory							
Only A Hobo	Great White Wonder (dble & single)	Twenty Four	Bob Dylan Volume 1	"			
Seven Curses		V.D. Waltz					
The Cough Song	Stealin'	And Now Your Mouth Cries Whoops	Bob Dylan Volume 2				

CARNEGIE HALL CONCERT

This is very much of an improvement on the New York Town Hall concert of six months earlier, though "John Brown" and "Davey Moore" have still not been exorcised from the act. As at the Town Hall concert, in spite of his nervousness he establishes a rapport with the audience who react very enthusiastically, especially to the protest stuff.

There are two unique things in the set, one of them is a song with, to my mind, a title that is attractive in itself - "Dusty Old Fairgrounds". Unfortunately, the song is not really up to much; one of the disappointing things is that it really is about dusty old fairgrounds - a whole list of them. Dylan introduces it as a route song and that is just what it is - an itinerary set to music. The tune sounds as though it is either going to evolve into something better or it is already a basically good tune that Dylan happens to be doing one of his leave-out-the-subtleties jobs on.

The other unique item is "Last Thoughts On Woody Guthrie", an eight-minute poem which Dylan recites at break-neck pace after explaining that he has been asked to provide a brief piece for a book on Woody Guthrie. He asks the audience to bear with him because he has not managed to stick to the original terms of reference, and indeed he has not. The last line of the poem's many lines is definitely about Guthrie; whether the rest of the poem, which takes the form of an inventory of hassles, is about him is difficult to say.

"Lay Down Your Weary Tune" must also have been very unfamiliar ground for the audience and probably had not long been written. The rendering here is fairly gentle and restrained compared to the studio version (see "Another Side Of ..." Out-takes) but both are equally good. "Percy's Song" is nicely done too, with Dylan opting for putting that superb squiggle in the third line. And in defence, or at least mitigation, of his tune stealing I should point out that in introducing the song he does mention that he took the melody from Paul Clayton.

"Seven Curses" is the last song on the tape; it is another efficient rendering but does not quite reach the immaculate standard of the "Times ..." out take. The audience must have been very disappointed that it did not appear on the next album just the same.

An error often made about this concert is that "New Orleans Rag" was included. This error arose because Columbia recorded the concert for a live album and then in the editing inserted the New York Town Hall version of "New Orleans Rag". The album was not released but did get as far as going on an acetate. A tape of this escaped and was later used to produce the bootleg album.

As to why Columbia did not release the album, it seems likely that "Last Thoughts On Woody Guthrie" was seen as too much of a risk. This could be one of the instances in which Columbia was right.

THE STEVE ALLEN SHOW

Although Steve Allen is painfully over-the-top in introducing Dylan here I do find it admirable the way he pursues Dylan and pins him down over his typically ambiguous introduction to "Hattie Carroll".

Dylan says something to the effect that he got the story from the newspapers and only changed the words. Instead of pretending to understand what he means, as a lot of people, including myself, would have done, Steve Allen says 'what do you mean - you just changed the

CARNEGIE HALL CONCERT   Mono PA tape   Date Recorded: October 1963

Song Titles	Records on which appearing		
When The Ship Comes In	Are You Now Or Have You Ever Been? - (His Gotham Ingress)		
John Brown	"		
Who Killed Davey Moore?	1000 Miles Behind / Best Of Great White Wonder	Great White Wonder Part 2 / John Birch Society Blues	Twenty Four / Dylan - (Don't) Look Back (triple) / At Home
Last Thoughts On Woody Guthrie (poem)	Are You Now Or Have You Ever Been? - (His Gotham Ingress)		
Lay Down Your Weary Tune	"		
Dusty Old Fairgrounds	"	Seems Like A Freeze Out	Dusty Old Fairgrounds
Percy's Song	"		
Seven Curses	"		

words?'. He does not actually get a very satisfactory answer, but it is a good try.

The rendering of the song itself by Dylan is not nearly as good as the album version. It lacks the control and, instead of moving between sadness and anger, comes across as just bad-tempered. It is still good - it gets a properly enthusiastic response from the audience - but it just does not stand up next to the perfection of the "Times ..." version.

One dubiously unique item in the programme is Steve Allen's recitation of the poem about Hibbing on the back of the "Times ..." cover. Ostensibly done on the spur of the moment, a piano accompaniment creeps in after a few lines with timing that is immaculate. It is not quite as bad as you might think. Better than "Three Angels".

STEVE ALLEN TV SHOW   Mono (not on disc) Date Recorded: February 1964
Song Title
The Lonesome Death Of Hattie Carroll (plus chat)

"ANOTHER SIDE OF BOB DYLAN" OUT-TAKES

There is some beautiful stuff here. In fact everything on this tape has something to recommend it, with the exception perhaps of "East Laredo" which is an apparently semi-improvised piano solo of Mexican flavour played extremely badly. It seems to be practically accepted as a fact that by the end of the "Another Side..." sessions Dylan had consumed something in the region of two bottles of Beaujolais, and one imagines that "East Laredo" might have been his final gesture before the day caught up with him.

But it was a brilliant day. Around twenty tracks recorded, many of them classics, and that is just the ones we know about. It illustrates that the use of the word 'genius' in referring to Dylan is not just something that has arisen out of the semantic excesses of pop journalism - it is a fair enough description to use in relation to a large portion of his work.

"New Orleans Rag" is not a work of genius but the versions here are good, vital, thumping music. The first take lasts for little more than a verse, but just in that time a whole atmosphere is set up. Even so, it is completely eclipsed by the second take which, with the aid of a rollicking, stomping piano, simply becomes a first class rock number (which is perhaps why it was left off the album). The lyrics are about a young man having his mind changed about visiting a lady of pleasure when he sees the string of shattered individuals emerging from her place of business. It is the sort of thing that could easily not have worked - it did not work at the New York Town Hall concert - but something intangible, perhaps the genuinely stoned tone of Dylan's voice, makes this version a hundred per cent successful down to the brilliant harmonica imitation of a man out of breath which ends it.

Although there are two versions of "Denise Denise" listed on the chart these are in fact one and the same performance. The difference between them is simply that one has maraccas dubbed on and one does not. It is possible that these are official Columbia maraccas but they could equally belong to an anonymous collector wishing to cause a little ripple among other collectors. The song itself is not that good but again it gets some sort of zest just from the pervasive vitality in Dylan's voice.

I do not know if "That's Alright Mama" was ever intended by Dylan to be an album track, and I do not know if Columbia would have allowed it anyway at that time, not being self penned. But the piano on it is remarkable - very unusual both rhythmically and simply in the order of the notes. The most analogous music I can think of would be parts of the soundtrack of "Spartacus" where they used what the sleeve notes claimed to be genuine ancient Roman rhythms. The effect with Dylan's performance here is that he seems to be continually teetering on the verge of breaking rhythm and blowing the whole thing. It is an inspired accompaniment for a very standard sort of song. It is a pity he did not use it for one of his own songs, though possibly he found later that he had forgotten how to play it.

"California" seems to be generally acknowledged as the prototype for "Outlaw Blues", especially as it contains a whole verse which wound up as part of the latter. Just the same, it can still be judged on its own merit, which is that with the combination of droll lyrics, thumping piano and the general sound of the "Another Side..." sessions it is an effective and entertaining number.

But everything pales before "I'll Keep It With Mine". Rolling Stone said this was written for Nico but I never understood whether they meant written for her to sing or that she was the girl in the song. Anyway, if Dylan was gentleman enough to leave the song off his own album in order that Nico could have exclusive rights to it that would certainly indicate that the numerous tales of his stepping all over other people to advance his career are not necessarily representative unless Dylan really did not realise how brilliant the song was.

To my mind it is the best song in the entire session, possibly the best thing he had written up to that point. It is performed perfectly too - even in the introduction where the piano momentarily loses the rhythm is perfect in its own way. And the lyrics form the least patronising way I have yet heard of saying 'I'm older than you - therefore I know better'.

The tune is exquisite. And it is exploited to its fullest extent by Dylan's superb singing and the way the piano and the voice change each other's roles from time to time. The whole thing is magnificent - Columbia should have made it public property years ago.

"Lay Down Your Weary Tune" is not in the same class but it is still an exceptional song. It is also an important song in the context of Dylan's rejection of protest. The lyrics are reminiscent in sentiment of "Chimes Of Freedom" in so far as they express awe at the beauty of nature. But this time Dylan compares the sounds of nature with vain strivings of composers and musicians, presumably such as himself. Ironically, but also imperatively I suppose, the song has a really good tune. It is slightly hymn-like, which is of course entirely appropriate, but it leaves one with the impression that it could be another of Dylan's borrowed jobs. Maybe not - either way it is a great song.

Another song which Dylan possibly did at these sessions is "Mama, You Been On My Mind". It is not included in the chart because the only Dylan version around seems to fit more convincingly in with the Witmark

ANOTHER SIDE OF BOB DYLAN OUT-TAKES   Mono   Date Recorded: June 1964

Song Titles	Records on which appearing									
	Great White Wonder (double only)	Bob Dylan Volume 2	Bob Dylan Volume 1	And Now Your Mouth Cries Whoops	Daddy Rolling Stone	Dylan - (Don't) Look Back (triple)	At Home	Best Of Great White Wonder	Help (double)	Bob Dylan - A Rare Batch Of Little White Wonder Volume 3
New Orleans Rag (fragment)	Stealin'									
New Orleans Rag (complete)										
Denise Denise *	Let Me Die In My Footsteps				Walking Down The Line					
Denise Denise (with maraccas) *										
That's Alright Mama (+ snatch of "Sally Free And Easy")	Great White Wonder Part 2	"		"	"	"		"		"
California (Goin' Down South)	The Villager	Seems Like A Freeze Out	Twenty Four					Best Of Great White Wonder		"
I'll Keep It With Mine	Great White Wonder Part 2	John Birch Society Blues		Joaquin Antique	"		At Home	"		"
East Laredo (East Laredo Blues)	"	"		Billion Dollar Bash						
Farewell									Help (double)	
Lay Down Your Weary Tune	The Villager	Seems Like A Freeze Out		"	"					"

* One of the versions of "Denise Denise" is reputed to be on an album of dubious existence titled "Hear Me Holler"

Demos. Possibly that is a mistake but, on the other hand, it is not unlikely that another tape exists that has not escaped from Columbia. As, indeed, it is not unlikely that the material listed in this book is simply the tip of the iceberg.

NEWPORT FOLK FESTIVAL 1964

So far "All I Really Want To Do" seems to be the only song to have surfaced from Newport '64. There is not a lot to say about it really. It is a great song, Dylan does it cheerfully and well, and the audience is appreciative. Maybe not as appreciative as they would have been to, say, "God On Our Side", (apparently "Another Side Of Bob Dylan" was considered by some folk freaks at the time of its release to be frivolous and unacceptable) but as this is the only track on the tape it is hard to judge.

The latter observation is in fact rendered redundant if you accept the recent claim by some collectors that "All I Really Want To Do" does not come from Newport '64 at all but Newport '65. Although it is acknowledged that it certainly did not form part of Dylan's main set in '65 it is reckoned that he may have performed it the previous day when a lot of the performers were doing one-off bits and pieces. At present I cannot find enough evidence to support this, so I am leaving it under '64.

NEWPORT FOLK FESTIVAL 1964 Mono PA tape Date Recorded: July 1964	
Song Title	Record on which appearing
All I Really Want To Do	St. Valentine's Day Massacre And More

JOAN BAEZ CONCERT, FOREST HILLS Mono Audience tape (not on disc) Date Recorded: August 1964
Song Titles
Mama/Daddy You Been On My Mind It Ain't Me Babe With God On Our Side

HALLOWEEN CONCERT 1964

Dylan was in very playful mood for this concert - there is none of the nervousness of the Carnegie Hall Concert of a year previously and as a result the whole thing is much more of an entertainment. In his whimsical raps he mocks a variety of things including his own songs; but he maintains a healthy respect for the audience and it is always he and they laughing together, never at each other.

The performances themselves are mostly very good - it is the "Another Side" voice and it moves from pathos to jokeyness while hardly seeming to change. Something that really works well is "John Birch Society Blues" done à la "I Shall Be Free Number 10". Dylan introduces it as "John Birch Paranoid Blues" and slips in various lyric changes which make for a nice sense of spontaneity.

The jokeyness in the voice is perfect also for "If You Gotta Go, Go Now", a song that was possibly getting its first public airing and which was quite controversial at the time. Strangely enough even when Manfred Mann had a hit with it in England there was never any fuss compared to the storm over the Stones' "Let's Spend The Night Together". Presumably "If You Gotta Go, Go Now" sounded like an ordinary pop title and so the repression brigade did not bother to seek it out and listen to it. Anyway, the Philharmonic audience obviously appreciated it. The applause is loud and the humour meets with guffaws rather than chuckles.

Another event which causes much amusement is where Dylan forgets the first line of "I Don't Believe You". He plays the introduction and then just keeps strumming. After a while he stops and says: 'Oh God ... here's the second verse of it ..... hey, does anybody know the first verse of this song?' Somebody in the audience yells out the first line and then he gets going. Pretty cool, you must admit.

More apparently spontaneous lyric changes occur in "World War III Blues", though the one trouble with such lyric re-vamps is that the verses that Dylan does not change make for a slight anti-climax. Just the same, by this time he could not really go wrong with the audience - they are right there with him whatever he says or does. In fact the only point in the concert where the audience is a little unsure how to react is earlier on when in introducing "Who Killed Davey Moore?" Dylan says 'This is ... er... this is a song about a boxer ... a boxer ... it's got nothing to do with boxing, it's just a song about a boxer ... (laughs) and ... er ... (laughs) ... it's ... er ... it's not even have anything to do with a boxer really ... it's got nothin' to do with *nothin'* ... (sniggers) ...well, I put all these words together - that's all ... this is ... er ... taken out of the newspapers ... nothing has been changed except the words.'

One wonders if Dylan felt a need to put the song down because of his move away from protest. On the other hand neither "Hattie Carroll" nor "Hard Rain" comes in for the same treatment, so perhaps he was just feeling negative about that particular song. Why he bothered to include it at all, when its lack of merit is only highlighted by the quality of the rest of the music, is hard to understand. Perhaps Dylan, or even more likely Grossman, his manager, felt that there had to be a couple of very specific protest songs in the set as opposed to songs of general protest like "The Times They Are A-Changin' ".

Towards the end of the concert Dylan calls Joan Baez on to the stage. She does "Silver Dagger" with Dylan on harmonica and they do three numbers as duets. As at Newport '63, musically it does not seem to harmonise and their timing is seldom synchronised. But the vibes of the whole thing are tremendous. The audience is obviously pleased that Joan Baez is there and the emotional rapport between her and Dylan is very evident but at the same time does not exclude anyone.

It is a very refreshing concert throughout but for me *the* most refreshing specific thing is Dylan's comment in response to someone in the audience yelling out a request. Having much sympathy with how insurance clerks, car assembly workers, supermarket check-out girls and various other people must feel when they read performers moaning in the music press about what a hard life it is being a superstar, it is gratifying to hear Dylan say: 'I'll do anything ... hope I never have to make a living'.

HALLOWEEN CONCERT, PHILHARMONIC HALL,
NEW YORK   Stereo PA tape
Date Recorded: October 31, 1964

Song Titles	Records on which appearing	
The Times They Are A-Changin'	All Hallows Eve 1964	
Spanish Harlem Incident	"	
Talkin' John Birch Society Blues	"	Basics In G Minor (EP)
To Ramona	"	
Who Killed Davey Moore?	"	Snack
Gates Of Eden	"	
If You Gotta Go, Go Now	"	
It's Alright Ma (I'm Only Bleeding)	"	
I Don't Believe You	"	
Mr. Tambourine Man	"	
A Hard Rain's A-Gonna Fall	"	
Talkin' World War III Blues	"	
Don't Think Twice, It's All Right	"	
The Lonesome Death Of Hattie Carroll	"	
Mama You Been On My Mind *1	"	Basics In G Minor (EP)
Silver Dagger *2		
With God On Our Side *1	"	
It Ain't Me Babe *1	"	"
All I Really Want To Do	"	Snack

*1 Plus Joan Baez
*2 Joan Baez - vocal, Bob Dylan - harmonica

SAN JOSE AUDITORIUM, CALIFORNIA
Mono Audience tape·(not on disc)
Date Recorded: November 1964

Song Titles
Gates Of Eden
If You Gotta Go, Go Now
It's Alright Ma (I'm Only Bleeding)
World War III Blues
Don't Think Twice, It's All Right
Mama/Daddy You Been On My Mind (with Joan Baez)

BERKELEY UNIVERSITY, CALIFORNIA
Mono Audience tape (not on disc)
Date Recorded: November 1964

Song Titles
The Times They Are A-Changin'
Talkin' John Birch Society Blues
To Ramona
Gates Of Eden
If You Gotta Go, Go Now
It's Alright Ma (I'm Only Bleeding)
Mr. Tambourine Man
A Hard Rain's A-Gonna Fall
World War III Blues
Don't Think Twice, It's All Right

"BRING IT ALL BACK HOME" OUT-TAKES

It is interesting that in the poem on the "Bring It All Back Home" sleeve Dylan says he has given up making any attempt at perfection. Assuming that he recorded the officially released version of "She Belongs To Me" - a performance that was totally and utterly perfect - before he wrote the poem then these session out-takes bear out what he is saying.

The best example is "Love Minus Zero". The out-take is not as polished as the version that was released, either from the point of view of Dylan's singing or of Bruce Langthorne's guitar work - in fact it sounds like a try-out for both of them. But the point is that it is more tuneful than the final version. And if Dylan had been more of a perfectionist he would have presumably gone on and done a third take - this time combining maximum tunefulness with maximum polish, unless of course to his taste the tune of the released version was the better one.

The out-take of "It's All Over Now, Baby Blue" indicates that this could well be the case. It indicates in fact that Dylan's tastes in melody at the time may have been positively perverse, because the out-take is just much better tunewise than the released version. Whereas on the latter the first two lines of each verse are not much more than a one note shout tapering down the scale at the end, the same lines on the out-take start working their way down the scale much earlier on and do so much more melodiously. Admittedly there is no trace of the Langthorne guitar on the out-take, but dubbing that on would not have been a problem. The only reason I can think of as to why the other take was used is that those first two lines, while less tuneful, are very distinctive merely on the basis of the raucous way they are put across. It is possibly relevant that the song books quote the lyrics exactly as they are on the out-take while the lyrics of the released version differ slightly from the song books. This would indicate that the inclusion on the album of the latter rather than the former was a last minute decision.

As I have implied, I have no arguments over "She Belongs To Me" - the released version is superior in every way to the out-take. But it is still fair to say that the out-take is brilliant. It loses a lot from not having that typewriter drum which graces the released version, but the vocal is excellent and so too is Bruce Langthorne's guitar which is slightly more rhythm orientated here and provides a loping-along effect in between each vocal line. It is beautiful guitar work - but again Langhorne just does not quite attain the perfection he gets on the final take. Specifically he does not achieve the climax that he gets on the latter - that superb phrase just before the start of the second line of the final verse where the guitar goes up in a manner that heralds that this *has* to be the last verse.

Bruce Langhorne was obviously a very important factor all round in the coming about of "Bringing It All Back Home". Apart from adding dimensions to every song he played on he is very much a symbol of Dylan's first major steps towards electric music. "Bringing It All Back Home" was not quite an electric album. While certainly a risky proposition to put before purists, it was still just about categoriseable as folk music. And this is the only reason I can think of why "If You Gotta Go, Go Now" was omitted. It just could not be seen as folk, regardless of the way Dylan was doing it at concerts the studio version is outright rock. It was released in Europe as a single but not until over two years after it was recorded. The first single to include electric instruments apart from "Mixed Up Confusion"/"Corrina Corrina" which was withdrawn soon after release, was "Subterranean Homesick Blues", which itself received a dubious response from folk fans but which slipped through because it could be considered a protest song and had easily audible acoustic guitar.

All extremely silly. If "If You Gotta Go, Go Now" had been included on "Bringing It All Back Home" it would have made a brilliant L.P. even better.

THE LES CRANE SHOW

This tape is a great disappointment - not from the point of view of Dylan's performance or of the sound quality but of Bruce Langhorne's accompaniment. Before I had heard it, when I read that Bruce Langhorne was on not only "Baby Blue" but "It's Alright Ma" as well, I thought how can you fit an electric guitar into "It's Alright Ma"? It must be amazing.

In reality it sounds as if Dylan suggested the idea of Langhorne doing the accompaniment about ten seconds before the programme started, and then moved his capo up a fret when Langhorne was not looking. It literally sounds as though they are each playing different songs.

"Baby Blue" is a trifle better. Langhorne tries a countryish approach, totally different from the album version. Given some rehearsal it might have worked quite well but as it stands it is too halting and tentative to be a positive contribution. In fact from time to time he gives up and reverts to the album arrangement, but sallies forth again after a few bars. It just does not seem possible that someone who made such a stupendous contribution to "Bringing It All Back Home" could play as badly as this.

As to the chat, Dylan is now on the way into his 'interviews as an art-form' period. Les Crane is not what you would call an intellectual and he tends to get a little demolished. Mind you, he does latch on. When he asks Dylan what he spends his money on and Dylan replies 'boots, bananas, fruit and pears,' it is clear he does not believe him.

Towards the end of the tape it becomes apparent that there are other people in the chat circle, and these include Tommy Sands, quite well known in the late fifties as a pop singer - now turned actor. They are all actually very tolerant of the fact that Dylan is getting all the laughs but I really feel for Tommy Sands when, on suggesting that Dylan could have a film career ahead of him, Dylan responds that he is already making a film in a subway tunnel with a script by Allen Ginsberg in which he plays his mother.

LES CRANE SHOW W.A.B.C. TV, NEW YORK
Mono (not on disc)
Date Recorded: February 1965

Song Titles
It's All Over Now Baby Blue (with Bruce Langhorne)
It's Alright Ma (I'm Only Bleeding)   "

Plus extensive chat

DON'T LOOK BACK (BACK-STAGE DOCUMENTARY ON THE '65 TOUR, MADE BY D.A.PENNEBAKER)

There is an entire book devoted to stills and dialogue from this film. The film is now unavailable and so is the book. The latter quotes one critic's opinion of the film as '... the neighbourhood brat blowing his nose for ninety minutes'. Of course the person who said that could have been one of the journalists psychologically maimed by Dylan in the film.

It is a very entertaining film - very funny in places and, as far as it is possible to tell, very impartial in the picture it draws of Dylan. In one way it is hard to understand how it was ever approved by Dylan and/or Grossman. Dylan does come over as pretty much of a slob. Not even a consistent slob - he gives much kinder responses to the naive questions of the attractive female journalist (Maureen Cleave, I think) than he does to the naive questions of the middle-aged male journalists.

The classic scene of the film for me is Dylan's reply when the individual who is supposed to have thrown a glass manages, during the verbal machine-gunning Dylan's giving him, to get in the bitter little interjection: 'You're a big noise - you know?'. 'I know it, man - I *know* I'm a big noise!' replies our Bobby.

The film is not really about music. There are no complete songs as such and what there is is fairly standard stuff. Unique items are restricted to sing-alongs of "Lost Highway" and "I'm So Lonesome I Could Cry". At the time the Joan Baez hotel room rendering of "Love Is Just A Four Letter Word" was quite a bonus but it has now been superceded by a couple of complete versions by her. I suppose you could say that Dylan playing the typewriter while Joan Baez sings "Percy's Song" (beautifully) is unique but then as far as Dylan's contribution goes, you might as *well* have a recording of him blowing his nose.

CIVIC AUDITORIUM, LOS ANGELES
Mono Audience tape (not on disc)
Date Recorded: April 1965

Song Titles

To Ramona
Gates Of Eden
If You Gotta Go, Go Now
It's Alright Ma (I'm Only Bleeding)
Love Minus Zero/No Limit
Mr. Tambourine Man
Don't Think Twice, It's All Right
With God On Our Side
She Belongs To Me
It Ain't Me Babe
The Lonesome Death Of Hattie Carroll
All I Really Want To Do
It's All Over Now Baby Blue

B.B.C. BROADCAST

I remember watching the two programmes they split this set-up into and feeling undecided about what I thought of them. Dylan was really mute. During the entire hour the only thing he said, apart from a straight introduction to "Boots Of Spanish Leather", was just before "It's Alright Ma" when he mumbled 'This is called "It's Alright Ma - I'm Only Bleeding" - Ho ho ho. It's a funny song'.

The performances are good but not as good as the American concerts of the previous few months or, the '65 Albert Hall concert. Half the trouble, I think, was the studio set-up; the B.B.C. had what they called a 'specially invited audience' - about a hundred people sitting there 'taking this talented young man extremely seriously'. It was not their fault - they probably felt as screwed up by the situation as Dylan did.

DON'T LOOK BACK   Mono tape from projector
Most of film made during May 1965

Song Titles	Source	Record on which appearing
All I Really Want To Do	Unknown, May 1965	
Only A Pawn In Their Game	Greenwood, Mississippi, Civil Rights Rally, July 1963	
The Times They Are A-Changin' (2 fragments)	Sheffield, May 1965	Don't Look Back
To Ramona	"	"
The Lonesome Death Of Hattie Carroll	Leicester, May 1965	"
Percy's Song *1	Nottingham Hotel, May 1965	
Love Is Just A Four Letter Word *1	"	
Lost Highway *2	"	"
I'm So Lonesome I Could Cry	"	"
Unknown song (piano & just audible vocal)	Unknown, May 1965	"
Don't Think Twice, It's All Right	Newcastle, May 1965	"
Piano solo	London Hotel, May 1965	"
To Sing For You *3	"	"
It's All Over Now Baby Blue	"	"
The Times They Are A-Changin'	Royal Albert Hall, May 1965	"
Talkin' World War III Blues	"	"
It's Alright Ma (I'm Only Bleeding)	"	"
Gates Of Eden	"	"
Love Minus Zero/No Limit	"	"

*1 Joan Baez only
*2 Bob Dylan with Joan Baez and others
*3 Donovan
There are also extracts from the "Bringing It All Back
Home" LP, but as this is an official album these are not
included in the chart. A certain amount of conjecture has
been involved in establishing some of the sources above;
thus some may be incorrect.
All tracks are fragments.

I am trying to remember what my reaction was to Dylan's actual appearance. I was quite impressed by the fact that he was the only performer around who did not have a variation on the Beatle hair style and he had this terrible Italian suit on if I remember rightly - the sort Burtons were selling for twelve pounds in the late fifties.

I watched one of the programmes at a party and the people there provided a fairly typical cross section of attitudes towards Dylan. Some people thought Dylan was very good, some thought he wrote good songs

ROYAL ALBERT HALL Mono Audience tape Date Recorded: May 1965		
Song Titles	Records on which appearing	
The Times They Are A-Changin' *		
To Ramona		
Gates Of Eden *		Long Time Gone (EPs)
If You Gotta Go, Go Now	Bob Dylan In Concert Volume 2	"
Mr. Tambourine Man	"	"
Talkin' World War III Blues *		
Don't Think Twice, It's All Right		
With God On Our Side		
She Belongs To Me		
It Ain't Me Babe		
The Lonesome Death Of Hattie Carroll		
All I Really Want To Do		
It's All Over Now Baby Blue		
It's Alright Ma (I'm Only Bleeding) *		
Love Minus Zero/No Limit *		
* A tape of partially PA quality of fragments of these songs exists in the form of the soundtrack of the film "Don't Look Back" (see previous chart)		

but 'he should leave other people to sing them' and a few got disproportionately angry about him. I think some people felt threatened by Dylan in the same way that a lot of our parents' generation felt threatened by Jagger.

BBC BROADCAST   Mono
Date Recorded: June 1965

Song Titles	Records on which appearing	
Hollis Brown	BBC Broadcast	
Mr. Tambourine Man	"	
Gates Of Eden	"	Help (double)
If You Gotta Go, Go Now	"	" (incomplete)
The Lonesome Death Of Hattie Carroll	"	
It Ain't Me Babe	"	
Love Minus Zero/No Limit	"	
One Too Many Mornings	"	
Boots Of Spanish Leather	"	
It's Alright Ma (I'm Only Bleeding)	"	
She Belongs To Me	"	
It's All Over Now, Baby Blue	"	

THE "HELP" TAPE (Reputedly with the Beatles)   Mono
Date Recorded: Reputedly 1965

Song Title	Records on which appearing			
Help	Help *	Long Time Gone (EPs)	Basics In G Minor	Help (double)

* On two different single albums of this title; the existence of one of them is uncertain

This tape is almost certainly neither Dylan nor the Beatles

Coming back to the performances, they are only not outstanding in relation to some of Dylan's other performances. If this was the only tape of Dylan that anyone had, his brilliance would still be obvious from it. The harmonica is even above average in places, especially on "One Too Many Mornings" which is very good all round.

But regardless of the precise standard of the performances, somewhere or other there is the original film of this and it is a piece of history. So why have not the B.B.C. filled up a Whistle Test with it? Is there one of these long-arm Dylan management bars on showing it? Have they lost it, destroyed it or has it simply not occurred to them that some people might like to see it again? After all they repeated Elton John in concert.

MIAMI SALES CONFERENCE MESSAGE/JOHN MAYALL SESSION MAY 1965

Rumours around for a long time of an extensive session with John Mayall's Band (including Eric Clapton) have now been clarified by the gentleman who engineered the session. He tells us that a session lasting some five hours did indeed take place in May 1965 in C.B.S.'s Bond Street studio but that no complete tracks were laid down - just a large number of intros and incomplete attempts, during many of which the tape was not even rolling. Of the material recorded only the sales message and a snatch of "If You Gotta Go, Go Now" have found their way into circulation. Following the session the tapes seem to have gone straight back to the States.

According to the engineer, one of the main reasons for the session not getting off the ground was that Dylan did not seem keen to be there at all. It appears that the presence of a lady singer in the studio was influencing his mood more towards the endocrinal than the cerebral. It also seems that the position of the piano caused considerable angst with Dylan repeatedly ordering it to be moved from one side of the studio to the other.

The short tape in circulation is not unamusing. It comes in at the point where somebody is asking Dylan to do the sales message again and Dylan responding that has forgotten what he said. Upon being reminded what he said he rejoins, 'No, I didn't say that - you said that.' After some argument he manages to lay down an uncharacteristically trite message to the effect of, 'Thanks for selling so many of my records - please keep it up.'

Then comes the attempt at "If You Gotta Go, Go Now". Dylan does a one-two-three count-in but all that is forthcoming is the sardonic comment from a member of the band, "Do it in tune!", and from another, in a Lancashire accent, 'You haven't worked much with bands, have you?' To this Dylan replies, 'I won't take a count, you start... I'll come in.' They eventually get going but the fragment they play is not what you would call tight and there is no trace of Mayall or Clapton. After one verse Dylan yells, 'We'll fade it here - *fade it out* - FADE IT OUT!' There is a little more argument with the control room and then that's it.

"HIGHWAY 61 REVISITED" OUT-TAKES

I think Rolling Stone referred to "Highway 61 Revisited" as 'the album that changed the world'. Absolutely right - even if Tony Palmer does think it was Donovan and the Byrds who were responsible for the lyric revolution of the mid-sixties. Leaving Dylan out of "All You Need Is Love" was a bit like making a film about the Bible and writing Jesus Christ out of the script.

BRINGING IT ALL BACK HOME OUT-TAKES   Mono   Date Recorded: December 1964

Song Titles	Records on which appearing							
It's All Over Now, Baby Blue	Stealin'	Great White Wonder Part 2	And Now Your Mouth Cries Whoops	Dylan - (Don't) Look Back (triple)	Joaquin Antique	Aspects Of Bob Dylan On Tour Volume 1		Bob Dylan - A Rare Batch Of Little White Wonder Volume 3
She Belongs To Me	"	"	Now Your Mouth Cries Wolf *1	"	"	"	Best Of Great White Wonder	Help
Love Minus Zero/No Limit	"	"	"	"	"	"	"	"
If You Gotta Go, Go Now		Great White Wonder (double & single)	"	Bob Dylan In Concert Volume 2		At Home		Deleted Single (different mix) *2

*1 This album also released as one half of a double album titled "Barbed Wire Blues"
*2 Official Recording

HIGHWAY 61 REVISITED OUT-TAKES   Mono   Date Recorded: Mid 1965

Song Titles	Records on which appearing						
Can You Please Crawl Out Your Window (1st take)							
Can You Please Crawl Out Your Window (2nd take) *1	Great White Wonder Part 2	Stealin'	Now Your Mouth Cries Wolf	Dylan - (Don't) Look Back (triple)	Aspects Of Bob Dylan On Tour Volume 2	At Home	Bob Dylan - A Rare Batch Of Little White Wonder Volume 3
Killing Me Alive	Great White Wonder (double only)	" *2	"	Help	Bob Dylan In Concert Volume 2	Best Of Great White Wonder	"
It Takes A Lot To Laugh, It Takes A Train To Cry	Great White Wonder Part 2	"	"				
From A Buick 6	Seems Like A Freeze Out	"	And Now Your Mouth Cries Whoops				

*1 This take was mistakenly released as a single under the title "Positively 4th Street" and was available in the Los Angeles area only because the error occurred at the Los Angeles pressing plant; it was withdrawn after two days but as it followed "Like A Rolling Stone" it probably sold quite a few copies in those two days
*2 Some versions of "Stealin'" do not include "Killing Me Alive"

"Highway 61" was an amazing album - is still an amazing album. The range of reaction when it came out was incredible. A lot of people in the music press seemed to get obsessed with the notion that it was against the law to write a song eleven minutes long. It was not till a few years later, when Dylan really was producing some dubious stuff, that the press decided that he could do no wrong. Many who had not previously been interested in Dylan thought the album was great. But I met very few former Dylan freaks who had a good word to say about it. They were using words like 'commercialised', 'sell-out', etc., and when you said 'Yes, yes - but do you like it?', they dismissed the question as irrelevant. I knew one girl who had thought Dylan's acoustic albums were marvellous but who, when I asked her what she thought of Dylan's new electric stuff, turned on me and snarled, 'I *HATE* Bob Dylan!'

Of course, many people started feeling more relaxed about the whole thing when the term 'folk rock' was invented. 'Folk rock' - I mean, I *ask* you. No wonder Dylan fell off his bike.

Turning to the "Highway 61" out-takes, it was right that they were not included in the album. That is not necessarily a criticism of them - it is just that it would be hard to improve on the format of the album as it stands. As a matter of interest someone did at one stage try to improve it; for a while "From A Buick 6" was replaced by the out-take of it. Why Columbia should go to the trouble of remastering the whole of one side of an album just for the sake of including this much weaker version of the song I cannot understand, but, anyway, they quickly thought better of it and went back to the original master, unless this was just another of Columbia's mix-ups.

Incidentally the album lost a lot when it was again remastered, this time for stereo. "It Takes A Lot To Laugh" lost some of its crispness, and the balance was messed up by the piano track being too loud. The stereo version also goes on for too long and gets into the bit where Dylan was running out of things to play on his harmonica. "Desolation Row" lost some of its clear, crystal quality, and the sound of the drums on "Just Like Tom Thumb's Blues" became totally different to the original mono version. So a decent tape collection should really include a tape of the original mono "Highway 61", unless you actually have a good condition copy of the album itself. Sadly this is even more applicable to "Blonde On Blonde" and, to a lesser extent, "Bringing It All Back Home".

I think take two of "Please Crawl Out Your Window" is of a good enough standard to have gone on the album but I can see that somehow it just would not fit. It was for a while officially available in the Los Angeles area as a mistake single under the title "Positively 4th Street" but it was withdrawn fairly quickly. The later fast version which was released as a single under its correct title was such a totally different arrangement that it virtually ceased to be the same song. The "Highway 61" out-take has a much more mellow sound which includes a fine xylophone phrase (which was subsequently used in the introduction of Glen Cambell's version of "Galveston") and some beautiful guitar work presumably by Mike Bloomfield. The first take is much the same in approach but is very unpolished and, in places, very out of tune.

The out-take of "It Takes A Lot To Laugh" just cannot be compared to the released version. Again, to all intents and purposes, it is a different song. It is fast and tuneless and the lyrics are only a pale shadow of those of the final version. It is strange that when Dylan performed the song at the '65 Newport Folk Festival it was the inferior version he chose, yet by that time "Highway 61" must have already been completed.

The words of the last verse of "Killing Me Alive" are a joke about the song just being a riff. The song *is* a straight twelve bar but it is not *just* a riff. The rhythm, for a start, is very unusual; pounding, but with a note played on the organ every fourth beat that somehow seems to correspond to the upstroke on a guitar. I would assume that it is very much a Dylan-Bloomfield-Kooper work-out with a lot improvised including the lyrics, some of which come from, or later found their way into, "Just Like Tom Thumb's Blues". Bloomfield and Kooper's virtuosoing is very much to the fore and it seems that Dylan is just enjoying the novelty of the whole electric thing. It is good - it is a pity there does not seem to be a tape around that does not lose treble and/or volume after the second verse.

One further point I should deal with is the question of whether takes of "She's Your Lover Now" and "I Wanna Be Your Lover Baby" were done at the "Highway 61" sessions. Scaduto, in his tapeography, reckons these were, but I cannot find any trace of any versions of these songs apart from those done at the L.A. session with the Band. I certainly live in hope but for the moment all I am willing to concede is that "I Wanna Be Your Lover Baby" as listed on the L.A. Band session chart could possibly have come from the "Highway 61" sessions - the sound would fit together.

In a way it would be sad to discover that there was a "Highway 61" out-take of "She's Your Lover Now". The song is so inspired that its non-inclusion would shatter the perfection of what up to now must stand as one of the most perfect albums ever.

NEWPORT FOLK FESTIVAL 1965

This is the famous first live electric performance where Dylan, with the Butterfield Blues Band backing him, was supposedly booed. You cannot actually hear precisely whether it is booing on the tape though there is certainly a distinct lack of applause on the electric numbers compared with the enthusiasm which greets "Mr. Tambourine Man" and "Baby Blue". There are occasional shouts from the audience but it is hard to tell whether they are negative or positive comments. One story about the performance is that there was a misunderstanding which arose from Dylan's voice being drowned by the backing. Some people in the audience shouted out that they could not hear and others in the audience thought they were cat-calling and joined in. Anyway, the electric performance ends somewhat peremptorily after three numbers with Dylan saying, 'Let's go, man - that's all'.

He then comes back, after a short gap, and goes into a completely acoustic "Baby Blue" which meets with unqualified approval. He follows this with "Mr. Tambourine Man" after asking the audience, 'Has anybody got an E harmonica? - *AIR*nibody?' Nobody apparently has and "Tambourine Man" winds up in F. It is the last number in the set and gets enraptured applause from the audience whom one can imagine saying something like 'Welcome back to the fold'.

It is not that surprising that the Newport audience was nonplussed by the electric numbers. Dylan chucked them right in at the deep end. The opener, "Maggie's Farm" is done as a hard rock number with Bloomfield's guitar doing very similar stuff to its contribution on the album version of "Tombstone Blues", but sounding a lot more vicious. Perhaps the audience would have had time to acclimatise if "Like A Rolling Stone" had been done first instead of second. The Butterfield Blues Band does not get anywhere near the sound of the single, and there is also a point where Dylan slurs for a few lines to disguise the fact that he has forgotten some of the words. Just the same, if you did not have the official version to compare it to, it would come across as a good performance. And no short-comings in the arrangements could disguise the fact that it is a brilliant song.

It is a pity Dylan chose the fast version of "It Takes A Lot To Laugh" as the next number. Even if you try to judge this in isolation, away from the beautiful album version, it still does not have much to offer. Like "Maggie's Farm" the vocal, to all intents and purposes, is a one note shout, but does not have the latter's humour in the lyrics to offset the lack of melody. Also as on "Maggie's Farm", Bloomfield is doing his "Tombstone Blues" stuff, but by now it is wearing a bit thin.

Even if this was not the Newport Folk Festival, the songs Dylan chose to do electrically do not make for a good set; Although the sound quality of the recording is good, it is not a tape I would play for entertainment. It is tempting to wonder whether Dylan *knew* it was not a good set - I mean, did he *know* he had to be rejected? Ho ho.

NEWPORT FOLK FESTIVAL 1965 Stereo PA tape Date Recorded: July 1965		
Song Titles	Records on which appearing	
Maggie's Farm *	Passed Over And Rolling Thunder	St. Valentine's Day Massacre And More
Like A Rolling Stone *	"	
It Takes A Lot To Laugh, It Takes A Train To Cry *	"	
It's All Over Now, Baby Blue	"	
Mr. Tambourine Man	"	"
* With the Paul Butterfield Blues Band		

LOS ANGELES SESSION WITH THE BAND

This is what tape collecting is all about. This is essential, classic, superlative stuff. The heart bleeds to know that the available tape can only be a fraction of the whole session. There are just splinters of "Midnight Train" and the slow "Crawl Out Your Window", and it is highly likely that Dylan and The Band went on to record complete versions. "Number

One" is just a backing track - presumably the vocal track is in some vault somewhere. Possibly the rumoured, but never heard, "Church With No Upstairs" was done at this session; maybe, too, a studio version of the first electric number of the '66 Albert Hall Concert, generally known as "Tell Me Mama" but probably in reality titled something like "Spuriously Seventeen Widows".

The session could be a rehearsal. This would be confirmed by the fragment of the slow "Crawl Out Your Window" which appears here. As far as I can make out the better known, complete slow version had already been accidentally released as a single by the time the session took place, and the snippet here, although pleasant, is a bit untogether. There is also the point that "She's Your Lover Now" starts raggedly as well as finishing raggedly - if it was a genuine tape they would presumably have started again. "I Wanna Be Your Lover Baby" and "Visions Of Johanna" are without hitch, but then that brings us on to the matter of whether all the songs listed do come from this session. "I Wanna Be Your Lover Baby" could be a "Highway 61" out-take and the fast version of "Please Crawl

FOREST HILLS, NEW YORK, 1965
Mono Audience tape
Date Recorded: August 1965

Song Titles	Records on which appearing	
She Belongs To Me		
To Ramona		
Gates Of Eden		
Love Minus Zero/No Limit		
Desolation Row		
It's All Over Now, Baby Blue		
Mr. Tambourine Man		
Tombstone Blues *		
I Don't Believe You *	Friends Of Chile	Video Chile
From A Buick 6 *		
Just Like Tom Thumb's Blues *		
Maggie's Farm *		
It Ain't Me Babe *		
Ballad Of A Thin Man *		
Like A Rolling Stone *		

* With Robbie Robertson, Levon Helm, Al Kooper & Harvey Brooks

Out Your Window" could be a session in itself, could come from an unknown session, or perhaps even from the "Blonde On Blonde" sessions. On the other hand, some people think the L.A. tape is one and the same as the "Blonde On Blonde" out-takes. I do not think so because the sound is not right - anyway, I prefer to think that "Blonde On Blonde" out-takes exist in abundance somewhere on some incredible tape as yet to come to light.

"Visions Of Johanna" is pretty definitely from the L.A. session. It is completely different in arrangement from the official version and also has slightly, though some people think very significantly, differing lyrics. This particularly applies to a phrase in the last verse which caused the cut to be generally known as the 'nightingale's code' version. I am not going to read a lot into 'nightingale's code'. It could be very meaningful, it could mean bird shit or it could be the first phrase that came into Dylan's head that scanned and rhymed. Another difference is that the word 'gone' is substituted for 'returned' in the fiddler's final statement. This is reckoned by one Dylan critic - I cannot remember who - to change the whole sense of the song. The earlier L.A. session version he sees as ending in pessimism because everything being 'gone' as opposed to 'returned' indicates that there is now no chance that it will ever be repaid. The official version he sees as the polar opposite in that now everything has been paid back and the slate is clean. I would not like to say - he could well be right.

As to the arrangement, the main difference is the rhythm which relies heavily on maraccas and a piano pattern slightly reminiscent of the high-hat on the official version of "Sad Eyed Lady Of The Lowlands", and the organ which gives a much fuller support to the overall sound than the organ on the released version. A further difference is the lack of an aggressive lead guitar. I personally prefer the official version from every standpoint (the mono version that is - the mix has been ruined on the stereo version), especially the subtly menacing sound of the organ and that killer lead guitar. But many people prefer the L.A. version and there is no argument that it is easily up to official album standard.

"I Wanna Be Your Lover Baby" is a brief rocker that unashamedly rips off the Beatles' "I Wanna Be Your Man" for the chorus. But it works because, whereas the lyrics of the first three lines of the chorus are identical to the Beatles' song, the last line veers off at a tangent.

The lyrics of the verses are classic Dylan '65-'66. There is the typical mêlée of totally unrelated events involving totally unrelated weirdo characters and the whole effect, as usual, is quite superb.

"Please Crawl Out Your Window" has very science-fictionish lyrics and on the fast version, which was released as a single, the arrangement tends to heighten the sci-fi effect. For people who were unhappy about the "Highway 61" album, the release of "Please Crawl Out Your Window" added insult to injury. It is total rock, and this was really the first Dylan record where the lyrics were actually subjugated by, or, at least, incidental to the music. The lyrics anyway are something of a far cry from "God On Our Side", but add to that a Robbie Robertson lead guitar that was undeniably Cream-influenced and you start to see why Dylan felt somewhat paranoid about the whole thing. It is very tempting in fact to interpret the song's title as a challenge to the folkies to come out of their womb.

Now to "She's Your Lover Now". This song embodies totally what Dylan was all about circa '65-'66. The lyrics are wild, spontaneous, full of images, totally disrespectful of accepted pop lyric forms and hyper-vicious.

The song is addressing two people, one of them the singer's ex-girlfriend and the other the guy who has taken her over. There is a constant veering back and forth between bitter, though not entirely negative recrimination towards the girl, and pulverising put-downs of the man. In amongst the torrent of reproaches and insults there are some lines which, had the song been released officially, might have become famous simply for their semantic cleverness. As the song goes on it gets weirder and weirder - in places it is reminiscent of Hieronymous Bosch's "Garden Of Earthly Delights".

Unfortunately the performance ends prematurely and abruptly with Dylan exclaiming 'Why're ..... what?' Whether the song was about to end anyway or whether there was even more of this brilliant, ethereal stuff to come is not known. There may well be a tape of another version. It is very likely that somewhere a complete version exists because there is supposedly a tape in existence of a telephone conversation between Dylan and his producer, Bob Johnson, in which Johnson tells Dylan that Columbia are going to release "She's Your Lover Now" as a single. There was also a report in the music press in 1966 to this effect.

Why they did not release it is as hard to understand as most of Columbia's other decisions about Dylan singles. The L.A. version, at least, is musically brilliant. There is a very attractive basic layer of sound provided by the piano (I think played by Dylan), enhanced by discreetly inspired Garth Hudson organ. The drumming is fast and perfect with a lot of high-hat plus what are nearly, but not quite, drum rolls at various dramatic points in the song. The lead guitar is again very discreet; it plays totally different roles in various places in the song, all brilliantly, and overall Robbie Robertson makes it sound like three separate instruments (as far as I can tell). The arrangement is very melodious and well-integrated and has none of that slight air of 'we'll chuck in all the usual stuff' that you get with a couple of the "Blonde On Blonde" tracks. It also sounds as though "She's Your Lover Now" has been arranged on a very careful and formal basis rather than relying to any great extent on improvisation. The total effect is astounding. The only reasons that occur to me as to why it did not get on "Blonde On Blonde" are, one, that there is a line in the melody that is very close to a line from "One Of Us Must Know" and, two, that the unrestrained viciousness of the lyrics was considered to be likely to push Dylan's image a bit too far towards the misanthropic.

Another matter for conjecture is what happened to the vocal track for "Number One". It sounds tantalisingly as though complete it would make another gem. A very intricate one as well - the chord sequence covers practically half the song, and it is very hard to improvise your own vocal without getting lost. Mostly the problem is one of finding that what you thought was the end of a line is in fact the beginning of one. As there are no lyrics it is hard also to understand how anyone can know that its title is "Number One". Could it, one wonders, really be the legendary "Church With No Upstairs"?

On the subject of titles, it is difficult to see how the fragment of the prototype for "Temporary Like Achilles", usually known as "Midnight Train", got to receive the title "Medicine Sunday" or "Medicine Show" in some quarters. The words certainly mention a 'midnight train' but there is no trace of the words 'medicine', 'Sunday' or 'show'. The only way you could know a title like that would be if you read it straight off the Columbia can or if someone who had been at the session told you. Interesting implications there.

The actual song, which we shall call 'Midnight Train" for the sake of argument, promises to be really good, better, I think, than "Temporary Like Achilles". The tune of the chorus line is the same as the latter but the one verse you get to hear of "Midnight Train" has a much more attractive melody than its successor. The backing has a lot more vitality as well. It could, I am afraid, have been yet another gem.

All this brilliant material not released. What were Columbia up to? Putting something aside for a rainy day? The rainy day came - two lots of rainy days came. On the first occasion they put out "Bob Dylan's Greatest Hits" and on the second occasion "Dylan". Strange, isn't it?

MELBOURNE 1966

These tracks surfaced relatively recently from a disc recording that was made for an Australian radio show. Hence there are some crackles.

The performances are superb. Dylan sounds exhausted mentally and physically and does a lot of coughing, but the songs gain rather than lose from this. There is no hint of any antagonism from the audience as with a lot of the other '66 gigs but then this is from the acoustic half.

Dylan does not say a lot between numbers - he devotes most of his attention to guitar tuning - but what he does say is friendly and unantagonistic, again unlike elsewhere in '66. You really feel for the man when he says, 'This is called The *Fourrrrrrrth Taaaaaaaym Arouwwwnd*'. In reality it was probably about the forty-fourth but it is still absolutely fresh, and in some ways better than the "Blonde On Blonde" version.

More oedipal ambiguity appears with Dylan introducing "Visions Of Johanna" as "Mother Revisited". No lyric changes but nevertheless a grippingly atmospheric rendering.

It is all good stuff. It cannot really be faulted except on the grounds that the guitar is used in much the same style on every song. Of course that could have been a sort of lead-in to the electric half - like 'there's only so much I can do with an acoustic guitar'.

He does not actually say that. What he does say - and this is in the form of an apology for the time spent tuning up - is, 'This isn't my guitar - it could go outa tune all the time .....my guitar got broken here in Australia and I had to borrow this one ..... this is a good guitar but it's a folk music guitar ..... folk music guitar .....'

A good proportion of the audience catches on and laughs in response to this. It is a pity the electric half of the concert is not in circulation. I do not think there can have been any booing.

LIVERPOOL 1966

This is where CBS took the now much-sought-after single from. It was a good choice too. True to tradition, Liverpool welcomes electric Dylan with open arms. There is not a negative noise to be heard from the audience throughout and I would imagine that Dylan, with his respect for the Beatles, must have felt well-pleased.

Apart from "Just Like Tom Thumb's Blues", obviously taken from the single, the sound quality of the tape is good but a bit dry. I do not think it can have come across like that in the theatre - it is just the way it was mixed

LOS ANGELES BAND SESSION   Mono   Date Recorded: December 1965

Song Titles	Records on which appearing				
Can You Please Crawl Out Your Window (slow version - fragment)					Deleted Single *1
Can You Please Crawl Out Your Window (fast version)	Seems Like A Freeze Out		Now Your Mouth Cries Wolf	And Now Your Mouth Cries Whoops	
I Wanna Be Your Lover Baby	"	40 Red White And Blue Shoestrings	"	"	
Number One (backing track only)	"	Let Me Die In My Footsteps			I'm Ready *2
Midnight Train (fragment) *3		V.D. Waltz			Troubled Troubadour *4
Visions Of Johanna *5	Seems Like A Freeze Out	40 Red White And Blue Shoestrings	"	"	
She's Your Lover Now		40 Red White And Blue Shoestrings	"	"	Help

*1 Official Recording
*2 Existence of this album very uncertain
*3 Also known as "Medicine Sunday" - a prototype for "Temporary Like Achilles"
*4 This song not credited on the "Troubled Troubadour" cover slip; possibly it only appears on some versions of the album
*5 At the time, "Visions Of Johanna" was titled "Seems Like A Freeze Out"

WESTCHESTER COUNTY CENTER, NEW YORK
Mono Audience tape (not on disc)
Date Recorded: February 1966

Song Titles
She Belongs To Me
To Ramona
Visions Of Johanna
It's All Over Now, Baby Blue
Desolation Row
Love Minus Zero/No Limit
Mr. Tambourine Man
Tell Me Mama *
I Don't Believe You *

* With the Hawks

HEMPSTEAD, NEW YORK   Mono   Audience tape (not on disc)   Date Recorded: Feb 1966

Song Titles
She Belongs To Me
4th Time Around
Visions Of Johanna
It's All Over Now, Baby Blue
Desolation Row
Love Minus Zero/No Limit
Mr. Tambourine Man
Tell Me Mama *
I Don't Believe You *
Baby Let Me Follow You Down *
Just Like Tom Thumb's Blues *
Leopard-skin Pill-box Hat *
One Too Many Mornings *

* With the Hawks

in the recording. Anyway, it is still obvious that it is great music.

"Tell Me Mama" is an eminently suitable opening number and there is no excuse for the song not going on "Blonde On Blonde". As a collector's item the Liverpool version is a lot rarer than the Albert Hall version (see Royal Albert Hall) but does have the disadvantage of a short microphone failure on the vocal - though that has become something of a distinguishing mark now.

The Band, or The Hawks as they then were, are in tremendously tight and creative form. It foxes me how they manage to start on the same beat as Dylan, especially on "Tell Me Mama" - he plays a few chords on his Fender (I think it was a Fender) that do not sound much more than a doodle to test the tuning, you hear a few vague foot-stomps and a just audible 'One - two - three' and then suddenly they are all in together. It is a pin-point in time, yet they are all on it absolutely simultaneously. From then on every instrument except Dylan's guitar is a lead. But nobody is upstaging anyone - it is totally integrated, inspired rock music. In no way could Dylan or the Band be accused of specifically copying anybody. The sound is very different from most of the music on the scene at the time; apart from the fact that none of the Band's instruments is restricted to a background function, it has a much more fundamentally rock beat than was generally being used around '66, yet at the same time it has a very high melodic content. And into all this Dylan's vocals slide as if they have been one band for years.

The best example of the integration of the sound is "Just Like Tom Thumb's Blues" - possibly an unfair example because it is the only track to have been professionally mixed, but it is so good it has to be singled out. Of the four Liverpool tracks in circulation this is the one track that I prefer to its Albert Hall counter-part. There is one organ phrase in the intro that is different by a couple of notes, and the interplay between Dylan's vocal and Robbie Robertson's lead guitar is just that bit more scintillating. Listen to the second verse - the *interplay* is just sixth sense.

"One Too Many Mornings" is the number which lends itself least to the sound and it is still excellent. "Like A Rolling Stone" was made for the sound and it goes beyond excellence. It is spoilt slightly on all the tapes I have heard by a badly spliced-on ending that, if it does not actually come from another concert, was recorded on another tape recorder that was running slow. So what you get in the final instrumental bars is an out-of-rhythm change into an alien sounding key. Still, the first seven minutes are perfect. (This is not the much-rumoured nine-minute version - the existence of that has not been proved.) It is slower than the official version but the extra time is made complete use of by Dylan screwing the maximum emphasis from each and every word. And slow as it is, the music still had that sort of rare thump that makes you not only want to stamp your feet but throw your whole body into the thing and celebrate being human. You could not do *that* to "God On Our Side".

DUBLIN ADELPHI 1966

There is a slight controversy among some collectors as to whether this really is Dublin. One of my fellow appreciators went through the music papers for the time and reckons that this tape matches what Dylan was reported as saying between numbers at one of the Albert Hall concerts. I would like to think this was really the missing acoustic half of the Albert Hall tape. That way you have one complete '66 gig.

Either way, these tracks are essential collectors' items. For my money "Visions Of Johanna", "Fourth Time Around" and "Just Like A Woman" are respectively the best versions of these songs anywhere in circulation, officially or unofficially. They do not have the "Blonde On Blonde" sneer in the vocals, and though that sneer is now part of our heritage, I still prefer the slightly less cynical sound of the "Highway 61" voice.

The Dublin vocals are about half-way between the two, so they are what you might call optimum classic Dylan. As with the Melbourne tape the guitar remains much the same for all the tracks, yet if you take each track in isolation the guitar is attractive and quite OK for the song. Anyway the merit of all the songs is so fundamental that they would lend themselves to practically any sort of arrangement, from unaccompanied to the full might of the Top of the Pops orchestra.

Coming back to the voice, it occurs to me that the sneer is a lot more in evidence on the Albert Hall tape than here and this may be an indication that these tracks cannot therefore be attributed to the Albert Hall. One thing I do know for sure is that these six tracks could not possibly have come from the *other* Albert Hall concert. I cannot remember whether it was the first or second night but I was at the *other* Albert Hall concert and "Tambourine Man" was very different from this. Throughout Dylan spat out the 'T' in 'tambourine' with an emphasis that came close to hatred. The song certainly was not the mellow affair it is here. I can also remember that in introducing "Visions Of Johanna" Dylan said something like, 'This is what some people would call a drurg (drug) song. I just wanna say that I've no idea what a *drurg* song is. I wouldn't know how to go about writing a *drurg* song.' At this point someone yelled out: 'We're with you, Bob', but Dylan was unimpressed and simply responded with a bored 'All rait'.

Coming back to the Dublin version of "Tambourine Man", there is one facet that this tape lacks compared with the audience tape of the concert. That is that on the audience tape Dylan's harmonica solo is somehow given a unique and stunning sound by the acoustics of the theatre. A sort of build-up of sound seems to take place and gives rise to a feeling of bells ringing all round the auditorium. It is breathtakingly beautiful and literally the perfect evocation of "Chimes Of Freedom". The P.A. tape misses all this.

I say P.A. tape, but a friend of mine somewhat expert in these matters claims that what has been assumed to be a P.A. tape could well be a very good audience tape. I disagree with him; I think it is a C.B.S. tape slightly dulled by copying. And on the subject of sound quality, it is a pity that Trade Mark of Quality do not seem to have made nearly such a good job of mastering "While The Establishment Burns" as they did "Burn Some More". "Tambourine Man" and "Baby Blue" on the latter are of very acceptable quality at least on all the copies of the album I have come across. But, with regard to the other four tracks, I have yet to hear a copy of "While The Establishment Burns" that does not crackle. The whole area of bootlegs of this tape is somewhat fraught. There are some versions with tracks missing, some with tracks fading before the end, some with clunks on "Visions Of Johanna" and some not, etc. "Black Nite Crash" - the one that fades - was, legend has it, copied from the T.M.Q. "While The Establishment Burns", and in the process added its own set of crackles.

If Dylan had not gone back to Columbia from Asylum the above hazards would not probably now be of such great concern to record collectors. There was a widespread rumour that Columbia were all set to release an entire '66 gig as their follow-up to "Dylan". It has also been suggested that by the time they got Dylan back they had got as far as printing the covers. Ah well.....

MELBOURNE, AUSTRALIA Mono PA tape Date Recorded: 19th April, 1966	
Song Title	Record on which appearing
She Belongs To Me (incomplete)	
4th Time Around	Bob Dylan In Melbourne, Australia *
Visions Of Johanna	"
It's All Over Now, Baby Blue	"
Desolation Row	"

* A European version of this album was produced, copied from the original Trade Mark of Quality album

LIVERPOOL Mono PA tape Date Recorded: 14th May, 1966			
Song Titles	Records on which appearing		
Tell Me Mama			
Just Like Tom Thumb's Blues	Burn Some More	40 Red White And Blue Shoestrings	Deleted Single *
One Too Many Mornings	"		
Like A Rolling Stone	"		

All with the Hawks
* Official Recording - B-side of "I Want You"

ROYAL ALBERT HALL 1966

To quote Grandad in Jack Rosenthal's "Barmizvah Boy", 'What can you say about perfection?'

The music is great, brilliant, stunning - all the superlatives you can think of. Dylan seethes with resentment towards the audience and it is translated into singing that is tight, searing and - dare I say it? - apocalyptic.

"Tell Me Mama" is not nearly such a friendly song as it was at Liverpool and the increased viciousness is, of course, an improvement.

Before "I Don't Believe You", Dylan plays a few bars of it on the harmonica, then says 'This is called "I Don't Believe You". It used to be like that - now it goes like this.' He stamps his foot four times and The Band comes in with the sort of immediacy you get from tipping a whole table full of crockery and cutlery into the sink all at once. It does not seem possible that the song was written for an acoustic guitar.

"Baby Let Me Follow You Down" is a slower starter but soon gets there. "Tom Thumb's Blues" just lags slightly behind the Liverpool version but it is still incredibly good. "Leopard-skin Pill-box Hat" is undoubtedly the best version of the song in circulation. It leaves the official version standing and I think a good part of the credit has to be attributed to Robbie Robertson's lead guitar. All power to Dylan's elbow for playing lead on the album version but it was just a little sedate compared with what Robbie Robertson unleashes here.

It is just prior to "One Too Many Mornings" that something happens to indicate that it is only a minority of the audience who are looking askance on Dylan's electrification. A few people start slow-hand clapping and to shut them up Dylan employs the rather ingenious device of muttering incomprehensible nonsense into the microphone until curiosity overcomes the slow-hand clappers and they stop in order to catch what he is saying. At this point the mutterings become 'I just wish you wouldn't clap so loud'. A much larger portion of the audience then bursts into applause indicating that they are on Dylan's side.

"One Too Many Mornings" comes into its own as a rock song much more than the Liverpool version did and again it is the sad acid in Dylan's voice that does it. So it is surprising that, with the mood Dylan is in, he does not appear to sing the song *at* the audience. It is faultlessly done but the vocal is surprisingly unaggressive.

Not so "Like a Rolling Stone". This is the occasion of the famous incident where a member of the audience, for reasons best known to himself, yells out 'Judas'. Other people are yelling things as well but nothing comprehensible, and it would appear that it is in answer to the 'Judas' accusation that Dylan responds, 'I don't be*lieve* you ..... Your're a *LIAR* ..... (moving back from the microphone) ..... you're a *FUCKING* LIAR'. At which point the Band crashes in and "Like A Rolling Stone" lets everyone know why the gentleman with a penchant for biblical analogy is talking through his sound-hole.

A word here perhaps about the other Albert Hall concert, no tape of which is in circulation. I cannot remember too much of what Dylan said in the first half because I was so amazed by the new songs, i.e., "Visions Of Johanna", "Fourth Time Around" and "Just Like A Woman". I recall that in response to some heckling over the time he spent tuning up he said something like 'It's for your benefit I'm doing this - if you're bored why don't you go outside and read some books?' Then in the second half he became steadily more sarcastic. His introduction to "I Don't Believe You" was something to this effect: 'I get accused of dis*miss*ing my old songs ..... well that's naart tchoo..... I *lurrrrrve* my old songs'. The tone of the voice, as it was with all the rapps, was totally bored. As he moved over to the piano to do "Mr. Jones" he growled, 'Awh, it's all the same stuff'.

What he was doing was tarring the whole audience with the brush he should have reserved for the few individuals who were actually not appreciating the music. There were one or two people cat-calling but the majority responded to each number with enthusiastic applause. I felt quite upset about being put in the same category as the oafs who came to heckle. Apart from anything else "Highway 61" had been out for six months and

DUBLIN ADELPHI	Mono	PA tape	Date Recorded: 5th May, 1966		
Song Title	Records on which appearing				
Mr. Tambourine Man	Burn Some More				
It's All Over Now, Baby Blue	"				
Visions Of Johanna	While The Establish-ment Burns	Black Nite Crash	Zimmerman - Live From The Berkeley Community Theater *1	Zimmerman - Looking Back (double) *3	
4th Time Around	"	"	"	"	
Just Like A Woman	"	"	"	"	Aspects Of Bob Dylan On Tour Volume 2
Desolation Row	"	(incomplete)	" *2	"	

*1 Title used in error
*2 "Desolation Row" omitted on some versions
*3 Also released as two single albums, "Zimmerman - Looking Back 1 & 2"

there had been ample coverage in the press about the gigs having an electric half - so if they did not like electric music they should not have come. And here was Dylan treating the appreciators in the same way as the louts.

At one point I was half-considering attempting to get back-stage afterwards and explain the true situation to him, but could think of no particular reason why Dylan should be pleased to see me. In fact things ended reasonably OK because Dylan's assumptions about the audience were proved wrong by a mass demand for an encore after "Like A Rolling Stone". He did not do one but after his initial gesture of dropping his harmonica holder disparagingly into the audience, he did come back and say 'Thank eyoo'. After that he momentarily lost his sense of direction and had to be shown the stage exit. It was a funny, sad little moment.

Concerning how the Albert Hall tape came into circulation, legend has it that a young man greatly impressed with the concert simply wrote to C.B.S. to ask them if they would send him a tape of it. According to the legend, they answered him most mysteriously - i.e., they sent him a tape - and the rest is history.

EAT THE DOCUMENT

Not many people saw this film and, as the tape in circulation is a diabolical quality audience job, there is little to say about it except that most of the unknown songs sound, from what you can hear of them, as though they were actually written around '66. And, again, from what can be heard of them, they sound incredibly good.

The first one is sung to an acoustic guitar only and has a breezy sort of tune with very clever and attractive cadence. It is virtually complete as far as I can gather, though there is a lengthy break in the middle. The sound quality of the tape makes it impossible to understand the lyrics as it does with all the other unknown songs.

The next one is a pretty short excerpt only, but you can hear enough to realise that it has a really good tune. In places it sounds vaguely like "Just Like A Woman" but I am reasonably sure it is a totally different song. It starts out with just an acoustic guitar and then something that could be a violin or possibly an organ comes in. What you can hear of it is very attractive.

Shortly after this comes a snatch of something with a full electric backing that is presumably provided by The Band. This track, like all the other unknown songs, is almost certainly not live. So, if it is a studio job, is this another contender for the title of "Church With No Upstairs"? (Incidentally, none of the unknown songs here seems to have a chord sequence remotely resembling "Number One", the backing track from the L.A. session.) Again, from what you can hear, it sounds like a really good tune.

Following this there is something which sounds like Robbie Robertson and Garth Hudson practising, but whether it is a Dylan song they are working on is doubtful. Then for a while all the songs become familiar though some of the performances of them are *not*. They are all fairly obviously from '66 gigs, but which gigs there is no way of telling. The most interesting of them is a version of "Just Like Tom Thumb's Blues" that has the organ taking a rather different approach from the well-known '66 tour versions. I know that 'swirling' is a word that is applied frequently to Garth Hudson's organ work, but all I can say about the organ on this track is that it is more swirling than usual.

Song Titles	Records on which appearing			
	Royal Albert Hall *	Zimmerman - Royal Albert Hall	Zimmerman - Looking Back (double)	
Tell Me Mama				
I Don't Believe You	"	"	"	
Baby Let Me Follow You Down	"	"	"	
Just Like Tom Thumb's Blues	"	"	"	Aspects Of Bob Dylan On Tour Volume 1
Leopard-skin Pill-box Hat	"	"	"	"
One Too Many Mornings	"	"	"	
Ballad Of A Thin Man (Also exists in stereo)	"	"	"	Bridgett's Album – A Vinyl Headstone Almost In Place
Like A Rolling Stone (Also exists in stereo)	"	"	"	"

* Also released under the title "In 1966 There Was A Concert"; it is also believed that 200 copies were pressed under the title "Now Your Mouth Cries Wolf" (not to be confused with the more widely known record of that title)

Towards the end of the tape we get two more unknowns. The first may not be a Dylan song and could in fact be an old song that I am unfamiliar with. Anyway it is a good tune again. The last one sounds like a Dylan song but it is hard to tell anything else about it at all - even whether it is any good or not, though I expect it is.

As to the content of the film apart from the songs, it was supposed, I believe, to be a similar sort of thing to "Don't Look Back". There are certainly a lot of snips from the '66 tour but in between the songs it gives the impression of being a lot weirder than its predecessor. At one point it does sound as though someone is getting one of Dylan's verbal hammerings, though he seems to be putting up a better fight than any of the "Don't Look Back" victims. But apart from that and the songs, the tape in circulation could be from a film of a day down a coal mine.

What happened to the film is a mystery. It was shown once as far as I know, and that was a press showing. The review I read gave the impression that the reviewer was determined not to commit himself until he had read what all the other reviewers had to say about it.

THE BASEMENT TAPE

More than anything else it was this tape that got the whole tape and bootleg scene going. Possibly it was designed to do so. It is certainly possible that these tracks were recorded nowhere near the basement of Big Pink in West Saugerties as is claimed. If they were, it seems very unlikely, in view of the full stereo of the tracks on the official album, that they were recorded, as is also claimed, on a domestic tape recorder using just two microphones. The whole matter smacks just a bit too much of legend manufacturing.

I do know that when, in 1968, it became apparent, from articles in the music press and from the release of a spate of singles of Dylan songs by other artists, that new Dylan material had been made available to various music industry people which was not available to me as a Dylan appreciator of some years' standing, I became extremely annoyed. If Jonathan King had a copy of the Basement Tape, I determined that I certainly had a right to one and, along with myriads of other appreciators, set out in search of a copy. In the meantime some people latched on to an obvious demand so that, not long after my search for a tape was fulfilled, "Great White Wonder" and "Troubled Troubadour" started appearing in various places.

What else, you might ask, did Dylan expect?

The Basement Tape certainly cannot have been withheld from release for reasons of lack of merit. It includes some of the best things Dylan has ever done. Which brings us on to the scandalous matter of the selection of tracks for the official album. What sort of a sick joke is it to have Quinn the Eskimo on the cover but not on the record? It is very odd indeed that there should have been such devastatingly glaring omissions, especially as in the 1975 interview with Mary Travers Dylan said that the Basement Tape was going to be put out 'in its entirety'. It is almost as though someone at Columbia actually had an interest in keeping the bootleg scene going.

Apart from the numerous songs that were left out altogether, they also selected a couple of wrong takes. "Tears Of Rage" on the official album not only lacks an introduction, it also has Richard Manuel singing grossly out-of-time and off-key harmonies. The version on "Great White

DUBLIN ADELPHI   Mono   Audience tape
Date Recorded: 5th May, 1966

Song Titles	Record on which appearing
Mr. Tambourine Man	Bob Dylan In Concert Volume 2
It's All Over Now, Baby Blue	"
Visions Of Johanna	
4th Time Around	
Just Like A Woman	
Desolation Row	

BRISTOL COLSTON HALL   Mono   Audience tape
Date Recorded: 10th May, 1966

Song Titles	Record on which appearing
She Belongs To Me	
4th Time Around	
Visions Of Johanna	
It's All Over Now, Baby Blue	
Desolation Row	
Just Like A Woman	
Mr. Tambourine Man	
Tell Me Mama *	Bob Dylan In Concert Volume 1
I Don't Believe You *	"
Baby Let Me Follow You Down *	"
Just Like Tom Thumb's Blues *	
Leopard-skin Pill-box Hat *	
One Too Many Mornings *	"
Ballad Of A Thin Man *	
Like A Rolling Stone *	"
* With the Hawks	

Wonder", on the other hand, has a beautiful guitar intro, Richard Manuel spot-on, and everything else perfect as well. The official "Too Much Of Nothing" is admittedly interesting because it was not in circulation previous to the album's release. But compared with the very different "Great White Wonder" take of the song it is not much more than an extemely tentative, un-worked-out rehearsal.

However, these are relatively minor quibbles compared with the question of why "I Shall Be Released", "Mighty Quinn", "I'm Not There", "Get Your Rocks Off" and last, but absolutely not least, "Sign On The Cross", were not, in any shape or form, included on the album. (The non-inclusion of the Dylan rendering of "Don't Ya Tell Henry" is easier to understand because the track is just an alcoholic cacophony.)

Everyone is presumably familiar with "I Shall Be Released" as a song. Suffice it to say then that the Dylan Basement version is, of the abundance of versions around by various people, the best. Apart from a superb vocal, it has some of the most beautiful Robbie Robertson guitar work in existence. There is absolutely no comparison with the "More Greatest Hits" track.

Likewise the Isle of Wight version of "Mighty Quinn" on "Self Portrait" is nothing more than a dying ember of the originals. Both Basement takes are very good but take 2 is that bit more distinctive for its fine acoustic guitar sound plus a very unusual introduction played on what sounds like a recorder.

"I'm Not There" is a strange song. It has something of the structure of some of the stuff on the first Leonard Cohen LP in that each verse is a lot

---

EDINBURGH   Mono   Audience tape (not on disc)   Date Recorded: 20th May, 1966

Song Titles
She Belongs To Me
4th Time Around
Visions Of Johanna
It's All Over Now, Baby Blue
Desolation Row
Just Like A Woman
Mr. Tambourine Man
Tell Me Mama *
I Don't Believe You *
Baby Let Me Follow You Down *
Just Like Tom Thumb's Blues *
Leopard-skin Pill-box Hat *
One Too Many Mornings *
Ballad Of A Thin Man *
Like A Rolling Stone *

* With the Hawks

of short lines sung without any break and going on longer than expected. The words, as far as they can be comprehended, are apparently a sort of pang of conscience about the nature of a relationship with a lady whom Dylan refers to as his neighbour. In places you get the impression that he is making the words up as he goes along. It is possible, even, that the incomprehensible bits are not real words at all but slurrings to fill in where inspiration temporarily runs out. The song needs some more work done on it but it is still basically very good and should have gone on the album. Unfortunately all the tapes of it start some way into the song. Possibly several verses are missed but, as what is left is over five minutes long, it is more likely that it is just the introduction that has been cut off.

"Get Your Rocks Off" is not one of Dylan's greatest compositions but as a semi-throwaway track it is quite funny. Like much of the Basement Tape it is simply made up of a string of non-sequiturs.

"Get Your Rocks Off" and "I'm Not There" are two of the rarer Basement Tape songs in that they did not appear on a lot of the demo tapes and acetates that originally came over to this country, and their bootleg appearances are very limited compared with those of the basic fourteen songs which made up the original acetate. (These were "Million Dollar Bash", "Yea Heavy", "Mrs. Henry", "Down In The Flood", "Lo And Behold", "Tiny Montgomery", "This Wheel's On Fire", "You Ain't Goin' Nowhere", "I Shall Be Released", "Too Much Of Nothing" (take 2), "Tears Of Rage" (take 3), "Mighty Quinn" (take 2), "Nothing Was

EAT THE DOCUMENT (not on disc)	Mono	Audience tape Filmed around May 1966
Song Titles		
Tell Me Mama (incomplete) *1		
Unknown Song (interrupted)		
Unknown Song (incomplete)		
Like A Rolling Stone (2 fragments) *1		
I Still Miss Someone (fragment) *2		
Jam (organ & electric guitar - short fragment) *3		
I Don't Believe You (interrupted) *1		
Ballad Of A Thin Man (interrupted) *1		
Just Like Tom Thumb's Blues (incomplete) *1		
Baby Let Me Follow You Down (fragment) *1		
Mr. Tambourine Man (interrupted)		
One Too Many Mornings (fragment) *1		
Unknown Song (incomplete)		
Unknown Song (fragment)		
*1 With the Hawks		
*2 Several unidentified voices with piano		
*3 Robbie Robertson & Garth Hudson		

Delivered" (take 1), and "Open The Door Homer" (take 3).) Also rel-
atively rare were "Apple Suckling Tree", "Odds And Ends" and
"Clothesline Saga" which, oddly enough, were included on "Troubled
Troubadour" but not credited on the cover slip. (Possibly early versions of
"Troubled Troubadour" did not include these tracks, but I have not come
across a copy that does not.)

Not on any acetates, as far as is known, were "Don't Ya Tell Henry" and
"Sign On The Cross". These tracks are generally categorised as part of the
Basement Tape but are reckoned to have been recorded possibly a short
time later than the main body of material. The strange thing is that, prior
to the release of the official album these were the only tracks available in
stereo. It is a very crude sort of stereo, in fact, with individual vocals and
instruments restricted exclusively in most cases to either one channel or
the other. Now that *is* the sort of effect you would get from recording on a
domestic machine as opposed to in a studio. So perhaps "Don't Ya Tell
Henry" and "Sign On The Cross" are the *true* Basement Tape.

But the strangest thing of all is that "Sign On The Cross" has never
been bootlegged. It is this inexplicable omission which embodies the
reason why it is better to be a tape collector than a bootleg collector -
because "Sign On The Cross" is probably the best thing on the entire
Basement Tape. It is a beautiful tune enhanced stunningly by a rich
swelling organ that gives you the impression that Garth Hudson could not
play a note a micro-second out of place if he tried, and a lead guitar of such
perfect mellowness, restraint and sympathy that it must put Robbie
Robertson alongside Bruce Langborne for the award of best lead guitar on
any Dylan track. If, as it is reputed, Robbie Robertson was involved in the
track selection for the official "Basement Tapes" album he must be a
person of remarkably little conceit to have allowed the omission of "Sign
On The Cross" plus the two best lead guitar runner-ups, "I Shall Be
Released" and "Tears Of Rage", take 3, from the final listing.

Whether "Sign On The Cross" is a religious song is ambiguous. Either
way, the lyrics are weirdly evocative. The last verse, and the break
preceding it where a passage of lyrics is spoken to the music, are put across
in an uncharacteristically manic and euphoric manner by Dylan. But to
read into this the notion that some sort of religious awakening is going on
is probably a shade unwise in view of Dylan's reputed habit of keeping a
little alcohol on hand at recording sessions.

It is possible that there are more Basement songs than are in circulation.
The appearance of the previously unknown "Goin' To Acapulco" on the
official album, while obviously a taunt to the bootleggers, may or may not
be the tip of yet another iceberg. What is probable is that there are a lot
more takes in existence of the already known songs. In his Rolling Stone
article Greil Marcus mentioned (rather ambiguously) a rock version of
"Tears Of Rage". From the context it seems that what he is referring to
would only be a snippet - just the same, it is an interesting thought. It
seems likely also that there are other versions of "I Shall Be Released",
"Down In The Flood", "You Ain't Goin' Nowhere", "This Wheel's On
Fire" and most of the other songs of which one version only is in circulation - it is doubtful that Dylan and The Band managed to obtain the standard they did on these without a few rehearsals.

One last point to mention is that, with regard to the different mixes of
"This Wheel's On Fire" and "You Ain't Goin' Nowhere" used on the

Dylan at Madison Square Garden, New York City, 1978.
(Photo by Billie Mudry)

THE BASEMENT TAPE (Continued)

Mono (except where indicated or where track appears on official album) Date Recorded: 1967

Records on which appearing

Song Titles	The Acetate	Waters Of Oblivion	Troubled Troubadour	Great White Wonder (double only)	Motorcycle	A Taste Of The Special Stash		Little White Wonder	Million Dollar Bash	At Home	Great White Wonder (double & single)	Help (double) / The Basement Tapes *2
Tears Of Rage (take 2)												
Mighty Quinn (take 1)									Million Dollar Bash			
Mighty Quinn (take 2)	"	"	"	"	Motorcycle	A Taste Of The Special Stash		Little White Wonder		"	Great White Wonder (double & single)	Help (double)
Nothing Was Delivered (take 1)	" *1								"			
Nothing Was Delivered (take 2)	"	"	"	"	"	"	Daddy Rolling Stone	"		"		The Basement Tapes *2
Open The Door Homer (take 1)												
Open The Door Homer (take 2)			"			"			"			
Open The Door Homer (take 3)	"	"	"	"		"		"		"		"
Apple Suckling Tree (take 1 – incomplete)	" *1	V.D. Waltz	"									
Apple Suckling Tree (take 2)												"
Clothes Line Saga (Talkin' Clothes Line Blues)	" *1	"	"									"
I'm Not There (incomplete)	" *1	"								Valentino Type Tangos		
Odds And Ends	" *1	"	"									"
Get Your Rocks Off	" *1	"										
Sign On The Cross *3												
Don't Ya Tell Henry *3		"								"		
Goin To Acapulco		"										"

*1 On some versions of the album only
*2 Official Recording
*3 Available in stereo

THE BASEMENT TAPE

Mono (except where indicated or where track appears on official album)   Date Recorded: 1967

Records on which appearing

Song Titles	The Acetate	Waters Of Oblivion	Troubled Troubadour	Great White Wonder Part 2	Motorcycle	A Taste Of The Special Stash	Little White Wonder	Million Dollar Bash	At Home	1000 Miles Behind	Billion Dollar Bash	The Basement Tapes *
Million Dollar Bash	"	"	"	"	"	"	"	"	"	"	"	"
Yea! Heavy And A Bottle Of Bread	"	"	"	"	"	"	"	"	"	"	"	"
Please Mrs. Henry	"	"	"	"	"	Daddy Rolling Stone		"	"	"	"	"
Down In The Flood	"	"	"	"		"	"	"				"
Lo And Behold	"	"	"	"	"	"	"	"	"		"	"
Tiny Montgomery	"	"	"	"	"	"	"	"				"
This Wheel's On Fire	"	"	"	"	"	"	"	"		Great White Wonder (double & single)		" (different mix)
You Ain't Goin' Nowhere	"	"	"	"	"	"	"	"	"		"	" (different mix)
I Shall Be Released	"	"	"			"	"	"	"	Great White Wonder (double only)		
Too Much Of Nothing (take 1)	"	"						"	"	Great White Wonder		"
Too Much Of Nothing (take 2)			"			"		"				
Tears Of Rage (take 1 - incomplete)								"				
Tears Of Rage (take 2)					"	"	"					"

* Official Recording

Continued...

official album, I have to admit that this is one instance where I cannot fault Columbia. I know a lot of people disagree, but in my opinion the remixes are better. Just the same, it is a minor blessing in the context of the gross mess that the official album embodied.

WOODY GUTHRIE MEMORIAL CONCERT

There were two Woody Guthrie Memorial Concerts - one at Carnegie Hall in 1968 in which Dylan appeared and one at the Hollywood Bowl in 1970. Recordings from the two were shuffled and released on two separate albums, part one on Columbia and part two on Warner Brothers. All the Dylan contributions are on the first one, which   is why it is the only one of the two that shops tend to stock. One thing that did not get onto either album was Odetta leading a mass rendering of "This Train" in which Dylan does a verse, and this is only in circulation as an audience tape.

His appearance at the Carnegie Hall '68 concert was a very isolated occasion for Dylan, and he turned up looking somewhat scholarly with hair parted in the middle and a beard. He was backed by The Band, who did a good job, but Dylan's vocals did not really do the song justice. "Dear Mrs. Roosevelt" is quite reasonable, but "Ain't Got No Home" is a bit lacking while "Grand Coulee Dam" is completely stripped of its tune.

"This Train" is good and rousing and also quite amusing where Odetta is trying to persuade Dylan to do his verse. The whole song gets delayed while he makes up his mind and into her words 'Come on, Bob' Odetta manages to squeeze beautifully the inflection of someone good-humouredly trying to persuade a recalcitrant seven year-old to do his scales.

JOHNNY CASH TV DOCUMENTARY

The Dylan-Cash association and Dylan's whole country phase could perhaps be seen as a sort of therapy period for Dylan. He was making pleasant, simple, undemanding music that was probably very enjoyable for all involved but it certainly was not a high creative spot in either his or Cash's musical career.

If you judge the Nashville tapes on that basis they are OK. If you judge them on the basis of what Dylan had produced before they leave rather a lot to be desired.

If you did not like what Dylan and Cash did to "Girl From The North Country" on "Nashville Skyline", you probably will not be too impressed with their version of "One Too Many Mornings", also included in the Cash Documentary. It is a lot better than the version from the actual Dylan-Cash recording session (see Nashville Session) and Cash, at least, sticks to the original tune but - well, it is very difficult *not* to remember how good the "Times ..." version was.

JOHNNY CASH SHOW, ABC-TV

The duet with Cash here is similar to, but a little scrappier than the "Nashville Skyline" duet, but "I Threw It All Away" and "Living The Blues" are done solo with hardly any variation on the album versions and, as such, are of a very acceptable standard. The only place where this does not apply is the last line of the break in "I Threw It All Away" which fails to crystallise the whole break the way it does on the album.

A press report at the time said that one of the numbers was a second

Phil Ochs and Bob Dylan, 1974. (Photo by Chuck Pulin)

attempt. The reporter put this down to Dylan's nervousness. It must be a bit nerve-racking if you know that most of your audience remember you as an acid child with a square yard of barbed wire round your head and you now look like a General Motors' executive.

THE NASHVILLE SESSION WITH JOHNNY CASH

At one stage the idea of a joint Cash-Dylan official album was reputedly on the cards. The reason it was shelved is fairly self-evident from these tracks. On the whole, although some of the performances are fairly enjoyable the musical standard is not very high. Dylan's and Cash's voices do not blend that well together, they are seldom synchronised and Dylan's harmonies tend to be inimaginative to say the least. As for the backing tracks, even the abundance of key changes cannot prevent the incessant chung-tung chong-tung guitar sound from palling after a while.

Exceptions are "I Walk The Line" which has Dylan and Cash a bit more together than usual, with Dylan doing some relatively adventurous harmonies, and which is a really good song anyway, and "Big River". The latter has Dylan singing with much more of his old bite on the solo bits and, as Cash is in charge of the harmonies here, there are places where they synchronise very closely indeed. They manage to come up with a different backing for this one as well, and the whole thing moves very nicely.

"Ring Of Fire" is OK, but though I hate to say it, it would have been better if Dylan had stayed out of it. "You Are My Sunshine" and "Guess Things Happen That Way" are entertaining but primarily because you sit there wondering how much longer Dylan can keep singing on one note.

THE "SELF PORTRAIT" OUT-TAKES

Undoubtedly there are more "Self Portrait" out-takes than the two here but they have not surfaced. Or, at least, some of them have surfaced but are now less out-takes than genuine tracks on the "Dylan" album. Just the same, there is still probably a good few left in Columbia's vaults. I hate to lend my voice to all the bitching that has gone on about "Self Portrait" but if these versions of "Ring Of Fire" and "Folsom Prison Blues" are anything to go by I am happy for the remaining out-takes to stay where they are.

"Ring Of Fire" is a great song but Dylan sings it with absolutely no respect for the original tune. In fact what he seems to be doing is singing the harmony lines he did on the duet version with Cash (see Nashville Sessions). These were bad enough as harmonies - as a main melody they are an insult.

"Folsom Prison Blues" was not that strong a song to start with, though the original Cash version was OK. All Dylan can find to do with it is speed it up to a ludicrous rate as the end of the song approaches. If this was not the musicians playing a joke on him it must have been Dylan deciding he wanted to get this whole Nashville bit out of the way as soon as possible.

ISLE OF WIGHT

In an interview prior to the concert Dylan said that he and The Band might stay on stage for three hours. The fact that they only stayed on for one hour caused quite a lot of resentment, especially as no reason was given for this. Something Dylan said to A. J. Weberman in their renowned telephone conversation of some time later (see interviews and miscellaneous tapes) indicated that he had simply been freaked out by the sheer size of the crowd.

Freaked-out or not , there was none of the old Dylan crowd-baiting. As with the press prior to the concert, he was the epitome of politeness on stage even down to his opening remark, 'It's great to be here'. This, plus his baggy-suited, straight appearance made it seem it was not Bob Dylan at all. This impression was nourished by the fact that he sang the songs like one of those performers who sing Dylan songs with an obvious total lack of comprehension of the material. You know - they put all the emphasis in the wrong place and stick little twiddles in where they do not fit.

People have told me that the vibes at the concert were great, so I suppose it is unfair to criticise the music in isolation. Just the same, in isolation I personally find the music generally dire. The versions of "She Belongs To Me", "Like A Rolling Stone" and "Mighty Quinn" are not much short of criminal and most of the other songs are nothing more than pale shadows of the originals. Exceptions, and by exceptions I mean songs about which anything good can be found to be said, are "It Ain't Me Babe", "Ramona" and "I Pity The Poor Immigrant". The latter's particular virtue is Robbie Robertson's solo where he makes his guitar sound like a mandolin and then crashes in at just the right moment with a more standard rock riff. Robbie Robertson's guitar is also something of a saving grace on "Highway 61 Revisited" where he compromises on the original 'wheeeeeee' sounds with an excellent line somewhat similar to the intro on Creedence Clearwater's "Up Around The Bend".

"It Ain't Me, Babe" is good because, while hardly anything of the original tune remains, the new tune is very pleasant. "Ramona" is not a patch on the original but it is such a good song it manages to slide into the treatment Dylan gives it pretty well. "Minstrel Boy" is hard to judge. It was the only totally new song of the set and as no other version has surfaced it is impossible to tell whether it suffered similar loss of zest to most of the other numbers. The extra-folky chorus is terrible but the verse has a very nice tune and lyrics that, from what you can hear of them, sound fairly good. It is just possible I suppose that this may originally have been an undiscovered Basement song.

Given the general standard I suppose that "I Threw It All Away", "Mr. Tambourine Man" and "I Dreamed I Saw St. Augustine" have to be conceded as passable renderings. A few people also rave about "Wild Mountain Thyme". I cannot see it myself but at £30,000 an hour I suppose it is a question of 'if you've got the thyme I've got the money'.

```
WOODY  GUTHRIE  MEMORIAL  CONCERT,  CARNEGIE
HALL     Mono Audience tape (not on disc)
Date Recorded: 20th January, 1968
```

Song Title
This Train
With Odetta & rest of concert participants

WOODY GUTHRIE MEMORIAL CONCERT, CARNEGIE HALL

Date Recorded: 20th January, 1968

Song Title	Records on which appearing			Stereo	PA tape
I Ain't Got No Home *1	Bridgett's Album - A Vinyl Headstone Almost In Place	A Tribute To Woody Guthrie Part 1 *2	A Tribute To Woody Guthrie Highlights *2	A Tribute To Woody Guthrie (double) *2	
Dear Mrs. Roosevelt *1	"	"	"	"	
Grand Coulee Dam *1	"	"	"	"	The Music People *2
This Land Is Your Land *3	A Tribute To Woody Guthrie Part 2 *2			"	

*1 With the Crackers (The Band)
*2 Official Recordings
*3 Judy Collins - Dylan sings background vocals

JOHNNY CASH TV DOCUMENTARY Mono & Stereo Date Recorded: Jan 1969

Song Titles	Records on which appearing			
Girl From The North Country (stereo) *1	Nashville Skyline *2			
One Too Many Mornings (mono) *1	Long Time Gone (EPs)	1000 Miles Behind	Dylan - (Don't) Look Back (triple)	40 Red White And Blue Shoestrings
*1 With Johnny Cash *2 Official Recording				

JOHNNY CASH SHOW, ABC-TV Mono Date Recorded: May 1969

Song Titles	Records on which appearing		
I Threw It All Away	Joaquin Antique		
Living The Blues	"	Great White Wonder (double only)	Bob Dylan In Concert Volume 2
Girl From The North Country			

NASHVILLE SESSION WITH JOHNNY CASH
Stereo   Date Recorded: February 1969

Song Titles	Records on which appearing	
One Too Many Mornings	The Dylan Cash Session	Nashville Sunset
Good Ol' Mountain Dew	"	"
I Still Miss Someone	"	"
Careless Love	"	"
Matchbox	"	"
That's Alright Mama	"	"
Big River	"	"
I Walk The Line	"	"
You Are My Sunshine	"	"
Ring Of Fire	"	"
Guess Things Happen That Way	"	"
Just A Closer Walk With Thee		"
'T' For Texas/Blue Yodell	"	"

All duets with Johnny Cash
Some editions of "The Dylan Cash Session" substitute "Just A Closer Walk With Thee" for "Blue Yodell"

SELF PORTRAIT OUT-TAKES   Mono
Date Recorded: June 1969

Song Titles	Records on which appearing	
Ring Of Fire	Let Me Die In My Footsteps	70 Dollar Robbery
Folsom Prison Blues	"	"

THE GEORGE HARRISON SESSION

There is *somebody* singing with George Harrison on these two songs but he is very much in the background. The only circumstantial evidence in support of its being Dylan is that he gets composing credit on George Harrison's official version of "I'd Have You Any Time". Anyway, the tracks here are not more than try-outs, so they do not embody one of the more tantalising Dylan mysteries.

ISLE OF WIGHT   Mono (except tracks available on official albums)   Date Recorded: 31st August, 1969

Song Titles	Records on which appearing			
She Belongs To Me	Isle Of Wight (incomplete)	Bob Dylan In Concert Volume 1	Self Portrait *1	Dylan - (Don't) Look Back (triple)
I Threw It All Away	Isle Of Wight			"
Maggie's Farm	"			70 Dollar Robbery
Wild Mountain Thyme		Daddy Rolling Stone	V.D. Waltz	"
It Ain't Me Babe	"	"	‥	"
To Ramona	"	"		
Lay Lady Lay	(incomplete)			
Highway 61 Revisited	Isle Of Wight	Bob Dylan In Concert Volume 1		
One Too Many Mornings	"			
I Pity The Poor Immigrant	(incomplete)			
Like A Rolling Stone	Isle Of Wight	Picnic *2	Self Portrait *1	
I'll Be Your Baby Tonight	" (incomplete)			
Mighty Quinn		More Bob Dylan Greatest Hits *1	"	
Minstrel Boy	Isle Of Wight	Daddy Rolling Stone		
Rainy Day Women Nos. 12 & 35	(incomplete)	Bob Dylan In Concert Volume 1		
Mr. Tambourine Man	Isle Of Wight (fragment) *3			
I Dreamed I Saw St. Augustine	Isle Of Wight *3 / " *3			

*1 Official Recording
*2 Existence uncertain
*3 Not on some versions

```
┌─────────────────────────────────────────────────────────┐
│ GEORGE HARRISON SESSION    Stereo                         │
│ Date Recorded: Probably 1969                              │
├──────────────────────────┬──────────────────────────────┤
│ Song Titles              │ Records on which appearing     │
├──────────────────────────┼──────────────────────────────┤
│ Every Time Somebody      │ Get Together Watching          │
│ Comes To Town            │        *1   Rainbows *2        │
├──────────────────────────┼──────────────────────────────┤
│ I'd Have You Any Time    │      "            "            │
├──────────────────────────┴──────────────────────────────┤
│ *1 Beatles bootleg EP                                     │
│ *2 Beatles bootleg of which there is also rumoured        │
│ to be an EP version; some versions do not have            │
│ these two tracks included                                 │
│ Whether Dylan is really on these tracks is hard           │
│ to tell                                                   │
└─────────────────────────────────────────────────────────┘
```

FANFARE - EARL SCRUGGS' TV DOCUMENTARY

"Nashville Skyline Rag" as performed on this programme was released officially (see chart) but does not measure up to the original Dylan album version. "East Virginia Blues" was not released but is quite good. Dylan's vocal is a shade too quiet but the tune still gets across and is nicely set off by the assortment of banjos and guitars that form the backing.

Earl Scruggs introduces the song (I assume it is Earl Scruggs) by saying 'Bob, why don't we do one that we can all sing together - something like "East Virginia Blues" '. As you would expect, Dylan does not come back with an equally well-rehearsed spontaneous rejoinder but goes straight into the song without even an acknowledging mumble.

BANGLADESH FIRST SHOW

Although PA recordings of two songs from the first show are in circulation, the sound quality is not up to the standard of the Apple album because, apart from having been taped from a radio programme, the recording equipment at the concert was apparently not as finely adjusted for the first show as it was for the second.

But sound quality aside, Dylan is definitely getting his inspiration back and the performances here are very good. "Hard Rain" maybe just has the edge on the second show version and George Harrison's lead seems to bear more relevance to the song the first time round. I cannot think of any particular reason why Dylan chose to drop "Love Minus Zero" for the second show. This version moves very well, Dylan's acoustic guitar is excellent and the other four superstars backing him get a more integrated sound than on some of the later tracks.

There are a number of bootlegs purporting to include first show Bangladesh tracks but as far as I can ascertain all these are in fact from the second show apart from a diabolical recording of "Love Minus Zero" which appears on the generally diabolical "Help" album. From a collector's point of view it must be acknowledged that Dylan gets very good coverage on the official Bangladesh album and anyway this is one area where bootlegging really is somewhat unethical.

FANFARE – EARL SCRUGGS TV DOCUMENTARY Mono & Stereo Date Recorded: 1970		
Song Titles	Records on which appearing	
Nashville Skyline Rag (stereo)	Earl Scruggs, His Family & Friends *	
East Virginia Blues	V.D. Waltz	70 Dollar Robbery
* Official Recording		

BANGLADESH FIRST SHOW Stereo PA tape Date Recorded: 1st August, 1971	
Song Titles	Record on which appearing
Love Minus Zero/No Limit	Help
A Hard Rain's A-Gonna Fall	

BANGLADESH FIRST SHOW   Mono Audience tape (not on disc) Date Recorded: 1st August, 1971
Song Titles
A Hard Rain's A-Gonna Fall
It Takes A Lot To Laugh, It Takes A Train To Cry
Blowin' In The Wind
Love Minus Zero/No Limit
Just Like A Woman

PAT GARRETT & BILLY THE KID

Somewhere, presumably, someone has a complete tape of the film soundtrack. But as it stands at the moment the only one being circulated is about ten minutes of highlights. Why record companies choose to call records soundtrack albums when they include different performances from those in the film is strange. However, possibly collectors are happy with a ten minute tape. It has a very slightly differing version of "Knockin' On Heaven's Door" plus another three "Billy" 's. Six "Billy" 's, pleasant as the song is, are probably enough for anyone. My only regret is that the tape does not include the bit in the film where Dylan has to keep repeating 'Beef stoo'.

BANGLADESH SECOND SHOW   Mono   Audience tape
Date Recorded: 1st August, 1971

Song Titles	Records on which appearing		
A Hard Rain's A-Gonna Fall	George Harrison, Bob Dylan, Leon Russell, Eric Clapton		
It Takes A Lot To Laugh, It Takes A Train To Cry	"		
Blowin' In The Wind	"		
Mr. Tambourine Man	"	Concert For Bangladesh	Madison Square Garden August 1st 1971 Afternoon Concert *1
Just Like A Woman	"	"	" *2

*1 This track could not be from the afternoon concert as Dylan did not perform it then
*2 This track is more likely to have come from the evening concert than the afternoon concert, hence its inclusion on this chart
The albums on this chart have been released under a number of different titles (see discography)
Dylan's set for the second Bangladesh show appears in its entirety on "The Concert For Bangladesh" triple album on Apple Records.

As to actual session out-takes nothing has leaked out but there are reports of several more variations on "Billy" plus the following titles: "Turkey Number 2", Turkey In The Straw", "Billy Surrenders" (alternative title "Speedball"), "Pico's Blues" and "Holly's Song".

Some of these tracks, according to a report in Rolling Stone by somebody who was actually at the sessions, are really excellent. The fact that they were not used, plus the fact that M.G.M. sold the soundtrack to Columbia at a time when Dylan's contract with Columbia had actually expired, may have contributed to Dylan's reputed disillusionment with the whole project.

BILLY THE KID   Mono   (not on disc) Date Recorded: 1973
Song Titles
Instrumental (fragment) Billy (fragment) Billy (fragment) Knockin' On Heaven's Door (fragment) Billy (fragment)
A bootleg EP titled "Alias", which purports to contain music from the actual soundtrack of "Pat Garrett And Billy The Kid", is in existence but it would seem to have been copied from the official album rather than to contain the above performances

THE 1974 TOUR WITH THE BAND

With the '74 tour collectors suddenly became posed with a problem they had not hitherto experienced with Dylan material, i.e., an over-abundance. It was a twenty-six city tour and tape recorders were out like flies. So there are thousands of tapes of varying levels of sound quality.

The matter is complicated by the famous but elusive White Bear Albums - eighteen doubles released within six weeks of each concert respectively and each only available, at least initially, in the surrounding area of the concert from which it was taken. As opposed to all the other '74 tour bootlegs, all the White Bear Albums are reputed to be mastered from tapes recorded direct from the P.A. systems. I have never actually seen or heard a copy of a White Bear Album but I understand the sound quality is second only to the official album, though still leaves a margin of doubt as to whether it was mastered from P.A. or audience recordings. Either way, it is strange that, given the organisation that must have been required to mount such a massive and efficient operation, there does not seem to have been any real attempt to export the albums. Just who, one wonders, are the people behind the White Bear?

Coming back to the question of the sheer bulk of tapes in circulation, the only feasible way to cover the area here is to simply list those performances

CHICAGO – THE AMPHITHEATER Mono/Stereo* Date Recorded: 3rd January, 1974

Song Titles	Records on which appearing		
	On The Road Again		
Hero Blues	On The Road Again		
Lay Lady Lay	"		
Tough Mama	"	Lovesongs For America	Drunken Minstrel
It Ain't Me Babe	"	"	
Leopard-skin Pill-box Hat	"	"	
All Along The Watchtower	"		Aspects Of Bob Dylan On Tour Volume 1
Ballad Of A Thin Man	"		
I Don't Believe You	"		
The Times They Are A-Changin'	"		
Song To Woody	"		"
The Lonesome Death Of Hattie Carroll	"		"
Except You	"		"
It's Alright Ma (I'm Only Bleeding)	"	Joaquin Antique On The Road 1974-1975	"
Forever Young	"	Lovesongs For America	
Something There Is About You	"	"	
Like A Rolling Stone	"	"	
The Weight	"		
Most Likely You Go Your Way	"		

* There are many 1974 tour tapes circulating in both mono and stereo and all appear to be audience tapes; if the White Bear albums do exist and they are indeed PA tapes, then PA tapes must exist; but none seem to be in circulation which appear on albums. With regard to material not on albums I ask the reader to assume that if there is one specific gig he is interested in, it is a safe bet that somebody somewhere will have a tape of it. As to the concerts actually listed here there will certainly be quite a lot of errors and omissions, for which I apologise, but information as to what was done where and when in 1974 becomes more confused as the time recedes.

As to attempting individual critiques of the concerts there is a lack of space in this book, inclination on my part, and point generally. The concerts do not seem to have varied that much - the Chicago gigs maybe get more people's votes than most, but in general they all seem to have been much the same from the point of view of Dylan's and The Band's performance and of the audience's response. The latter is universally ecstatic to the point where you feel that if someone had put a dead cat on stage and called it Bob Dylan the reaction would have been the same. According to a quote from Bill Graham, who organised the tour, Dylan himself was a little suspicious at first of the degree of enthusiasm. Apparently when he asked Dylan why he did not do encores even though they were demanded he replied that the audience only called for an encore because it was the thing to do. So the next night, at the end of the last song, Bill Graham ordered the house lights to be turned on so that Dylan could see the audience's faces. It was after that apparently that he started doing an encore every time.

I personally find most of the '74 tour performances I have heard slightly sterile. Dylan was churning it out night after night, sometimes in the afternoons as well, and that is just what it sounds like. 'Glazed' is the word for his voice most of the time. On the whole The Band's sets are a lot better.

For me the best thing to have come out of the tour is "Except You", probably written around the time of "Planet Waves" and done at a number of concerts including Chicago, from which comes the most bootlegged version. It is a fairly good tune with some quite biting lyrics. A studio version is rumoured but to date nothing has happened to substantiate the rumour.

Apart from "Except You" and odd exceptions such as the inclusion of "Hero Blues" at Chicago, "As I Went Out One Morning" at Toronto, "Desolation Row" at St. Louis and "Visions Of Johanna" at Denver, the choice of material was very predictable throughout the tour. In a conversation with Dylan, Paul Simon was once quoted as saying that he got fed up with audiences expecting him to do "Sounds Of Silence", "Homeward Bound" and all his other best known stuff time after time. Dylan was reported as responding that if he went to a Paul Simon concert those would be the songs *he'd* like to hear him do. So possibly, just for once, in amongst all the misconceptions audiences have about Dylan, we have here a little misconception that Dylan has about audiences.

'BLOOD ON THE TRACKS' SESSIONS

'Blood on the Tracks' originally appeared in the States with different versions of five of the songs, but only on test pressings. Why Dylan decided to do these five again and release the album as it now stands is not clear, but a few people must have got hold of the originals and must be very proud owners of albums that are now worth a fortune. (The original covers, in case you are wondering, are two a penny.)

Unfortunately the most common tape in circulation was taken from a

CHICAGO – THE AMPHITHEATER	Date Recorded: 4th January, 1974	
Song Titles	Records on which appearing	
	Second Time Around	Chicago
Hero Blues		
Lay Lady Lay	Second Time Around	Chicago
Just Like Tom Thumb's Blues	"	
It Ain't Me Babe	"	"
Tough Mama	"	
Ballad Of A Thin Man	"	"
All Along The Watchtower	"	"
Leopard-skin Pill-box Hat	"	"
Knockin' On Heaven's Door		
The Times They Are A-Changin'	"	
Love Minus Zero/No Limit	"	
The Lonesome Death Of Hattie Carroll	"	
Except You	"	
It's Alright Ma (I'm Only Bleeding)	"	
Forever Young	"	"
Something There Is About You		"
Like A Rolling Stone	"	"
Most Likely You Go Your Way		"

A performance of "Maggie's Farm" also appears on the album "Second Time Around" but does not seem to have come from this concert copy with a jump on "Idiot Wind". (Tapes without the jump *are* around, but they are rare.) All the bootlegs were mastered from tapes with the jump and record collectors experienced a certain amount of confusion over whether or not the jump was actually a fault in their own copies of these bootlegs. This confusion was added to by the fact that the first bootleg "Joaquin Antique" did have a fault of its own on all copies - a stick on "Idiot Wind" not long after the jump. I personally found out the truth about this to my cost through trying to persuade a perfectly good copy of "Joaquin Antique" not to jump. Korneyphone in fact withdrew the album because of the stick and it immediately became one of the most valuable bootlegs in existence. The value was subsequently brought down a little by the release of "Passed Over & Rolling Thunder" which contained all five tracks, but copies of "Joaquin Antique" still command a high price, partially because of their simple rarity value and partially because the tracks have a slightly different sound to that of the later albums.

PHILADELPHIA - THE SPECTRUM - 1st Show Date Recorded: 6th January, 1974	
Song Titles	Record on which appearing
Hollis Brown	Epitaph To Amerika
Lay Lady Lay	"
Just Like Tom Thumb's Blues	"
It Ain't Me Babe	"
Tough Mama	"
Ballad Of A Thin Man	"
All Along The Watchtower	"
Leopard-skin Pill-box Hat	"
Knockin' On Heaven's Door	"
To Ramona	"
Mama You Been On My Mind	"
The Lonesome Death Of Hattie Carroll	"
Except You	"
It's Alright Ma (I'm Only Bleeding)	"
I Don't Believe You	"
Forever Young	"
Something There Is About You	"
Like A Rolling Stone	"

Returning to the actual music I think it is true to say that replacing the original "If You See Her Say Hello" and "Lily, Rosemary And The Jack Of Hearts" was a good move. The originals have only a rather uninteresting acoustic guitar plus bass accompaniment, the tunes are not nearly as worked out as the later versions and Dylan sings them in a rather sickly sweet accent. The toned down version of this accent worked well on "You're Gonna Make Me Lonesome When You Go" but it is especially unsuccessful on "If You See Her Say Hello".

PHILADELPHIA - THE SPECTRUM - 2nd Show Date Recorded: 6th January, 1974	
Song Titles	Record on which appearing
Rainy Day Women Nos. 12 & 35	40 Red White And Blue Shoestrings *
Lay Lady Lay	"
Just Like Tom Thumb's Blues	"
It Ain't Me Babe	"
I Don't Believe You	"
Ballad Of A Thin Man	"
All Along The Watchtower	"
Leopard-skin Pill-box Hat	"
Knockin' On Heaven's Door	"
The Times They Are A-Changin'	"
It's All Over Now, Baby Blue	"
Song To Woody	"
Mr. Tambourine Man	"
Except You	"
It's Alright Ma (I'm Only Bleeding)	"
Forever Young	"
Something There Is About You	"
Like A Rolling Stone	"
Most Likely You Go Your Way	"
* Not to be confused with earlier album of the same title	

"Tangled Up In Blue" is different, but just about as good as the final version. The difference lies again in the simple acoustic backing plus one or two lyric changes. These include relating the first half of the song's story in the third person as opposed to the first person. One possible reason why the track was withdrawn is that a racket goes on throughout caused, apparently, by Dylan's jacket buttons rattling against the back of his guitar.

The other two originals are in something of a different category in that they have beautiful mellow backings provided by Eric Weissberg's Deliverance. It is hard to choose between the original and the final version of "You're A Big Girl Now" - they are both exceptionally good. This applies also to "Idiot Wind" but in this case the two versions are absolutely poles apart in concept and arrangement. Whereas the final version is virtually a rock song, the original is very gentle musically. The gentleness is deceptive because the words gain vitriol in being sung mildly; nevertheless the difference would have been easily wide enough to justify leaving both versions on the album. Further justification would have been provided by the fairly drastic lyric changes in the last two verses.

"Idiot Wind" is reckoned to be concerned at least partially with media distortion. Is it possible, one wonders, that the idiot wind is Columbia's publicity machine? New Musical Express recently reported that, when Dylan returned to Columbia after his sojourn with Asylum, he wanted to do a triple album but the company did not think the market could take it. Of course, what is more important than the question of whether Dylan wrote "Idiot Wind" as a reaction to this is the question of what happened to the rest of the songs that would have made up the triple. That is if the N.M.E. report is not of a similar fantasy nature to their claim to have got hold of the lost Dylan album, "Snow Over Interstate 80".

FRIENDS OF CHILE
The only positive thing that can be said of Dylan's contribution to the Chile Benefit is that he deserves credit simply for taking part in the concert.

Other than that the singing is horrific. Reputedly Dylan was so smashed that he fell off the stage. It all adds to the legend, doesn't it?

THE OTHER END CLUB (WITH JACK ELLIOT)
Here you have yet another example of why, if you want a truly representative Dylan collection, you cannot stop with the official stuff. This was an impromptu appearance on Jack Elliot's spot at the Other End Club but, after the duet on "Pretty Boy Floyd", instead of some standard impromptu number what we get is the one and only available performance of a song known to collectors as "St. John The Evangelist", probably the most brilliant thing Dylan had done for years. Beautiful, eerie, easily-as-good-as-"Blonde-on-Blonde" lyrics and a tune that is unusual and perfect.

The performance took place shortly before Dylan went into the studios to record "Desire". The only reason I can think of why it did not go on the album, apart from the usual Dylan contrariness, is that the lyrics are a marital good-bye. But it having been excluded, if old patterns repeat themselves, I doubt whether we shall ever see it officially now.

PHILADELPHIA – THE SPECTRUM	Date Recorded: 7th January, 1974	
Song Titles	Records on which appearing	
Rainy Day Women Nos. 12 & 35	In The Waters Of Oblivion	
Lay Lady Lay	"	
Just Like Tom Thumb's Blues	"	
It Ain't Me Babe	"	
I Don't Believe You	"	
Ballad Of A Thin Man	"	
All Along The Watchtower	"	
Hollis Brown	"	
Knockin' On Heaven's Door	"	
Just Like A Woman	"	
Girl From The North Country	"	Drunken Minstrel
Wedding Song	"	"
Except You	"	
It's Alright Ma (I'm Only Bleeding)	"	
Forever Young	"	
Something There Is About You	"	
Like A Rolling Stone	"	
Most Likely You Go Your Way	"	

A performance of "The Times They Are A-Changin'" appears on the album "In The Waters Of Oblivion" but does not seem to have come from this concert; this album is not to be confused with the earlier album titled "Waters Of Oblivion"

TORONTO – MAPLE LEAF GARDENS	Date Recorded: 10th January, 1974
Song Titles	Records on which appearing
Most Likely You Go Your Way	Great American Hawks
I Don't Believe You	"
As I Went Out One Morning	"
Lay Lady Lay	"
Just Like Tom Thumb's Blues	"
Ballad Of A Thin Man	"
All Along The Watchtower	"
Hollis Brown	"
Knockin' On Heaven's Door	"
The Times They Are A-Changin'	"
Don't Think Twice, It's All Right	"
Gates Of Eden	"
Love Minus Zero/No Limit	" Drunken Minstrel
It's Alright Ma (I'm Only Bleeding)	"
Forever Young	"
Something There Is About You	"
Like A Rolling Stone	"

MONTREAL – THE FORUM Date Recorded: 11th January, 1974	
Song Titles	Records on which appearing
Most Likely You Go Your Way	Ceremonies For The Horsemen
Lay Lady Lay	"
Just Like Tom Thumb's Blues	"
I Don't Believe You	"
It Ain't Me Babe	"
Ballad Of A Thin Man	"
All Along The Watchtower	"
Hollis Brown	"
Knockin' On Heaven's Door	"
The Times They Are A-Changin'	"
Gates Of Eden	"
Except You	" Drunken Minstrel
It' Alright Ma (I'm Only Bleeding)	"
Don't Think Twice, It's All Right	"
Forever Young	"
Something There Is About You	"
Like A Rolling Stone	"
Most Likely You Go Your Way	" *

An isolated track from the Montreal concert of 12th January, "Blowin' In The Wind", appears on the album "Drunken Minstrel"
* It is unknown whether the reprise of "Most Likely You Go Your Way" is included on the White Bear albums

BOSTON – BOSTON GARDENS – 1st Show   Date Recorded: 14th January, 1974

Song Titles	Records on which appearing	
Rainy Day Women Nos. 12 & 35	Sand And Ashes	Boston 1974 – Dylan & The Band Return
Lay Lady Lay	"	"
Just Like Tom Thumb's Blues	"	"
It Ain't Me Babe	"	"
I Don't Believe You	"	"
Ballad Of A Thin Man	"	"
All Along The Watchtower	"	"
Hollis Brown	"	"
Knockin' On Heaven's Door	"	"
The Times They Are A-Changin'	"	"
Don't Think Twice, It's All Right	"	"
Gates Of Eden	"	"
Just Like A Woman	"	"
It's Alright Ma (I'm Only Bleeding)	"	"
Forever Young	"	"
Something There Is About You	"	"
Like A Rolling Stone	"	"
Most Likely You Go Your Way	"	"

BOSTON - BOSTON GARDENS - 2nd Show Date Recorded: 14th January, 1974	
Song Titles	Record on which appearing
Most Likely You Go Your Way	Swansong
Lay Lady Lay	"
Just Like Tom Thumb's Blues	"
Rainy Day Women Nos. 12 & 35	"
It Ain't Me Babe	"
Ballad Of A Thin Man	"
All Along The Watchtower	"
Hollis Brown	"
Knockin' On Heaven's Door	"
Blowin' In The Wind	
Don't Think Twice, It's All Right	"
Gates Of Eden	"
Love Minus Zero/No Limit	"
It's Alright Ma (I'm Only Bleeding)	"
Forever Young	"
Something There Is ABout You	"
Like A Rolling Stone	"
Most Likely You Go Your Way	

JOHN HAMMOND TV SHOW

This is where "Hurricane" as shown on "The Old Grey Whistle Test" came from. Why the B.B.C. did not show the complete Dylan performance is a little hard to understand, but then they cut off Jackson Browne in the middle of "The Pretender" when there was not even another programme to follow.

Having chosen to show only half of the Dylan set, I suppose "Hurricane" was the obvious choice. But from a collector's point of view the other half would have been a lot better. Apart from the way Dylan sings 'Champyan uv thur wirrrld', it is not very different from the single version. "Oh Sister", on the other hand, was not available in this country in any form at the time, and "Simple Twist Of Fate" is different from the album version both backing-wise and lyric-wise.

Dylan introduced "Oh Sister" rather aggressively with the words, 'This is for someone watching tonight I know - she knows who she is'. On a recent L.P. Joan Baez sang a self-penned song called "Oh Brother" in which she accuses some unspecified person of presumption.

It was very strange to see the man himself on the T.V. screen. The old charisma still oozed even if it was a little restricted by black and white striped trousers.

WASHINGTON – CAPITOL CENTER Date Recorded: 15th January, 1974	
Song Titles	Record on which appearing
Most Likely You Go Your Way	Tarantula XI
Lay Lady Lay	"
Just Like Tom Thumb's Blues	"
I Don't Believe You	"
It Ain't Me Babe	"
Ballad Of A Thin Man	"
All Along The Watchtower	"
Hollis Brown	"
Knockin' On Heaven's Door	"
The Times They Are A-Changin'	"
Don't Think Twice, It's All Right	"
Wedding Song	"
Just Like A Woman	"
It's Alright Ma (I'm Only Bleeding)	"
Forever Young	"
Something There Is About You	"
Like A Rolling Stone	"
Most Likely You Go Your Way	

THE ROLLING THUNDER REVUE

The Rolling Thunder Revue ran for a long time. Nothing short of an encyclopedia would serve to categorise the tapes that were made. So as with the '74 tour the run-down in this book will be on the basis simply of those performances that have got on to disc.

As to appraising the Revue I can only make the generalised statement that from what I have heard on tape and from reports generally it seems to have been a much more vital and spontaneous thing than the '74 tour. This was presumably Dylan's intention in keeping the arrangements relatively informal, though possibly he was also hoping that lack of notice as to the where and when of concerts might help to thwart 'White Bear'. There are in fact rumours of a couple of Rolling Thunder 'White Bear' albums but whether these are true and, if they are, whether the albums are up to the standard of the '74 tour 'White Bear' albums, I have no idea.

A fair number of reasonable quality audience tape bootlegs have got to this country but apart from "Bridgett's Album - A Vinyl Headstone Almost In Place", the bootleg of the songs from the T.V. special not included in the official album, there have been no albums of P.A. quality.

I have not included a separate appraisal of the T.V. special because it seems a reasonable assumption that anyone interested enough in Dylan to buy this book is likely to have seen the programme. I thought "Deportees" was the most enjoyable thing in the show. Dylan's and Joan Baez's duetting has substantially improved since the '63-'64 days and it was nice to see her coping with him as well, both musically and emotionally.

Roger McGuinn's contribution was also rather good. I liked the way Dylan's face remained absolutely inscrutable while McGuinn worked his lyric revamp. It is a shame they faded the programme half-way through the number. I was looking forward to Dylan's revenge.

THE LAST WALTZ

This is from The Band's farewell concert which wound up as a film and album. At the time of writing neither had gone on release so it is not possible to comment on them here. A tape began circulating at a fairly early stage but, although it is of P.A. quality, the mix leaves a lot to be desired.

Dylan's contributions to the concert are punchy but he still sounds very much as he did on the '74 tour. On the other hand, The Band's backing is heavier than in '74 and each number is more distinctively arranged. The heaviness reaches a peak with the reprise of "Baby Let Me Follow You Down" which uses an intro not far removed from the Cream's "Sunshine Of Your Love". Robbie Robertson is in fine form generally and in places there are shades of the '66 Albert Hall concert. Particularly noteworthy is

WASHINGTON – CAPITOL CENTER Date Recorded: 16th January, 1974	
Song Titles	Record on which appearing
Most Likely You Go Your Way	Rare Spots
Lay Lady Lay	"
Just Like Tom Thumb's Blues	"
One Too Many Mornings	
It Ain't Me Babe	"
Ballad Of A Thin Man	"
All Along The Watchtower	"
Hollis Brown	"
Knockin' On Heaven's Door	"
The Times They Are A-Changin'	"
Don't Think Twice, It's All Right	"
Gates Of Eden	"
Except You	"
Forever Young	"
Something There Is About You	"
Like A Rolling Stone	"
Most Likely You Go Your Way	

his work on "Forever Young" where he gets a nice 'wall of sound' effect while maintaining a strong melodic content. Also with this number, unlike some of the others, Dylan shows some respect for the original tune - and it is a good one.

"I Shall Be Released" also has him sticking mostly to the original melody and again it is a strong, full sound. The chorus seems to involve all the concert's guests and, though a bit ragged, gets something of the feel of "Blowin' In The Wind" at the '63 Newport Folk Festival.

A device used twice in Dylan's set is that of running straight into the next number without waiting for applause (unless, of course, the tape has been cleverly spliced). It occurs where "Hazel" follows "Baby Let Me Follow You Down" and then again from "Forever Young" into the reprise of "Let Me Follow You Down". Perhaps Dylan's admiration for The Beatles' innovations finally got the better of him even if he did wait ten years to actually copy one.

There is more I could say about the tape but it is rather academic in view of the imminent release of the official album from the concert. Whether, of course, all the Dylan tracks will be used on the album is uncertain. It is The Band's concert and Dylan is just one of a whole load of superstar guests, but *the* one.

Interviews and Miscellaneous Tapes

December 1961 - Interview with Billy James of Columbia
December 1964 - Interview with Bob Blackmar at Long Beach, California
May 1965   - Swedish Radio interview
October 1965 - Interview with Allen Stone in Detroit
December 1965 - Los Angeles press conference
December 1965 - San Francisco press conference, K.Q.E.D.-T.V.
March 1966   - Interview for C.B.C.
? 1966   - Interview with Nat Hentoff for Playboy
? 1966   - Bob Fass phone-in
? 1966   - Stockholm press conference
January 1971 - Telephone conversation with A. J. Weberman.
                  This tape in fact found its way on to an official Broadside album entitled "Bob Dylan Versus A. J. Weberman" but Dylan had it withdrawn before it reached the shops.
                  See Official Discography - Miscellaneous.
November 1974 - Interview with Mary Travers. (Extracts from this appear on the bootleg E.P. "Basics In G Minor". Poor quality.)
1975   - Dylan's Los Angeles answerphone. Dylan (apparently) singing a little song asking people to leave a message when they 'hear that lonesome tone'. Appears on the E.P. "Valentino Type Tangos".

Song Titles	Records on which appearing	
	Mom's Apple Pie	Charlotte, N. Carolina
Most Likely You Go Your Way		"
Lay Lady Lay		"
Just Like Tom Thumb's Blues		"
Rainy Day Women Nos. 12 & 35		"
It Ain't Me Babe		"
Ballad Of A Thin Man		"
All Along The Watchtower		"
Hollis Brown		"
Knockin' On Heaven's Door		"
The Times They Are A-Changin'		"
Don't Think Twice, It's All Right		"
Gates Of Eden		"
Just Like A Woman		"
It's Alright Ma (I'm Only Bleeding)		"
Forever Young		"
Something There Is About You		"
Like A Rolling Stone		"
Most Likely You Go Your Way		

CHARLOTTE - COLLISEUM   Date Recorded: 17th January, 1974

MIAMI – HOLLYWOOD SPORTATORIUM	Date Recorded: 19th January, 1974	
Song Titles	Records on which appearing	
Most Likely You Go Your Way	Love Songs	Lovesongs For America
Lay Lady Lay	"	"
Just Like Tom Thumb's Blues	"	"
Leopard-skin Pill-box Hat	"	"
It Ain't Me Babe	"	"
Ballad Of A Thin Man	"	"
All Along The Watchtower	"	"
Hollis Brown	"	"
Knockin' On Heaven's Door	"	"
The Times They Are A-Changin'	"	"
Don't Think Twice, It's All Right	"	"
Gates Of Eden	"	"
Just Like A Woman	"	"
It's Alright Ma (I'm Only Bleeding)		"
Forever Young	"	"
Something There Is About You	"	"
Like A Rolling Stone	"	"
Most Likely You Go Your Way	"	"

The album "Love Songs" includes a performance of "Rainy Day Women Nos. 12 & 35" but it does not come from this concert

MEMPHIS – MID–SOUTH COLLISEUM Date Recorded: 23rd January, 1974	
Song Titles	Record on which appearing
Most Likely You Go Your Way	Long Distance Information
Lay Lady Lay	"
Just Like Tom Thumb's Blues	"
Rainy Day Women Nos. 12 & 35	"
It Ain't Me Babe	"
Ballad Of A Thin Man	"
All Along The Watchtower	"
Hollis Brown	"
Knockin' On Heaven's Door	"
The Times They Are A-Changin'	
Don't Think Twice, It's All Right	"
4th Time Around	"
Gates Of Eden	"
Just Like A Woman	"
It's Alright Ma (I'm Only Bleeding)	"
Forever Young	"
Something There Is About You	"
Like A Rolling Stone	"
Most Likely You Go Your Way	

Dylan on Unofficial Tapes of Other Artists' Performances

ROLLING THUNDER TOUR

With regards to other artists' contributions to the Rolling Thunder concerts, Dylan sometimes assisted with the back-up and sometimes did not. As there are numerous Rolling Thunder Tapes it would be too large an undertaking to catalogue here which instrument Dylan played on what performances.

FORT WORTH – COUNTY CENTER Date Recorded: 25th January, 1974	
Song Titles	Record on which appearing
Most Likely You Go Your Way	Pony Express
Lay Lady Lay	"
Just Like Tom Thumb's Blues	"
Rainy Day Women Nos. 12 & 35	"
It Ain't Me Babe	"
Ballad Of A Thin Man	"
All Along The Watchtower	"
Hollis Brown	"
Knockin' On Heaven's Door	"
The Times They Are A-Changin'	"
Don't Think Twice, It's All Right	"
Gates Of Eden	"
Just Like A Woman	"
It's Alright Ma (I'm Only Bleeding)	"
Forever Young	"
Something There Is About You	"
Like A Rolling Stone	"
Most Likely You Go Your Way	

ALLEN GINSBERG SESSIONS 1971-72

Tapes of what was to be Allen Ginsberg's Apple album entitled 'Holy Soul Jelly Roll' are in circulation with Dylan, Happy Traum and Dave Amran assisting with accompaniments. Dylan does back-up vocals on "See You In San Diego" and "Nurse's Song", guitar accompaniment on some William Blake poems plus guitar and over-dubs of piano and organ on "September On Jessore Road". The reason for the album's non-release was reputedly either that Ginsberg and Dylan lost interest or that the language was considered too avant-garde.

NASSAU - COLLISEUM
Date Recorded: 28th January, 1974

Song Titles	Record on which appearing
Most Likely You Go Your Way	Live In The Big Apple
Lay Lady Lay	"
Just Like Tom Thumb's Blues	"
Rainy Day Women Nos. 12 & 35	"
It Ain't Me Babe	"
Ballad Of A Thin Man	"
All Along The Watchtower	"
Hollis Brown	"
Knockin' On Heaven's Door	"
The Times They Are A-Changin'	"
Don't Think Twice, It's All Right	"
Gates Of Eden	"
Just Like A Woman	"
It's Alright Ma (I'm Only Bleeding)	"
Forever Young	"
Something There Is About You	"
Like A Rolling Stone	"
Most Likely You Go Your Way	

NEW YORK - MADISON SQUARE GARDEN
Date Recorded: 30th January, 1974

"Knockin' On Heaven's Door" from this concert
appears on the official album, "Before The Flood"

ANN ARBOR - NOTRE DAME
Date Recorded: 2nd February, 1974

Song Titles	Record on which appearing
Most Likely You Go Your Way	It's Been A Long Long Time
Lay Lady Lay	"
Just Like Tom Thumb's Blues	"
Rainy Day Women Nos. 12 & 35	"
It Ain't Me Babe	"
Ballad Of A Thin Man	"
All Along The Watchtower	"
Hollis Brown	"
Knockin' On Heaven's Door	"
The Times They Are A-Changin'	"
Don't Think Twice, It's All Right	."
Gates Of Eden	"
Just Like A Woman	"
It's Alright Ma (I'm Only Bleeding)	"
Forever Young	"
Highway 61 Revisited	"
Like A Rolling Stone	"
Most Likely You Go Your Way	

ST. LOUIS - ARENA
Date Recorded: 4th February, 1974

Two Dylan performances from this concert, "A Hard Rain's A-Gonna Fall" and "Desolation Row" make an isolated appearance on the album "On The Road 1974-1975"

DENVER - COLLISEUM
Date Recorded: 6th February, 1974

"Visions Of Johanna" and "Wedding Song" from this concert appear on the album "On The Road 1974-1975"

LOS ANGELES FORUM – 1st Show   Date Recorded: 14th February, 1974

Song Titles	Records on which appearing				
	St. Valentine's Day Massacre	Bridgett's Album *1			
Most Likely You Go Your Way	St. Valentine's Day Massacre				
Lay Lady Lay	"				
Just Like Tom Thumb's Blues	"	"			
Rainy Day Women Nos. 12 & 35	"	"			
It Ain't Me Babe	"				
Ballad Of A Thin Man	"				Before The Flood *3
All Along The Watchtower	"	"			"
Hollis Brown	"				
Knockin' On Heaven's Door	"				St. Valentine's Day Massacre & More
She Belongs To Me	"				
It's All Over Now, Baby Blue	"		On The Road 1974-1975	St. Valentine's Day Massacre (triple) *2	
The Times They Are A-Changin'	"		"		
Just Like A Woman	"	"	"		
It's Alright Ma (I'm Only Bleeding)	"	"	"		
Forever Young	"				
Highway 61 Revisited	"	"	"		
Like A Rolling Stone	"	"	"		
Blowin' In The Wind	"				Before The Flood *4

*1 This album was also released under the titles "Live In 1974" and "The Last Bash"
*2 This triple album was also released as a double plus a single; the single album, titled "St. Valentine's Day Massacre: Acoustic", contains "It's All Over Now, Baby Blue" from this concert
*3 Official Recording
*4 "Blowin' In The Wind" on this album is a splice of the version from this concert and the version from the LA 13th February concert; tracks on the official album also from the 13th February are "Lay Lady Lay", "Rainy Day Women Nos. 12 & 35" and "Like A Rolling Stone"

LOS ANGELES FORUM – 2nd Show   Date Recorded: 14th February, 1974

Song Titles	Records on which appearing			Before The Flood *2
	St. Valentine's Day Massacre (triple) *1	St. Valentine's Day Massacre & More		
Most Likely You Go Your Way	"	"		
Lay Lady Lay	"	"		
Just Like Tom Thumb's Blues	"	"		
Rainy Day Women Nos. 12 & 35	"	"		"
It Ain't Me Babe	"	"		
Ballad Of A Thin Man	"	"		
All Along The Watchtower	"	"		
Hollis Brown	"	"	High Voltage *3	
Mr. Tambourine Man	"	"		
Knockin' On Heaven's Door	"	"		
She Belongs To Me	"	"	On The Road 1974-1975	"
Just Like A Woman	"	"		
Gates Of Eden	"	"		"
Don't Think Twice, It's All Right	"	"		"
It's Alright Ma (I'm Only Bleeding)	"	"		
Forever Young	"	"		"
Highway 61 Revisited	"	"		
Like A Rolling Stone	"	"		
Maggie's Farm	"	"		
Blowin' In The Wind	"	"		

*1 This album was also sold as a single – "St. Valentine's Day Massacre: Acoustic" plus a double – "St. Valentine's Day Massacre: Electric"

*2 Official Recording

*3 Possibly other tracks on this album come from the LA concerts but it's hard to determine precise source

This was the last concert of the 1974 tour

FRIENDS OF CHILE Mono PA tape Date Recorded: May 1974		
Song Titles	Records on which appearing	
Deportees *		
North Country Blues	Friends Of Chile	Video Chile
Spanish Is The Loving Tongue	"	"
Blowin' In The Wind (incomplete)	"	"
* With Arlo Guthrie		

SNACK BENEFIT Stereo Date Recorded: 23rd March, 1975	
Song Titles	Record on which appearing
Are You Ready For The Country?	S.N.A.C.K. *1
Ain't That A Lot Of Love	"
Looking For A Love	"
Loving You (Is Sweeter Than Ever)	"
I Want You	"
The Weight	"
Helpless/Knockin' On Heaven's Door *2	"
Will The Circle Be Unbroken	"
With Neil Young, Garth Hudson, Levon Helm, Rick Danko, Tim Drummond & Ben Keith *1 Although the concert was broadcast in stereo on FM radio, the bootleg is an audience tape *2 Sung as 'Knockin' on the dragon's door'	

BLOOD ON THE TRACKS OUT-TAKES   Stereo   Date Recorded: 1974

Song Titles	Records on which appearing		
	Joaquin Antique	Passed Over And Rolling Thunder	Blood-Takes
Tangled Up In Blue		"	"
Lily, Rosemary And The Jack Of Hearts	"	"	"
If You See Her Say Hello	"	"	"
You're A Big Girl Now	"	"	"
Idiot Wind	"	"	"

These tracks, which are different takes from the well-known versions, appeared on test pressing copies of "Blood On The Tracks"

OTHER END CLUB Mono Could be Audience or PA tape Date Recorded: July 1975	
Song Titles	Record on which appearing
Pretty Boy Floyd *1 St. John The Evangelist	Valentino Type Tangos (EP) *2
*1 With Jack Elliott *2 Under the title "Abandoned Love"	

Bob Dylan and The Band, 1972. (Photo by Chuck Pulin)

JOHN HAMMOND TV SHOW   Stereo
Date Recorded: 1975

Song Titles	Records on which appearing		
Hurricane	Passed Over And Rolling Thunder	Blood-Takes	Bob Dylan In Concerto (EP) *
Oh Sister	"	"	
Simple Twist Of Fate	"	"	"

* Only a fragment of "Hurricane" is included on this disc

ROLLING THUNDER TV SPECIAL, FORT COLLINS
Mono except tracks featured on official album   Date Recorded: 23rd May, 1976

Song Titles	Records on which appearing
A Hard Rain's A-Gonna Fall *1	Bridgett's Album - A Vinyl Headstone Almost In Place
Blowin' In The Wind *1	"
Railroad Boy *1	"
Deportees *1	"
I Pity The Poor Immigrant *1	"
Shelter From The Storm	Hard Rain *2
Maggie's Farm	"
One Too Many Mornings	"
Mozambique	Bridgett's Album - A Vinyl Headstone Almost In Place
Idiot Wind	Hard Rain
Knockin' On Heaven's Door (incomplete) *3	

*1 With Joan Baez
*2 Official Recording
*3 With Roger McGuinn

PROVIDENCE, RHODE ISLAND - CIVIC CENTER
Mono/Stereo *   Audience tape
Date Recorded: 4th November, 1975

Song Titles	Records on which appearing	
When I Paint My Masterpiece		
It Ain't Me Babe	Passed Over And Rolling Thunder	
A Hard Rain's A-Gonna Fall		
Romance In Durango		
Isis		
The Times They Are A-Changin'		
Never Let Me Go	"	
I Dreamed I Saw St. Augustine	"	
I Shall Be Released	"	
It's Alright Ma (I'm Only Bleeding)		
Oh Sister		
Hurricane		
One More Cup Of Coffee		
Sara		
Just Like A Woman	"	Bob Dylan In Concerto (EP)
Knockin' On Heaven's Door	"	"
This Land Is Your Land		

The version of "Knockin' On Heaven's Door" on the
album "The Hurricane Carter Benefit" is credited
as coming from Providence, Rhode Island, but this
appears to be incorrect
* As with the 1974 tour tapes, many Rolling
Thunder tapes are circulating in both mono and
stereo

BOSTON MUSIC HALL - 1st Show
Audience tape
Date Recorded: 21st November, 1975

Song Titles	Record on which appearing
When I Paint My Masterpiece	
It Ain't Me Babe	The Night The Revue Came To Boston
The Lonesome Death Of Hattie Carroll	"
It Takes A Lot To Laugh, It Takes A Train To Cry	"
Romance In Durango	"
Isis	"
Blowin' In The Wind	
The Water Is Wide (Sink Or Swim)	
Mama You Been On My Mind	
Down In The Mine (Dark As A Dungeon)	
I Shall Be Released	
Mr. Tambourine Man	
Simple Twist Of Fate	"
Oh Sister	"
Hurricane	"
One More Cup Of Coffee	"
Sara	
Just Like A Woman	
Knockin' On Heaven's Door	
This Land Is Your Land	

HARTFORD CIVIC CENTER   Audience tape
Date Recorded: 24th November, 1975

Song Titles	Record on which appearing
When I Paint My Masterpiece	Hold The Fort For What It's Worth
It Ain't Me Babe	
The Lonesome Death Of Hattie Carroll	
Tonight I'll Be Staying Here With You	
A Hard Rain's A-Gonna Fall	
Romance In Durango	
Isis	
Blowin' In The Wind	"
Dark As A Dungeon (Down In The Mine) *	
Mama You Been On My Mind *	
Never Let Me Go *	
I Shall Be Released *	
Love Minus Zero/No Limit	
Simple Twist Of Fate	
Oh Sister	
Hurricane	
One More Cup Of Coffee	
Sara	
Just Like A Woman	
Knockin' On Heaven's Door	
This Land Is Your Land	

* With Joan Baez

BANGOR, MAINE - MUNICIPAL AUDITORIUM
Audience tape
Date Recorded: 27th November, 1975

Song Titles	Records on which appearing
When I Paint My Masterpiece	
It Ain't Me Babe	Bangor, Maine
The Lonesome Death Of Hattie Carroll	
Tonight I'll Be Staying Here With You	
A Hard Rain's A-Gonna Fall	"
Romance In Durango	"
Isis	
The Times They Are A-Changin'	
I Dreamed I Saw St. Augustine	
Mama You Been On My Mind *	"
Dark As A Dungeon (Down In The Mine) *	
I Shall Be Released *	"
I Don't Believe You	
Simple Twist Of Fate	"
Oh Sister	
Hurricane	
One More Cup Of Coffee	"
Sara	
Just Like A Woman	"
Knockin' On Heaven's Door	
This Land Is Your Land	The Hurricane Carter Benefit

* With Joan Baez

HURRICANE CARTER BENEFIT - NEW YORK

NEW YORK, MADISON SQUARE GARDEN
HURRICANE CARTER BENEFIT   Audience tape
Date Recorded: 8th December, 1965

Song Titles	Record on which appearing
When I Paint My Masterpiece	The Hurricane Carter Benefit
It Ain't Me Babe	"
The Lonesome Death Of Hattie Carroll	"
Tonight I'll Be Staying Here With You	"
It Takes A Lot To Laugh, It Takes A Train To Cry	"
The Times They Are A-Changin'	"
Dark As A Dungeon (Down In The Mine)	"
Mama You Been On My Mind	"
Never Let Me Go	"
I Dreamed I Saw St. Augustine	"
Romance In Durango	"
Oh Sister	"
Hurricane	"
Isis	"
One More Cup Of Coffee	"
Sara	"
Just Like A Woman	"
Love Minus Zero/No Limit	
Simple Twist Of Fate	
Knockin' On Heaven's Door	
This Land Is Your Land	

FORT WORTH, TEXAS - COUNTY CENTER
Audience tape
Date Recorded: 16th May, 1976

Song Titles	Record on which appearing
Mr. Tambourine Man	
It Ain't Me Babe	Hold The Fort For What It's Worth
Where Did Vincent Van Gogh? *1	"
Maggie's Farm	
One Too Many Mornings	"
Mozambique	"
Isis	"
Blowin' In The Wind	
Railroad Boy *2	" *3
Deportees *2	"
I Pity The Poor Immigrant *2	"
Shelter From The Storm	"
I Threw It All Away	
Memphis Blues Again	"
Oh Sister	"
You're A Big Girl Now	"
You're Gonna Make Me Lonesome	"
When You Go	
Lay Lady Lay	"
Going Going Gone	"
Idiot Wind	"
Knockin' On Heaven's Door	
Gotta Travel On	

*1 With Bobby Neuwirth
*2 With Joan Baez
*3 This song titles "Dying Of Love" on the album sleeve

THE LAST WALTZ (THE BAND'S FAREWELL CONCERT), WINTERLAND, SAN FRANCISCO Stereo PA tape Date Recorded: 25th October, 1976	
Song Title	Record on which appearing
Baby Let Me Follow You Down	The Last Waltz*1
Hazel	
I Don't Believe You	"
Forever Young	"
Baby Let Me Follow You Down (reprise)	"
I Shall Be Released *2	
*1 Official Recording *2 With rest of concert participants	

Rumours

THE PITTSBURG RADIO TAPE
Supposedly including the titles, "Hard Time Blues", "Jack Of Diamonds", "Hard Travellin' ", "Snakeskin Blues", "Stuck Inside The Twilight Zone", "Death Letter Blues", and "Mr. Ragamuffin Man", it is 99.9% certain that this tape is a put-on.

"GREAT WHITE WONDER VOLUME 2"
Rumours of a completely different "Great White Wonder II", containing titles such as "Your Letter", "Never", "I Can't Live Without You" and "Because I Care", started simply because some versions of "Great White Wonder" used false titles on the labels in order to avoid customs problems.

THE BANDS' NEW YEAR'S EVE CONCERT, CARNEGIE HALL, DECEMBER '71
Scaduto reckons that there is a tape of Dylan and The Band doing "Please Mrs. Henry" and "Like A Rolling Stone" from this concert. Rolling Stone reported that the concert was recorded but that Dylan's set was "Down In The Flood", "When I Paint My Masterpiece", "Don't Ya Tell Henry" and "Like A Rolling Stone". Either way, no tape has surfaced.

RENALDO AND CLARA Filmed: 1976	
Song Titles	Record on which appearing
When I Paint My Masterpiece	
Kaw-Liga	
Isis	Four Songs From Renaldo And Clara *
Ballad In Plain D	
In The Pines	
Hava Nagilah	
A Hard Rain's A-Gonna Fall	
People Get Ready	"
I Want You	
Need A New Sun Rising	
Salt Pork West Virginia	
Mule Skinner Blues	
What Will You Do When Jesus Comes?	
Fast Speaking Woman	
Little Moses	
It Ain't Me Babe	"
Knockin' On Heaven's Door	
Hurricane	
She Belongs To Me	
Catfish	
It Takes A Lot To Laugh, It Takes A Train To Cry	
Diamonds And Rust	
If You See Her Say Hello	
Romance In Durango	
One,Too Many Mornings	
Time Of The Preacher	
House Of The Rising Sun	
One More Cup Of Coffee	
Good Love Is Hard To Find	
Harmonium Improvisation	
Eight Miles High	
Chestnut Mare	
Sara	
The Water Is Wide (Sink Or Swim)	
Patty's Gone To Laredo	
Suzanne	
Never Let Me Go	"
Sad Eyed Lady Of The Lowlands	
Tangled Up In Blues	
Hollywood Waltz	
Just Like A Woman	

It is thought that this track listing may not be absolutely
complete and is not in the precise order of the soundtrack
Several of the performances are not by Bob Dylan
* Official promotional 12" EP

THE STEPHEN PICKERING COLLECTION

It is rumoured that Stephen Pickering, the author, claims to have in his collection the following items:

Dylan demos of "Love Is Just A Four Letter Word", "Farewell Angelina", and "Wanted Man";

"Planet Waves" out-takes of "Except You" and "Forever Young";

A Canadian TV request programme including "The Times They Are A-Changing' ", "Hattie Carroll", "World War III Blues", "Hard Rain", "Girl From The North Country" and "Restless Farewell";

"Billy The Kid" out-takes including "Holly's Song" and "Pico's Blues";

"New Morning" out-takes including "Jamaica Farewell" and "Take A Letter To Mary"(?);

Dylan singing Hebrew religious songs;

The whole of a '66 Australian concert in excellent sound quality;

A Dylan-Grateful Dead session reckoned to have taken place in 1972;

Some additional "Blood on the Tracks" out-takes with Eric Clapton;

"Desire" out-takes including "Golden Loom" and "Seven Days"

Some of these, like The Grateful Dead session and "Jamaica Farewell", have been talked about for a long time now. It is conceded by some collectors that Pickering could well be in possession of all these tapes; others think he is living in a fantasy world. In an interview with Dark Star Magazine Joan Baez said that Dylan had never made recordings of "Farewell Angelina" or "Love Is Just A Four Letter Word".

"SNOW OVER INTERSTATE 80"

The lost Christmas album of 1965 appears to have been a whimsical little jape played by the staff of New Musical Express on its readers.

"CHURCH WITH NO UPSTAIRS"

A 1966 song rumoured for some time but supported by little in the way of tangible evidence.

"HOLYLAND"

Another lost album, this time a prank by the staff of International Times.

"THE MASKED MARAUDERS"

A tangible enough album not very obliquely purporting to be a super-session involving Dylan, Jagger, McCartney and various others, but in reality the staff, this time, of Rolling Stone.

BOB JOHNSON-DYLAN PHONE CONVERSATION

This tape, alluded to in the appraisal of the L.A. Session, supposedly includes Bob Johnson telling Dylan that Columbia have decided to release "She's Your Lover Now" as a single. So far the tape has not surfaced.

GERDES FOLK CITY

Ten Dylan performances from here circa '61 are rumoured to be around but I know no one who actually has them.

"DOUG SAHM AND BAND" SESSIONS

Scaduto's tapeography intimated a number of takes not used on the album. While the existence of these is very likely, they have not appeared so far.

ISLE OF WIGHT REHEARSAL TAPE

A rumour was going around at one stage that Dylan and The Band hired a barn on the Isle of Wight for rehearsal and the person they rented it from slipped a tape recorder under the straw. No tape ever came to light as far as I know.

RED ROCKING CHAIR TAPE

The "Red Rocking Chair" is supposedly the name of a pub on the Isle of Wight where Dylan and The Band turned up and had a sing song. A person wrote to International Times claiming to have been there, recorded it, and even ripped off Dylan to the tune of £10 by agreeing to sell him the tapes and then giving him blank ones. Who knows.....?

"I FOUND IT IN AN ASH CAN" (TRASH CAN?)

Not an album at all but a collection of various performances, mostly not bootlegged, put together on one tape.

"PORTRAIT"

Again not an album but assorted tracks on a tape.

"UNDERSTAND YOUR MAN", "WANTED MAN"

These titles recur as songs recorded in the course of the Nashville Sessions with Cash but nobody seems to actually have them on tape.

"MR. TAMBOURINE MAN" WITH JACK ELLIOT

The demo of 'Tambourine Man' that was sent to The Byrds has been rumoured as having been cut with Jack Elliot. However, the tape has not leaked out.

4 NEW DYLAN SONGS CIRCA 1972-73

A writer called Ellen Sander was reported in 1973 to be in possession of a tape of Dylan singing four new songs recorded around the end of 1972. These reputedly had a "Freewheelin' " type of sound and included an anti-war song and a song that commented on Joni Mitchell.

Around the same time a Los Angeles radio station started playing a tape of what they were given to believe to be four new Dylan songs, but a person from New York 'phoned them eventually to say that the tape was a hoax perpetrated by himself.

It is not clear whether the two tapes are connected or not.

9 MINUTE "LIKE A ROLLING STONE"

The existence of a live 9 minute "Like A Rolling Stone" from an unspecified '66 gig has not been confirmed.

ELECTRIC "RAMBLIN', GAMBLIN' WILLIE"

A "Freewheelin' " out-take of "Ramblin', Gamblin' Willie" with some electric backing is reported, fairly reliably, as now being in circulation.

ADDITIONAL MINNESOTA HOTEL TAPE TRACKS

A number of these are reported to be in existence but this has not been confirmed.

"NEW MORNING" OUT-TAKES

Rumours of a number of these, including a 13 minute version of "Jamaica Farewell" have not been confirmed. However, a number of the tracks on "Dylan" seem likely, from the sound of the voice, to have been recorded at the "New Morning" sessions.

GRATEFUL DEAD SESSION

A tape of the Dylan-Grateful Dead session has been rumoured for some years but still has not come to light.

"LASSO FROM EL PASO" - KINKY FRIEDMAN

Dylan is rumoured to be on "Sold American" but other musicians involved in the recording have stated that Dylan took no part in any of the proceedings.

"THE LIVE ADVENTURES OF AL KOOPER AND MIKE BLOOMFIELD" - AL KOOPER AND MIKE BLOOMFIELD

A doubtful rumour exists that Dylan performed on this album under the name Roosevelt Gook. Extremely unlikely since any live appearance by Dylan at the time would have been reported in the media.

Versions by Other Artists of Dylan Songs of which no Performances by Dylan are in Circulation

BALLAD OF EASY RIDER (McGuinn-Dylan?): Version by The Byrds on the soundtrack of the film 'Easy Rider'. Also version by Fairport Convention on the album '(Guitar Vocal)' by Richard Thompson. Dylan reportedly co-wrote the song but declined to take credit.

CATFISH (Dylan-Levy): Version by Kinky Friedman on "Lasso From El Paso".

CHAMPAGNE ILLINOIS: Version by Carl Perkins.

FAREWELL ANGELINA: Joan Baez single (U.K. Fontana TF639). Also on the album "Farewell Angelina" (U.K. Vanguard SURL 19018) plus assorted compilations.

GOLDEN LOOM: Version by Roger McGuinn's Thunderbyrd on the album "Thunderbyrd".

I'D HAVE YOU ANY TIME (Dylan-Harrison): George Harrison on the album "All Things Must Pass".

JACK OF DIAMONDS (Dylan-Carruthers): This is the poem on the sleeve of "Another Side Of ....." set to music by Ben Carruthers. Single by Ben Carruthers and The Deep. Also version on the first Fairport Convention L.P. (U.K. Polydor 583035).

LONG DISTANCE OPERATOR: Version by The Band on the album "The Basement Tapes".

LOVE IS JUST A FOUR LETTER WORD: Joan Baez single. Also on the album "Any Day Now" (U.K. Vanguard 79306/7) plus assorted compilations. Live version on the album "From Every Stage" (U.K. A & M SP3704)

SIGN LANGUAGE: Eric Clapton on the album "No Reason To Cry" (U.K. RSO 2479179). Dylan duets with Clapton on this.

TROUBLED AND I DON'T KNOW WHY: Joan Baez unofficial live tape.

UP TO ME: Roger McGuinn on the album "Cardiff Rose". Written around the time of "Blood On The Tracks".

WALLFLOWER: Doug Sahm and Band on the album "Doug Sahm And Band" (U.K. Atlantic K40466). Dylan duets with Sahm on this.

WANTED MAN: Version by Johnny Cash.

Basic Official Discography
ALBUMS

BOB DYLAN	Stereo	Mono version deleted
THE FREEWHEELIN' BOB DYLAN	Stereo	Mono version deleted
THE TIMES THEY ARE A-CHANGIN'	Stereo	Mono version deleted
ANOTHER SIDE OF BOB DYLAN	Stereo	Mono version deleted
BRINGING IT ALL BACK HOME	Stereo	Mono version deleted

Stereo mixes slightly different to those on the mono version.

HIGHWAY 61 REVISITED   Stereo   Mono version deleted
Stereo mixes substantially different to the mono versions of the following tracks: "It Takes A Lot To Laugh, It Takes A Train To Cry", "Ballad Of A Thin Man", "Just Like Tom Thumb's Blues", "Desolation Row". Also difference in the length of some tracks.

BLONDE ON BLONDE   Stereo   Mono version deleted
Stereo mixes substantially different to the mono version of the following tracks: "Visions Of Johanna", "One Of Us Must Know", "Sad Eyed Lady Of The Lowlands". The stereo "One Of Us Must Know" includes an organ phrase just before the last verse which is not audible at all on the mono version.

BOB DYLAN'S GREATEST HITS   Stereo   Mono version deleted
Version with slightly different track listing released in some European countries.

BOB DYLAN'S GREATEST HITS VOLUME 2	Stereo	
BOB DYLAN GREATEST HITS VOLUME 3	Stereo	Europe only
GREATEST HITS	Stereo	Germany
JOHN WESLEY HARDING	Stereo	
NASHVILLE SKYLINE	Stereo	
SELF PORTRAIT	Stereo	
NEW MORNING	Stereo	
MORE BOB DYLAN GREATEST HITS	Stereo	
PAT GARRETT & BILLY THE KID SOUNDTRACK	Stereo	
DYLAN	Stereo	
PLANET WAVES	Stereo	
BEFORE THE FLOOD	Stereo	
BLOOD ON THE TRACKS	Stereo	
THE BASEMENT TAPES	Stereo	
DESIRE	Stereo	

Available in quadrophonic. Different mixes.

HARD RAIN	Stereo	
STREET LEGAL	Stereo	Mono version deleted
BOB DYLAN AT BUDOKAN	Stereo	
SLOW TRAIN COMING	Stereo	

SINGLES

1962 Mixed Up Confusion/Corrina Corrina	Mono	
1965 On The Road Again/Bob Dylan's 115th Dream	Mono	(USA only)
Gates Of Eden/She Belongs To Me	Mono	(USA only)

	The Times They Are A-Changin'/Honey Just Allow Me One More Chance	Mono	(USA only)
	Subterranean Homesick Blues/She Belongs To Me	Mono	(UK only)
	Subterranean Homesick Blues/The Times They Are A-Changin'	Mono	(Europe only)
	Maggie's Farm/On The Road Again	Mono	(UK only)
	Like A Rolling Stone/Gates Of Eden	Mono	
	Like A Rolling Stone Part 1/Like A Rolling Stone Part 2	Mono	(France only)
	Can You Please Crawl Out Your Window (slow version under incorrect title "Positively 4th Street")/From A Buick 6	Mono	(Los Angeles area only)
	Positively 4th Street/From A Buick 6	Mono	
	Can You Please Crawl Out Your Window/Highway 61 Revisited	Mono	
	One Of Us Must Know/Queen Jane Approximately	Mono	
1966	Rainy Day Women Nos. 12 & 35 (edited)/Pledging My Time (edited)	Mono	
	Mixed Up Confusion/Corrina Corrina	Mono	(Re-issue - Europe only)
	I Want You/Just Like Tom Thumb's Blues (Live at Liverpool 1966)	Mono	
	Just Like A Woman/Obviously 5 Believers	Mono	(USA only)
	Leopard-Skin Pill-Box Hat/Most Likely You Go Your Way...	Mono	
	Rainy Day Women Nos. 12 & 35/Like A Rolling Stone	Mono	(USA only)
1967	If You Gotta Go, Go Now/To Ramona	Mono	(Europe only)
	Just Like A Woman/I Want You	Mono	
1968	Drifter's Escape/John Wesley Harding	Mono	(Europe only)
	All Along The Watchtower/I'll Be Your Baby Tonight	Mono	(Europe only)
1969	I Threw It All Away/Drifter's Escape	Stereo	
	Lay Lady Lay/Peggy Day	Stereo	
	Tonight I'll Be Staying Here With You/Country Pie	Stereo	
	Blowin' In The Wind/Corrina Corrina	Stereo	(Italy only)
1970	Copper Kettle/Wigwam	Stereo	
1971	If Not For You/New Morning	Stereo	
	Watching The River Flow/Spanish Is The Loving Tongue (different from album version)	Stereo	
	George Jackson/George Jackson (Big Band Version)	Stereo	
1973	Knockin' On Heaven's Door/Turkey Chase	Stereo	
	A Fool Such As I/Lily Of The West	Stereo	
	Something There Is About You/Tough Mama	Stereo	
	Something There Is About You/Going Going Gone	Stereo	(France only)
1974	On A Night Like This/You Angel You	Stereo	

Most Likely You Go Your Way/Stagefright (The Band)	Stereo
It Ain't Me Babe/All Along The Watchtower	Stereo
1975 Tangled Up In Blue/If You See Her Say Hello	Stereo
Tears Of Rage/Million Dollar Bash	Stereo
Hurricane Part I/Hurricane Part II	Stereo (USA)
Hurricane Part I/Hurricane (complete - 33⅓ rpm)	Stereo (UK)
Mozambique/Oh Sister	Stereo
1977 Stuck Inside Of Mobile/Rita May	Stereo
1978 Baby Stop Crying/New Pony	Limited number on 12″ in UK. Stereo

Also released in USA only:

Positively 4th Street/Rainy Day Women Nos. 12 & 35	Mono

France only:

Just Like Tom Thumb's Blues/Ballad Of A Thin Man	Mono

E.P.S (MOSTLY DELETED)

With God On Our Side (Dylan and Baez)/The Bells Of Rhymney (Seeger)/Wagoner's Lad (Baez)	UK
Blowin' In The Wind (Dylan and Newport cast)/Oh Freedom (Baez)/Careless Love (Seeger)	UK
Ye Playboys And Playgirls (Dylan and Seeger)/Te Ador, Te Manha (Baez)/This Land Is My Land (Seeger)	UK
Don't Think Twice/Corrina Corrina/Blowin' In The Wind/When The Ship Comes In	UK
If You Gotta Go, Go Now/Mr. Tambourine Man (edited)/With God On Our Side	UK

A handful of these E.P.s were pressed but production stopped, apparently on Dylan's instructions.

One Too Many Mornings/It Ain't Me Babe/Spanish Harlem Incident/She Belongs To Me/Oxford Town	UK
Mr. Tambourine Man/Subterranean Homesick Blues/It's All Over Now Baby Blue	UK
Rainy Day Women/Pledging My Time/One Of Us Must Know	France
Blowin' In The Wind/Corrina Corrina/Don't Think Twice/Honey Just Allow Me One More Chance	France
With God On Our Side (split over two sides)/Motorpsycho Nitemare	France
I Want You/Obviously 5 Believers/Just Like A Woman	France
All I Really Want To Do/Oxford Town/To Ramona/Spanish Harlem Incident	France
Subterranean Homesick Blues/It Ain't Me Babe/The Times They Are A-Changin'	France
Positively 4th Street/Mr. Tambourine Man (fade after 2nd verse)/From A Buick 6/On The Road Again	France
Can You Please Crawl Out Your Window/Highway 61 Revisited/Tombstone Blues	France

Leopard-Skin Pill-Box Hat/Most Likely You Go Your Way ...../
Absolutely Sweet Marie   France

Rainy Day Women/Bob Dylan's Blues/Pledging My Time/Can You
Please Crawl Out Your Window   Germany

Leopard-Skin Pill-Box Hat/Most Likely You Go Your Way ...../Visions
Of Johanna   Germany

It Takes A Lot To Laugh/Outlaw Blues/Maggie's Farm/She Belongs
To Me   Germany

Positively 4th Street/Highway 61 Revisited/From A Buick 6/It Takes A
Lot To Laugh   Germany

I Want You/5th Dimension (The Byrds)/Hungry (Paul Revere)/I Am A
Rock (Simon & Garfunkel)   Germany

Mr. Tambourine Man/Subterranean Homesick Blues/On The Road   Australia

Blowin' In The Wind/Don't Think Twice/Corrina Corrina/Down The
Highway   Australia

The Times They Are A-Changin'/When The Ship Comes In/Only A
Pawn In Their Game/One Too Many Mornings   Australia

Like A Rolling Stone/Highway 61 Revisited/From A Buick 6   Australia

New Morning/Three Angels/The Man In Me/Wigwam   Australia

Lay Lady Lay/I Threw It All Away/Nashville Skyline Rag/Country Pie Australia

John Wesley Harding/The Wicked Messenger/I'll Be Your Baby
Tonight/All Along The Watchtower   Australia

A Hard Rain's A-Gonna Fall/If Not For You/Mighty Quinn/Watching
The River Flow   Australia

Rainy Day Women/Pledging My Time/Gates Of Eden   Portugal

Highway 61 Revisited/She Belongs To Me/Queen Jane Approximately   Portugal

Positively 4th Street/From A Buick 6/Like A Rolling Stone   Portugal

Dear Landlord/Down Along The Cove/Ballad Of Frankie Lee And
Judas Priest   Portugal

On The Road Again/Bob Dylan's 115th Dream/Gates Of Eden/She
Belongs To Me   USA

Rainy Day Women/Pledging My Time/One Of Us Must Know   Spain?

Albums Containing Dylan Tracks

BROADSIDE BALLADS VOLUME 1 - Various Artists
(USA - Broadside BR 301) Dylan under the name Blind Boy Grunt
Only A Hobo   Broadside Sessions, 1963
Talkin' Devil   Broadside Sessions, 1963
John Brown   Broadside Sessions, 1963
Let Me Die in My Footsteps (under the title "I   Broadside Sessions, 1963
    Will Not Go Down Under The Ground" -
    Happy Traum vocal, Dylan harmonica)

BROADSIDE REUNION - Various Artists
(USA - Folkways FR 5315) Dylan under the name Blind Boy Grunt
Train A-Travellin'   Broadside Sessions, 1963
I'd Hate To Be You On That Dreadful Day   Broadside Sessions, 1963
Emmett Till   W.B.A.I. Radio, 1962
Ballad Of Donald White   W.B.A.I. Radio, 1962
These tracks are not up to the usual level of official album sound quality.

EARL SCRUGGS: HIS FAMILY AND FRIENDS - Various Artists
(UK - CBS S64777)
Nashville Skyline Rag   Fanfare - Earl Scruggs' TV documentary 1970

EVENING CONCERTS AT NEWPORT VOLUME 1 - Various Artists
(UK - Fontana TFL 6138 Mono. USA - Vanguard Mono VRS 9148, Stereo VSD 79148)
Blowin' In The Wind   Newport Folk Festival 1963

NEWPORT BROADSIDE - Various Artists
(UK - Fontana TFL 6038 Mono. USA - Vanguard Mono VRS 9144, Stereo VSD 71944)
Ye Playboys And Playgirls (with Pete Seeger)   Newport Folk Festival, 1963
With God On Our Side (with Joan Baez)   Newport Folk Festival, 1963

THE LAST WALTZ - The Band's Farewell Concert
(UK - K66076 (3WS 3146))
Baby Let Me Follow You Down
I Don't Believe You
Forever Young
Baby Let Me Follow You Down (Reprise)
I Shall Be Released

THE CONCERT FOR BANGLADESH - Various Artists
Triple (UK - Apple STCX 3385 Stereo)
A Hard Rain's A Gonna   Concert for Bangladesh, 2nd Show August, 1971
   Fall
It Takes a Lot To Laugh,   Concert for Bangladesh, 2nd Show August, 1971
   It Takes A Train To
   Cry
Blowin' In The Wind   Concert for Bangladesh, 2nd Show August, 1971
Mr. Tambourine Man   Concert for Bangladesh, 2nd Show August, 1971
Just Like A Woman   Concert for Bangladesh, 2nd Show August, 1971

TRIBUTE TO WOODY GUTHRIE PART 1 - Various Artists
(UK - CBS 64861 Stereo)
I Ain't Got No   Woody Guthrie Memorial Concert, January 20th, 1968
   Home (with The
   Band)
Dear Mrs.   Woody Guthrie Memorial Concert, January 20th, 1968
   Roosevelt
Grand Coulee   Woody Guthrie Memorial Concert, January 20th, 1968
   Dam

TRIBUTE TO WOODY GUTHRIE PART 2 (Warner Bros. K46144)
Background vocals on Judy Collins' performance of "This Land Is Your Land".

TRIBUTE TO WOODY GUTHRIE - HIGHLIGHTS
(USA Columbia)
All three Dylan tracks from Part 1.

TRIBUTE TO WOODY GUTHRIE - Double
(USA - Warner Bros. ZW 3447)
Part 1 and Part 2 as one album.

WE SHALL OVERCOME - Various Artists
(USA - Folkways FH 5592)
Only A Pawn In Their   Washington Civil Rights March, August, 1963
   Game (incomplete - poor
   quality)

Samplers

All the Dylan tracks here are taken from other official albums.

ALL-STAR HOOTENANNY - Various Artists
(UK - CBS BPG 62217)
Blowin' In The Wind   - From "Freewheelin' "
Also Carolyn Hester's "Swing and Turn Jubilee" (Dylan on harmonica)

CBS SHOWCASE
(UK - CBS 66205)
Just Like A Woman   - From "Blonde On Blonde"
The Times They Are A-Changin'   - From "The Times They Are A-Changin' "

GREATEST FOLK SINGERS OF THE SIXTIES - Various Artists
Double (UK - Vanguard VSD 17/18)
Blowin' In The Wind   - From the Newport Folk Festival 1963
The mix on this compilation brings Dylan more to the fore compared to previous releases.

ROCK BUSTER - Various Artists
Double (UK - CBS PR 48/49)
Days Of '49   - From "Self Portrait"

THE MUSIC PEOPLE - Various Artists
(UK - CBS S66315)
Grand Coulee Dam   - From "A Tribute To Woody Guthrie
                                       Part 1"

THE ROCK MACHINE TURNS YOU ON - Various Artists
(UK - CBS SPR 22)
I'll Be Your Baby Tonight   - From "John Wesley Harding"

TODAY'S SOUNDS - Various Artists
(UK - CBS 62861)
I Want You   - From "Blonde On Blonde"
Just Like Woman   - From "Blonde On Blonde"
Rainy Day Women Nos. 12 & 35   - From "Blonde On Blonde"

Miscellaneous

BOB DYLAN VERSUS A. J. WEBERMAN - THE HISTORIC CONFRONTATION
(USA - Folkways FB 5322 (Broadside No. 12))
The famous telephone conversation between Dylan and his number one fan was on the verge of reaching the public via this official album when Dylan managed to get the whole thing stopped.

Dylan on Other Artists' Records

AL'S BIG DEAL UNCLAIMED FREIGHT: AN AL KOOPER ANTHOLOGY — Al Kooper Double (UK - CBS 88093)
"If Dogs Run Free" - the Dylan version from "New Morning".

BARRY GOLDBERG - Barry Goldberg (USA - ATCO SD 7040)
Back-up vocals plus percussion - "Stormy Weather Cowboy", "It's Not The Spotlight", "Silver Moon", "Minstrel Show", "Big City Woman".

CHRONICLES - Booker T. and Priscilla Jones (UK - A & M SP 4413)
Harmonica - "Crippled Cow".

CAROLYN HESTER - Carolyn Hester (UK - CBS SBPG 62033)
Harmonica on "Fly Away", "Come Back Baby", "Swing and Turn Jubilee".

COM'N BACK FOR MORE - David Blue (UK - Asylum SYL 9025)
Harmonica on "Who Love".

DEATH OF A LADIES' MAN - Leonard Cohen (UK - CBS 86042)
Background vocals on "Don't Go Home With Your Hard On" and "Iodine".

DICK FARINA AND ERIC VON SCHMIDT - Dick Farina and Eric Von Schmidt
(UK - Folklore F-LEUT/7)
Dylan under the name Blind Boy Grunt; harmonica and back-up vocals on "You
Can Always Tell", "Cocaine", "London Waltz", "Glory, Glory".

DOUG SAHM AND BAND - Doug Sahm (UK - Atlantic K 40466)
Guitar, vocal, harmonica and organ - "San Antone", "Wallflower", "Blues Stay
Away From Me", "Faded Love", "Me And Paul". "San Antone" released as a
single.

DISCONNECTED - The Dial-a-Poem Poets Double (USA - Giorno Poetry Systems
GPS 0003)
Piano and back-up vocals on "Jimmy Berman".

EARL SCRUGGS: HIS FAMILY & FRIENDS
See section on albums containing Dylan tracks.

ELECTION YEAR RAG - Steve Goodman Single (USA - Buddah BDA 326)
Piano and back-up vocals. This track also on the compilation album "The Essential
Steve Goodman".

JACK ELLIOT - Jack Elliot (USA - Vanguard VRS 9151)
Harmonica on "Will The Circle Be Unbroken".
Dylan rumoured to be on this track under the name Tedham Porterhouse.

MIDNIGHT SPECIAL - Harry Belafonte (UK - RCA Camden CDS 1100)
Harmonica on "Midnight Special".

MISS O'DELL - George Harrison Single (UK - Apple R 5988)
Dylan rumoured to be on this track on harmonica.

NO REASON TO CRY - Eric Clapton (UK - RSO 2479 179)
Duets on "Sign Language".

ROGER McGUINN - Roger McGuinn (UK - CBS 65274)
Harmonica on "I'm So Restless".

SOMEBODY ELSE'S TROUBLES - Steve Goodman (USA - Buddah BDS 5121)
Dylan under the name Robert Milkwood Thomas. Harmonica and back-up vocals
on "Somebody Else's Troubles". This track also on the compilation album "The
Essential Steve Goodman".

SONGS FOR THE NEW DEPRESSION - Bette Midler (UK -Atlantic K 50212)
Back-up vocals on "Buckets Of Rain".

TAKE A LITTLE WALK WITH ME - Tom Rush (UK - Electra EXL 308)
Dylan rumoured to be on piano under the name Roosevelt Gook - "You Can't
Judge A Book", "Who Do You Love?", "Money Honey".

THE BLUES PROJECT - Various Artists (USA - Electra EKS 7264)
Dylan under the name Bob Landy on "Downtown Blues".

THE BITTER END YEARS - Various Artists Triple (USA - Roxburg RXL 300)
Dylan rumoured to be on "Who Do You Love?" under the name Roosevelt Gook
(from the above Tom Rush album).

*THREE KINGS AND THE QUEEN - Big Joe Williams, Lornie Johnson,
Roosevelt Sykes and Victoria Spivey* (USA - Spivey LP 1004)
Back-up vocals on "Sitting On Top Of The World", harmonica on "Wichita".

TRIBUTE TO WOODY GUTHRIE PART 2 (Warner Bros. K46144)
Background vocals on Judy Collins' performance of "This Land Is Your Land".

*VOLUME TWO KINGS AND THE QUEEN - Big Joe Williams, Lornie Johnson,
Roosevelt Sykes, Victoria Spivey, plus Memphis Slim* (USA - Spivey LP 1014)
Dylan on harmonica on "It's Dangerous", "Big Joe" and "Victoria".

Bootleg Discography

Source, sound quality and, in the case of live material, whether taped direct from
the public address system or by a member of the audience, are inserted where
known. This will either take the form of a generalised statement about each album
or, where an album contains tracks of varying quality, source, etc., individual annotations against each track.

Abbreviations: E = excellent (sound quality); G = good; F = fair; M = medium;
P = poor; T = terrible; S = stereo; PA = mastered from a tape taken direct from
the public address system; A = mastered from an audience tape. Labels: T.M.Q.1
= the original Trade Mark of Quality Label which depicted a picture of an entire
pig; T.M.Q.2 = the label started by some of the original T.M.Q. personnel split-
ting off, depicting a pig's head wearing glasses and smoking a cigar; Z.A.P. = ZE
ANONYM PLATTENSPIELER (one of Kornyfone's many pseudonyms);
SODD = Singer's Original Double Disc (Kornyfone again); TAKRL = The
Amazing Kornyfone Record Label; TKRWM = The Kornyfone Records for the
Working Man (according to some sources these are a group of people who have pir-
ated the Kornyfone name); C.B.M. = Contraband Music; L.M.C. = ?; F.R.T. =
?. Blank Label - Berkeley Records are referred to as such because their records fre-
quently do not have a label name.

Please note that the sound quality ratings given assume a reasonable standard of
pressing. Where specific albums are known to have been badly pressed in quantity,
as opposed to the odd one or two, this is mentioned. Some labels, for example
Contraband, Phonygraph and Pirate, are infamous for their poor pressings. Generally T.M.Q., Kornyfone and Worlds Records albums maintain a reasonably high
standard of pressing.

Please also note that it is not possible to give information on where to obtain
bootlegs either here or in private correspondence because people seeking that
information could just as easily be representatives of the British Phonograph
Association as genuine Dylan collectors.

ACETATE, THE	see "The Acetate"
A COLLECTION OF PERFORMANCES FROM THEN AND NOW - subtitle for "Passed Over And Rolling Thunder"	
ALBERT HALL	see "Royal Albert Hall"
ALIAS (L.P.)	see "The Gaslight Tapes"
ALIAS (E.P.) Billy (4 versions) Knockin' On Heaven's Door 2 Instrumentals	All tracks from the sound track of "Pat Garrett And Billy The Kid". Possibly copied from the official album. Reput-edly stereo, medium to good quality.

ALL HALLOWS EVE 1964 - Double (T.M.Q.2, Kornyfone - SODD, Worlds Records)

Record 1	*Record 2*
The Times They Are A-Changin'	A Hard Rain's A-Gonna Fall
Spanish Harlem Incident	Talkin' World War III Blues
Talking John Birch Society Blues	Don't Think Twice, It's All Right
To Ramona	The Lonesome Death Of Hattie Carroll
Who Killed Davey Moore?	Mama You Been On My Mind (with Joan Baez)
Gates Of Eden	
If You Gotta Go, Go Now	With God On Our Side (with Joan Baez)
It's Alright Ma (I'm Only Bleeding)	
I Don't Believe You	It Ain't Me Babe (with Joan Baez)
Mr. Tambourine Man	All I Really Want To Do

All tracks from the Halloween Concert, Philharmonic Hall, New York, October 1964. Stereo, P.A. recording, excellent sound quality throughout.

AND NOW YOUR MOUTH CRIES WHOOPS (Kornyfone - TAKRL)

1	New Orleans Rag (Fragment)	G	"Another Side Of ....." out-take, June 1964
	That's Alright Mama	E	"
	Cocaine	G	Minnesota Hotel Tape, December 1961
	Stealin'	G	"
	Hard Times In New York	G	"
	Wade In The Water	E	"
	It's All over Now Baby Blue	E	"Bringing It All Back Home" out-take, December 1964
	The Cough Song	E	"Times ....." out-take, 1963
2	I Wanna Be Your Lover Baby	E	L.A. Band Session, December 1965
	Can You Please Crawl Out Your Window	G	"
	From A Buick 6	E	"Highway 61" out-take, 1965
	Visions Of Johanna	GL.A. Band Session, December 1965
	She's Your Lover Now	G	"

This album is in fact Side 2 of "Stealin' " backed on to Side 2 of "Seems Like a Freeze Out". It is relatively rare and appears to be the result of an error whereby Side 2 of "Stealin' " was used when the intention had been to use Side 1. The sister album, "Now Your Mouth Cries Wolf" represents the correction of this error. Both albums include the minor error of Side 1 on the cover slip being Side 2 on the record. Above listing is as per cover slip.

APPROXIMATELY (Rocalian Records) - Sides 2 and 4 of the double "Great White Wonder" (original track arrangement).

A RARE BATCH OF LITTLE WHITE WONDER - See "Bob Dylan - A Rare Batch Of Little White Wonder"

ARE YOU NOW OR HAVE YOU EVER BEEN (HIS GOTHAM INGRESS) (Kornyfone - TAKRL)

Last Thoughts On Woody Guthrie	PA	G	Carnegie Hall Concert, October 1963
Lay Down Your Weary Tune	PA	G	"
Dusty Old Fairgrounds	PA	G	"
John Brown	PA	G	"
When The Ship Comes In	PA	G	"
Who Killed Davey Moore?	PA	G	"
Percy's Song	PA	G	"
New Orleans Rag	PA	G	New York Town Hall Concert, April 1963

| Seven Curses | PA | G | Carnegie Hall Concert, October 1963 |

ASPECTS OF BOB DYLAN ON TOUR (R.S. Records)
(Two record set sold as double or two single albums)
Volume 1

It's All Over Now Baby Blue		G	"Bringing It All Back Home" out-take, December 1964
George Jackson		G	Single, November 1971
She Belongs To Me		G	"Bringing It All Back Home" out-take, December 1964
Leopard-Skin Pill-Box Hat	PA	G	Royal Albert Hall Concert, May 1966
Just Like Tom Thumb's Blues	PA	G	"
The Lonesome Death Of Hattie Carroll	A	M	Chicago Concert, January 3rd 1974
Song To Woody	A	M	"
Except You	A	M	"
All Along The Watchtower	A	M	"
Something There Is About You	A	M	"
Like A Rolling Stone	A	M	"
Most Likely You Go Your Way And I'll Go Mine	A	M	"

Volume 2

Talkin' Bear Mountain Picnic Massacre Disaster Blues		G	"Bob Dylan" out-take, 1962
Can You Please Crawl Out Your Window		G	"Highway 61" out-take (2nd take), 1965
It Ain't Me Babe			
I Shall Be Released		F	The Basement Tape, 1967
Just Like A Woman	PA	F	Dublin Adelphi Concert, May 1966
Talkin' John Birch Society Blues		G	The Original "Freewheelin' ", 1963
Most Likely You Go Your Way And I'll Go Mine	A	M	? Concert, 1974
Lay Lady Lay	A	M	? Concert, 1974
Forever Young	A	M	? Concert, 1974
Knockin' On Heaven's Door	A	M	? Concert, 1974
The Times They Are A-Changin'	A	M	? Concert, 1974
Don't Think Twice, It's All Right	A	M	? Concert, 1974
Just Like A Woman	A	M	? Concert, 1974

A TASTE OF THE SPECIAL STASH (Straight Records)

1 Down In The Flood   (under the title "Best Friend")
    Lo And Behold
    Tiny Montgomery   (under the title "Montgomery Says Hello")

    Open The Door Homer   (under the title "Open the Door Rachael")

    Nothing Was Delivered   (under the title "Nothing Will Do")
    This Wheel's On Fire   (under the title "Wheels of Fire")

2 You Ain't Goin' Nowhere
    Tears Of Rage
    Mighty Quinn
    Million Dollar Bash
    Yea! Heavy And A Bottle Of Bread   (under the title "Take Me Down To California")

Please Mrs. Henry
I Shall Be Released
All tracks medium quality, from the Basement Tape, 1967

AT HOME Double

Wade In The Water	Minnesota Hotel Tape, December 1961
Talkin' John Birch Society Blues	The Original "Freewheelin' ", 1963
Eternal Circle	"Times ....." out-take, 1963
I'm Ready (Not Dylan)	John Hammond?
Ramblin', Gamblin' Willie	The Original "Freewheelin' ", 1963
Stealin'	Minnesota Hotel Tape, December 1961
Million Dollar Bash	The Basement Tape, 1967
Please Mrs. Henry	"
You Ain't Goin' Nowhere	"
Too Much Of Nothing	"
I Shall Be Released	"
Tears Of Rage	"
This Wheel's On Fire	"
Cocaine (Incomplete)	Minnesota Hotel Tape, December 1961
Who Killed Davey Moore?	Carnegie Hall Concert, October 1963
Only A Hobo	"Times ....." out-take, 1963
I'll Keep It With Mine	"Another Side Of ....." out-take, June 1964
Hard Times In New York	Minnesota Hotel Tape, December 1961
Percy's Song	"Times ....." out-take, 1963
Yea! Heavy and A Bottle of Bread	The Basement Tape, 1967
Lo And Behold	"
Open The Door Richard	"
Mighty Quinn	"
Nothing Was Delivered	"
If You Gotta Go, Go Now	"Bringing It All Back Home" out-take, December 1964
Can You Please Crawl Out Your Window	"Highway 61" out-take (take 2), 1965

AT HOME Single

Wade In The Water	Minnesota Hotel Tape, December 1961
Cocaine (Incomplete)	"
Talkin' John Birch Society Blues	The Original "Freewheelin' ", 1963
Who Killed Davey Moore?	Carnegie Hall Concert, October 1963
Eternal Circle	"Times ....." out-take, 1963
Only A Hobo	"
New Orleans Rag	"Another Side Of ....." out-take, June 1964
I'm Ready (Not Dylan)	John Hammond?
I'll Keep It With Mine	"Another Side Of ....." out-take, June 1964
Ramblin' Gamblin' Willie	The Original "Freewheelin' ", 1963
Hard Times In New York	Minnesota Hotel Tape, December 1961
Percy's Song	"Times ....." out-take, 1963

A THOUSAND MILES BEHIND
(Full title: "The Great White Wonder ..... A Thousand Miles Behind .....")

1 Who Killed Davey Moore	Carnegie Hall Concert, October 1963
Moonshine Blues (under title "Whiskey Bottle")	Witmark Demo, 1963
Interview	Allen Stone Interview Detroit Oct 1965
Please Mrs. Henry	The Basement Tape, 1967
Million Dollar Bash	"

Yea! Heavy And A Bottle Of Bread (under title "Take Me Down To California")		"
Interview Part 2		Allen Stone Interview Detroit Oct 1965
Car Car (with Dave Van Ronk - under the title "Ride In The Car")		The Gaslight Tape (2), 1962

2	Ballad Of Donald White (under the title "Song To Donald White")		W.B.A.I. New York, May 1962
	Man On The Street (under the title "The Old Man In The Street")		The Gaslight Tape (2), 1962
	He Was A Friend of Mine		"
	Song To Woody		"
	One Too Many Mornings (with Johnny Cash)		Johnny Cash T.V. Documentary, 1969

A VINYL HEADSTONE ALMOST IN PLACE - Subtitle for "Bridgett's Album"

BANGLADESH (Bank Records) Possibly the same album as "Concert For Bangladesh"

BANGLADESH (Instant Analysis) - Same album as "George Harrison, Bob Dylan, Leon Russell, Eric Clapton"

BANGLADESH, CONCERT FOR - See "Concert for Bangladesh", "Madison Square Garden, August 1st 1971" and "George Harrison, Bob Dylan, Leon Russell, Eric Clapton".

BARBED WIRE BLUES Double (Kornyfone - SODD)
Combination of the two single albums "Ode For Barbara Allen" and "Now Your Mouth Cries Wolf".

BANGOR, MAINE (TKRWM)
(Full title: "Bob Dylan/The Rolling Thunder Revue - Bangor, Maine")

It Ain't Me Babe	I Don't Believe You
A Hard Rain's A-Gonna Fall	Simple Twist Of Fate
Romance In Durango	One More Cup Of Coffee
Mama You Been On My Mind	Sara
I Shall Be Released	Just Like A Woman
	Knockin' On Heaven's Door

All tracks from the Rolling Thunder Revue Concert, Bangor, Maine, 1975. Audience tape, fair quality.

BASICS IN G MINOR (E.P. Imitation Kornyfone label)

Help		P	Reputedly Dylan and Beatles, 1965
John Birch Society Blues	PA	P	Halloween Concert Philharmonic Hall, New York, 1965

Mama You Been On My Mind
(with Joan Baez)
It Ain't Me Babe (with Joan Baez)
Plus extracts from Mary Travers interview, 1974

BBC BROADCAST Double (T.M.Q. 1 & 2) Full title on T.M.Q.1: "G.W.W.-B.B.C. Broadcast"

1	Love Minus Zero/No Limit	3	Hollis Brown
	One Too Many Mornings		Mr. Tambourine Man
	Boots Of Spanish Leather		Gates Of Eden
2	It's Alright Ma (I'm Only Bleeding)	4	If You Gotta Go, Go Now
	She Belongs To Me		The Lonesome Death Of Hattie Carroll
	It's All Over Now Baby Blue		It Ain't Me Babe

All tracks from the B.B.C. Broadcasts 1965. Fair quality microphone recording.

BELIEVE WHAT YOU HEARD (Kornyfone - Z.A.P., Worlds Records)

1   Sink Or Swim (with Joan Baez)
    Mama You Been On My Mind
    (with Joan Baez)
    Down In The Mine (Dark As A
    Dungeon) (with Joan Baez)
    Sara
    I Shall Be Released
    Tangled Up In Blue

2   A Hard Rain's A-Gonna Fall
    Romance In Durango
    One More Cup Of Coffee
    Isis
    The Times They Are A-Changin'

Audience tape, fair quality, stereo. All tracks Rolling Thunder Revue, but which gigs not known.

BEST OF GREAT WHITE WONDER (T.M.Q. 1 and 2)
(Also released as "Great White Wonder Revisited" on Kornyfone-Z.A.P. Same master, generally slightly better pressings)

1	Worried Blues		F*	"Bob Dylan" out-take, 1962
	Tomorrow Is A Long Time	PA	G	New York Town Hall Concert, April 1963
	New Orleans Rag	PA	G	"
	Who Killed Davey Moore?	PA	G	Carnegie Hall Concert, October 1963
	Talkin' John Birch Society Blues		E	The Original "Freewheelin' ", 1963
	Mixed Up Confusion		G	"Freewheelin' " out-takes and
	Corrina Corrina		G	single, 1963
	Talkin' Bear Mountain Picnic Massacre Disaster Blues		F	"Bob Dylan" out-take, 1962
2	That's All Right Mama		G	"Another Side Of....." out-take, June 1964
	I'll Keep It With Mine		F*	"
	California		G	"
	Killing Me Alive		G	"Highway 61" out-take, 1965
	She Belongs To Me		G*	"Bringing It All Back Home" out-take, December 1964
	If You Gotta Go, Go Now		G*	"
	Love Minus Zero/No Limit		G*	"

Some of these tracks are better sound quality than they were on the bootlegs on which they first appeared, viz., "Talkin' John Birch" and "Tomorrow Is A Long Time" (better quality than on the official album).

Tracks marked * are of slightly inferior quality to other bootleg versions.

BILLION DOLLAR BASH (Existence of this album unconfirmed)

Million Dollar Bash	Basement Tape, 1967
Yea! Heavy And A Bottle Of Bread	"
Please Mrs. Henry	"
Lo And Behold	"
Tiny Montgomery	"
You Ain't Goin' Nowhere	"
Mixed Up Confusion (under title "Hung Over Hung Down Hung Up")	The Original "Freewheelin' ", 1963
East Laredo (under title "Pactulos Joe's Piano Solo")	"Another Side Of....." out-take, June 1964

Sound quality not known.

BLACK NITE CRASH (Paranoid Productions) - Some tracks as "While The Establishment Burns" but last track on each side fades. Also quality inferior (medium to fair).

BLIND BOY GRUNT (Blank label, T.M.Q. 1 & 2) Also released as "The Kindest Kut". T.M.Q. 1 full title: "G.W.W.-Blind Boy Grunt"

1	Hard Times In New York	E	Minnesota Hotel Tape, December 1961
	Baby Let Me Follow You Down	E	,,
	Sally Gal	E	,,
	Stealin'	E	,,
	Gospel Plow	E	,,
	Ballad Of Donald White	G	W.B.A.I. New York, May 1962
	Only A Hobo/Talkin' Devil	E	Broadside Sessions, 1963
	Wade In The Water	E	Minnesota Hotel Tape, December 1961
2	It's Hard To Be Blind (under title 'There Was A Time When I Was Blind')	E	Minnesota Hotel Tape, December 1961
	V.D. Blues	E	,,
	V.D. Waltz	E	,,
	V.D. City	E	,,
	V.D. Woman (V.D. Gunners Blues)	E	,,
	Cocaine	E	,,
	Omie Wise	E	,,
	John Brown	E	Broadside Sessions, 1963

BLOODTAKES (Shalom) - Side 2 and 3 of "Passed Over And Rolling Thunder"

BOB DYLAN IN CONCERT VOLUMES 1 & 2 - Double/2 Singles (Skand label) (This album was copied and released as 'Live Parts 1 and 2'. Inferior quality to the original)

Volume 1

1	Tell Me Mama	A	F	Bristol Colston Hall Concert, May 1966
	Baby Let Me Follow You Down	A	F	,,
	One Too Many Mornings	A	F	,,
	Like A Rolling Stone	A	F	,,
2	She Belongs To Me	A	F	Isle of Wight, August 31st, 1969
	Maggie's Farm	A	F	,,
	Highway 61 Revisited	A	F	,,
	One Too Many Mornings	A	F	,,
	Like A Rolling Stone	A	F	,,
	Mighty Quinn	A	F	,,
	Rainy Day Women Nos. 12 & 35	A	F	,,

Volume 2

1	Killing Me Alive		G	"Highway 61" out-take, 1965
	If You Gotta Go, Go Now		G	"Bringing It All Back Home" out-take, December 1964
	Mixed Up Confusion		G	"Freewheelin' " out-take + single, 1963
	Playboys And Playgirls (with Pete Seeger)	PA	G	Newport Folk Festival 1963
	With God On Our Side (with	PA	G	,,
2	Living The Blues		F	Johnny Cash TV Show, May 1969
	If You Gotta Go, Go Now	A	F	Royal Albert Hall Concert, May 1965
	Mr. Tambourine Man	A	F	,,
	I Don't Believe You	A	F	Bristol Colston Hall Concert, May 1966

BOB DYLAN IN CONCERT PART 1 - Swedish version of "Twenty Four"

BOB DYLAN IN CONCERT (E.P.) (Gong)

Simple Twist Of Fate	G	John Hammond TV Show, 1975
Hurricane (Fragment)	G	”
Just Like A Woman	A F	Rolling Thunder Revue
Knockin' On Heaven's Door	A F	Providence, Rhode Island, 1975

BOB DYLAN IN MELBOURNE AUSTRALIA (T.M.Q.1 - Deluxe)
Sub-titled: "The Enigmatic Story Of A Boy And His Dog ..... With A Cast Of Thousands"
This album was copied and released with the same cover design on the FYG label. There was very little loss of quality incurred in the copying.
1   4th Time Around
    Visions Of Johanna (introduced by Dylan as "Mother Revisited")
2   It's All Over Now Baby Blue
    Desolation Row
    All tracks from Melbourne Concert 1966. Sound quality basically good, but a lot of crackles.

BOB DYLAN/THE BAND — CHARLOTTE N. CAROLINA - See "Charlotte, N. Carolina"

BOB DYLAN THROUGH THE YEARS - Reputedly a quadruple album; nothing else known

BOB DYLAN/THE ROLLING THUNDER REVIEW — BANGOR, MAINE - See "Bangor Maine".

BOB DYLAN/THE ROLLING THUNDER REVIEW IN NEWHAVEN - Nothing known about this album.

BOB DYLAN — THE LITTLE WHITE WONDER (Buhay)
Volume 1

1 Who You Really Are	G	Banjo Tape with Happy Traum, January 1963
Candy Man	F	Minnesota Hotel Tape, December 1961
Emmett Till	G	W.B.A.I., New York, May 1962
California	G	"Another Side Of ....." out-take, June 1964
Only A Hobo	F	"Times ....." out-take, 1963
2 Baby Please Don't Go	G	Minnesota Hotel Tape, December 1961
Man of Constant Sorrow	G	”
I Ain't Got No Home	G	”
Farewell (Incorrectly titled "Farewell Angelina")	G	Banjo Tape with Happy Traum, January 1963
Poor Lazarus	F	Minnesota Hotel Tape, December 1961

Volume 2

1 Wade in the Water	E	Minnesota Hotel Tape, December 1961
V.D. Blues	G	”
New Orleans Rag (Fragment)	G	”
Baby Let Me Follow You Down	G	”
Cocaine	G	”
2 That's All Right Mama	E	"Another Side Of ....." out-take, June 1964
Stealin'	G	Minnesota Hotel Tape, December 1961
The Cough Song	E	"Times ....." out-take, 1963
Hard Times In New York	G	Minnesota Hotel Tape, December 1961
If I Cound Do It All Over I'd Do It All Over You	G	Banjo Tape with Happy Traum, January 1963

Volume 3

1	Sally Gal	G	Minnesota Hotel Tape, December 1961
	Long Time Gone	F	Witmark Demo, 1963
	Omie Wise	G	Minnesota Hotel Tape, December 1961
	Watcha Gonna Do	G	Witmark Demo, 1963
	John Brown	M	"
2	I Shall Be Free	F	Witmark Demo, 1963
	Ain't Gonna Grieve	F	"
	V.D. Woman (V.D. Gunners Blues)	G	Minnesota Hotel Tape, December 1961
	Nowadays (Long Ago, Far Away)	M	Witmark Demo, 1963
	See That My Grave Is Kept Clean	G	Minnesota Hotel Tape, December 1961

Whether these albums are bootlegs or legal is open to debate.

BOB DYLAN — A RARE BATCH OF LITTLE WHITE WONDER VOLUMES 1&2 (Joker) Same tracks respectively as "Bob Dylan - The Little White Wonder, Volumes 1 & 2". Some tracks inferior quality. One verse edited out of "If I Could Do It All Over".

BOB DYLAN — A RARE BATCH OF LITTLE WHITE WONDER VOLUME 3 (Joker)

Can You Please Crawl Out Your Window		G	"Highway 61" out-take (take 2), 1965
From A Buick 6		E	"
Lay Down Your Weary Tune		G	"Another Side Of ....." out-take, June 1964
Dusty Old Fairgrounds	PA	G	Carnegie Hall Concert, October 1963
It's All Over Now Baby Blue		E	"Bringing It All Back Home" out-take, December 1964
If You Gotta Go, Go Now		E	"
She Belongs To Me		E	"
Love Minus Zero/No Limit		E	"
It Takes A Lot to Laugh, It Takes A Train to Cry	E	E	"Highway 61" out-take, 1965
Killing Me Alive (Barbed Wire Fence)		G	"

The legality or not of the Joker albums is again debatable.

BOB DYLAN AND THE BAND LIVE (Live Records) - See "Royal Albert Hall"

BOSTON 1974 — DYLAN AND THE BAND RETURN - Double (Blank label - Berkeley)
Contains all the Dylan performances from the 14th January '74 concert at Boston Gardens (1st Show). Audience tape, medium quality throughout.
For further Boston 1974 albums see "Swansong" and "Sand and Ashes".

BOSTON, THE NIGHT THE REVUE CAME TO - See "The Night the Revue Came to Boston"

BRIDGETT'S ALBUM (T.M.Q.2)
There are two completely different "Bridgett's Albums". The first is a '74 tour album with tracks as follows:

It's All Over Now Baby Blue	Most Likely You Go Your Way And I'll Go Mine
The Times They Are A-Changin'	
Don't Think Twice, It's All Right	Rainy Day Women Nos. 12 & 35
Just Like A Woman	Hollis Brown
Love Minus Zero/No Limit	Highway 61 Revisited
It's Alright Ma (I'm Only Bleeding)	Like A Rolling Stone
	Blowin' in the Wind

All tracks reputedly from the Los Angeles Forum, 1st Show, February 14th 1974, except "Love Minus Zero" and "Don't Think Twice" the source of which is unknown. Medium quality, audience recording. This was ostensibly T.M.Q.'s farewell album.

The second "Bridgett's Album" is .....

BRIDGETT'S ALBUM — A VINYL HEADSTONE ALMOST IN PLACE (Kornyfone - TAKRL)

1	A Hard Rain's A-Gonna Fall (with Joan Baez)		G	Rolling Thunder T.V. Special, Fort Collins, shown September 1976
	Blowin' In The Wind (with Joan Baez)			
	Railroad Bill (with Joan Baez)			
	Deportees (with Joan Baez)			
	I Pity The Poor Immigrant (with Joan Baez)			
	Mozambique			
2	I Ain't Got No Home (with The Band)	PA	G	Woody Guthrie Memorial Concert, January 1968
	Dear Mrs. Roosevelt (with The Band)	PA	G	"
	Grand Coulee Dam (with The Band)	PA	G	"
	Ballad of A Thin Man (with The Band)	PA	G	Royal Albert Hall Concert, May 1966
	Like A Rolling Stone (with The Band)	PA	G	"

This was ostensibly TAKRL's farewell album.

BURN SOME MORE (T.M.Q. 1 & 2) T.M.Q.1 full title: "G.W.W.-Burn Some More"

1	Just Like Tom Thumb's Blues	PA	G	Liverpool Concert, May 1966
	One Too Many Mornings			"
	Like A Rolling Stone			"
	Mr. Tambourine Man	PA	F	Dublin Adelphi Concert, May 1966
	It's All Over Now Baby Blue			"
2	Lonesome River's Edge (Fragment)		G	Banjo Tape with Happy Traum, January 1963
	Who You Really Are (Incomplete)			"
	Bob Dylan's Dream			"
	? (Fragment)			"
	Farewell			"
	If I Could Do It All Over I'd Do It All Over You			"
	Masters Of War			"
	Keep Your Hands Off Her (Fragment)			"
	You Don't Do Me Like You Used To Do			"
	Goin' Back To Rome (Fragment)			"
	Stealin'			"

CAST OFF LUNGS AND RETOUCHED BADLANDS - Subtitle for "Lovesongs for America"

CEREMONIES FOR THE HORSEMEN - Double (White Bear). Existence unconfirmed. Contains all the Dylan performances from the January 11th '74 concert at the Forum, Montreal, except the reprise of "Most Likely You Go Your Way And I'll Go Mine". Stereo, good quality throughout. Could be a good audience tape or PA (reputedly).

CEREMONIES OF THE HORSEMAN (Highway Hi-fi, T.M.Q.2, Kornyfone - TAKRL)
Title on cover slip actually reads "*Ceremoies* of the Horseman" but this is assumed to be a printing error.

Only A Hobo	Hero Blues
If I Could Do It All Over I'd Do It All Over You	Don't Think Twice, It's All Right
	Oxford Town
Boots Of Spanish Leather	Hollis Brown (under title: "The Rise
Girl From The North Country	And Fall Of Hollis Brown")
Bob Dylan's Dream	Blowin' In The Wind
I Shall Be Free	When The Ship Comes In
Tomorrow Is A Long Time	The Times They Are A-Changin'

All tracks from the Witmark Demos, 1963. Excellent sound quality throughout.

CHARLOTTE, NORTH CAROLINA — BOB DYLAN/THE BAND - Double (Pirate, CBM)
Contains all the Dylan performances from the January 17th '74 concert at the Colliseum, Charlotte, plus The Band's 'Stage Fright'. Audience tape, medium quality throughout, poorly pressed. For further Charlotte '74 album see "Mom's Apple Pie".

CHILE, FRIENDS OF - See "Friends of Chile"

CHICAGO

Lay Lady Lay	Knockin' On Heaven's Door
It Ain't Me Babe	Forever Young
Ballad Of A Thin Man	Something There Is About You
All Along The Watchtower	Like A Rolling Stone
Leopard-Skin Pill-Box Hat	

All tracks from the January 4th 1974 concert at the Chicago Amphitheater. Sound quality not known.

CONCERT FOR BANGLADESH (F.R.T. Records)

My Sweet Lord -	Mr. Tambourine Man -
George Harrison	Dylan
Beware Of Darkness -	Just Like A Woman -
George Harrison	Dylan
While My Guitar Gently Weeps -	That's The Way God Planned It -
George Harrison	Billy Preston
Something -	It Don't Come Easy -
George Harrison	Ringo Starr
Bangladesh -	Jumpin' Jack Flash -
George Harrison	Leon Russell

All tracks probably from the Bangladesh 2nd Show - 'Mr. Tambourine Man' *definitely* is. Poor quality throughout. This album possibly also released as "Bangladesh" (Bang Records). In addition there may be some albums with the same tracks in a different order. For further Bangladesh concert bootlegs see "Madison Square Gardens, August 1st 1971" and "George Harrison, Bob Dylan, Leon Russell, Eric Clapton".

DADDY ROLLING STONE - Double (Skand)
Record 1

Rocks and Gravel	G	The Original "Freewheeling", 1963

Let Me Die In My Footsteps		"
Talkin' John Birch Society Blues		"
Stealin'	E	Minnesota Hotel Tape December 1961
Wade In The Water	E	"
In The Evening	G	"
Cocaine	G	"
I Was Young When I Left Home	G	"
Ramblin' Round	G	"
Hezekiah Jones	G	"
New Orleans Rag (Incomplete)		"Another Side Of ....." out-take, June 1964

Record 2

Tears Of Rage		G	The Basement Tape, 1967
Please Mrs. Henry		G	"
Open The Door Richard		G	"
Nothing Was Delivered		G	"
This Wheel's On Fire		G	"
You Ain't Going Nowhere		G	"
I Shall Be Released		G	"
Too Much Of Nothing		F	"
Wild Mountain Thyme	PA	F	Isle Of Wight Concert, August 31st 1969
To Ramona	PA	F	"
Minstrel Boy	PA	F	"

DEMO TAPES - See "The Demo Tapes"

DIRTY DRIVIN' RAIN - Alternative title for "Twenty Four"

DON'T LOOK BACK (T.M.W.1, Phonygraph): T.M.Q.1 Full Title: "G.W.W.-Don't Look Back"
Highlights from the sound-track of the film. Fair quality. Phonygraph versions poorer quality.

(DON'T) LOOK BACK - See "Dylan - (Don't) Look Back"

DRUNKEN MINSTREL

Blowin' In The Wind	Friends of Chile Concert, May 1974
Tough Mama	Chicago Concert, January 3rd 1974
Girl From The North Country	Philadelphia Concert, January 7th 1974
Wedding Song	"
Love Minus Zero/No Limit	Toronto Concert, January 10th 1974
Except You	Montreal Concert, January 11th 1974
Blowin' In The Wind	Montreal Concert, January 12th 1974

Nothing known about the sound quality of this album.

DUSTY OLD FAIRGROUNDS - Existence uncertain

Hezekiah Jones	?
Open The Door Homer	The Basement Tape, 1967
Tears Of Rage	"
Rocks And Gravel	"
One Too Many Mornings	?
Quit Your Low Down Ways	?
Train A-Travellin'	Broadside Sessions, 1963
Can You Please Crawl Out Your Window	?
Walkin' Down The Line	?
Farewell	?
Dusty Old Fairgrounds	Carnegie Hall Concert, 1963

DYLAN
Title used on some copies of "Great White Wonder Part 2" Double. Also released separately as "Dylan Volume 1" and "Dylan Volume 2".

DYLAN AND THE BAND RETURN - See "Boston 1974"

DYLAN CASH SESSION - See "The Dylan Cash Session"

DYLAN THROUGH THE YEARS - See "Bob Dylan Through the Years"

DYLAN '62 — ORIGINAL GASLIGHT-WITMARK ARCHIVES (FYG)

1	Ain't No More Cane On The Brazo		
	Handsome Molly	G	"
	John Brown	G	"
	Hollis Brown	G	"
	See That My Grave Is Kept Clean	G	"
	Cocaine	G	"
2	The Cuckoo Is A Pretty Bird	G	"
	Motherless Children	G	"
	Bound To Win	G	Witmark Demo, 1963
	Walls Of Redwing	G	"
	Let Me Die In My Footsteps (Fragment)	G	"
	Eternal Circle (Fragment)	G	"

DYLAN VOLUMES 1 AND 2 (CBM)
Two single albums equivalent to the 'Great White Wonder Part 2' double.

DYLAN — (DON'T) LOOK BACK Triple (SODDS - Great Sounds)

1	Ye Playboys And Playgirls (with Pete Seeger)	PA	GS	Newport Folk Festival, 1963
	With God On Our Side (with Joan Baez)	PA	GS	"
	Blowin' In The Wind		GS	Official album track (some loss of quality)
	Wild Mountain Thyme		F	Isle of Wight Concert, August 1969
	Car Car (with Dave Van Ronk)		M	The Gaslight Tape (2), 1963
	Only A Pawn In Their Game (under the title "Ballad of Edgar Meyers")		P	Washington Civil Rights March, August 1963
2	Percy's Song (under the title "Turn Turn")		G	"Times ....." out-take, 1963
	Wade In The Water		E	Minnesota Hotel Tape December 1961
	Cocaine (Incomplete)		G	"
	Talkin' John Birch Society Blues		G	The Original "Freewheelin' ", 1963
	Masters Of War		GS	Official album track (some loss of quality)
	A Hard Rain's A-Gonna Fall		GS	"
3	Who Killed Davey Moore?		G	Carnegie Hall Concert, October 1963
	I'll Keep It With Mine		F	"Another Side Of ....." out-take, June 1964
	One Too Many Mornings (with Johnny Cash)		G	Johnny Cash TV Documentary, January 1969

	Eternal Circle	E	"Times ....." out-take, 1963
	Love Minus Zero/No Limit	G	"Bringing It All Back Home" out-take, December 1964
	It's All Over Now Baby Blue	E	"
4	She Belongs To Me	F	Isle of Wight Concert, August 31st 1969
	She Belongs To Me	G	"Bringing It All Back Home" out-take, December 1964
	Maggie's Farm	F	Isle of Wight Concert, August 31st 1969
	Like A Rolling Stone	GS	Official Track (some loss of quality)
	Please Crawl Out Your Window	G	"Highway 61" out-take, 1965
	Absolutely Sweet Marie (Incomplete)	GS	Official track (some loss of quality)
5	Desolation Row	GS	Official track (some loss of quality)
	Visions Of Johanna	GS	"
	Positively 4th Street	GS	"
6	That's Alright Mama	E	"Another Side Of ....." out-take, June 1964
	I Want You	GS	Official track (some loss of quality)
	4th Time Around	GS	"
	As I Went Out One Morning	GS	"
	Girl From The North Country	GS	"
	Just Like A Woman	GS	"
	All Along The Watchtower	GS	"
	One Too Many Mornings	GS	"

Some of the tracks here not taken from official albums are in a mock form of stereo.

EARLY 60s REVISITED (T.M.Q.1)

1	Handsome Molly	F	Riverside Church, New York, July 1961
	Omie Wise (under the title "Naomi Wise")	F	"
	Poor Lazarus	F	"
	Mean Old Southern Train	G	"
	Acne (with Jack Elliot)	G	"
2	He Was A Friend Of Mine	G	Leeds Music Demo, 1962
	Man On The Street (Take 1 - incomplete)	G	"
	Hard Times In New York	G	"
	Poor Boy Blues	G	"
	Ballad For A Friend	G	"
	Man On The Street (Take 2)	G	"
	Standing On The Highway	G	"
	Talking Bear Mountain Picnic Massacre Disaster Blues	G	"

EPITAPH TO AMERICA - Double (White Bear). Existence unconfirmed.
Contains all the Dylan performances from the January 6th '74 1st Show at the Spectrum, Philadelphia. Stereo, good quality throughout, good audience recording or PA (reputedly).

FOREST HILLS 1965 - See "Friends of Chile"

FORT COLLINS - See "Bridgett's Album - A Vinyl Headstone Almost In Place"

FORT WORTH - See "Hold the Fort For What It's Worth"

FORTY RED WHITE AND BLUE SHOESTRINGS (Roach Records)

1	I Wanna Be Your Lover Baby	G		LA Session with The Band December 1965
	Number One	G		"
	Visions Of Johanna	F		"
	She's Your Lover Now	G		"
2	One Too Many Mornings (with Johnny Cash)	G		Johnny Cash TV Documentary, January 1969
	Let Me Die In My Footsteps	F		The Original 'Freewheelin', ' 1963
	Rocks And Gravel	G		"
	I'm Ready (Not Dylan)	G		John Hammond?
	Just Like Tom Thumb's Blues	PA	G	Liverpool Concert, 1966

FORTY RED WHITE AND BLUE SHOESTRINGS - Double (White Bear)
All the Dylan performances from the January 6th '74 concert 2nd show at the Spectrum, Philadelphia. Good quality. PA or good audience recording.

FRIENDS OF CHILE (Pirate, C.B.M.)

1	Sally Gal	A	M	Carnegie Hall Hootenanny September 1962
	Highway 51			"
	Talkin' John Birch Society Blues			"
	Hollis Brown			"
	North Country Blues	PA	M	Friends of Chile Benefit Concert, May 1974
	Spanish Is The Loving Tongue			"
	Blowin' In The Wind (incomplete)			"
	I Don't Believe You	A	P	Forest Hills Concert, August 1965

The cover slip lists "Hard Rain" as a track from the Chile Concert included in the album, but it is not in fact on the album, and it is dubious whether a tape of it exists or if it was even performed at the concert. Album generally badly pressed. Also released under the title "Forest Hills 1965".

GET TOGETHER (Beatles E.P. - Tobe Milo label)

Beatles Interview with Kenny Everett	ES
Cotton Fields - Beatles	ES
Every Time Somebody Comes to Town - Dylan and Harrison	P
I'd Have You Any Time - Dylan and Harrison	P
Loving Sacred Loving - Beatles and Rolling Stones	ES
Shapes Of Orange - Beatles and Rolling Stones	ES
Too Many Cooks - Beatles and Rolling Stones	ES

GASLIGHT TAPES, THE - See "The Gaslight Tapes"

GEORGE HARRISON, BOB DYLAN, LEON RUSSELL, ERIC CLAPTON
(Label not known, possibly SAD Productions)

My Sweet Lord -	It Takes A Lot To Laugh, It Takes A
George Harrison	Train To Cry -
Beware of Darkness -	Dylan
George Harrison	Blowin' In The Wind -
While My Guitar Gently Weeps -	Dylan
George Harrison	Mr. Tambourine Man -
Here Comes The Sun -	Dylan
George Harrison	Just Like A Woman -
Something -	Dylan
George Harrison	
Bangladesh -	
George Harrison	
A Hard Rain's A-Gonna Fall -	
Dylan	

All tracks from the Bangladesh Concert, August 1st 1971, probably 2nd show. Audience tape - fair quality. Also released under title "Bandladesh" (Instant Analysis) and "The Greatest Show On Earth" (Share Records).

GOTHAM INGRESS, HIS - See "Are You Now Or Have You Ever Been"

GREAT AMERICAN HAWKS - Double (White Bear) Existence unconfirmed.
All the Dylan performances from the January 10th '74 Concert at Maple Leaf Gardens, Toronto. Stereo, good quality. PA or good audience recording (reputedly).

GREAT WHITE WONDER - Double (Blank label, T.M.Q.1, Blank label - Berkeley Records, Contraband - also various anonymous labels who produced copies of very bad quality from the original album).
Which side backs on to which varies according to the label. The track listing below follows the original format. With the T.M.Q. version what below is Side 3 becomes Side 2 and vice versa.

1	Baby Please Don't Go	G	Minnesota Hotel Tape, December 1961
	Pete Seeger Chat	G	W.B.A.I., New York, May 1962
	Dink's Song	G	Minnesota Hotel Tape, December 1961
	See That My Grave Is Kept Clean	G	"
	East Grange, N.J.	G	"
	Man Of Constant Sorrow	G	"
2	New Orleans Rag (Fragment)	F	"Another Side Of ....." out-take, June 1964
	If You Gotta Go, Go Now	P	"Bringing It All Back Home" out-take, December 1964
	Only A Hobo	M	"Times ....." out-take, 1963
	Killing Me Alive	M	"Highway 61" out-take, 1965
	Mighty Quinn	M	The Basement Tape, 1967
	This Wheel's On Fire	M	"
3	Candy Man	F	Minnesota Hotel Tape, December 1961
	Ramblin' Round	G	"
	Hezekiah Jones (Black Cross)	F	"
	I Ain't Got No Home	G	"
	Emmett Till	G	"
	Poor Lazarus	F	"
4	I Shall Be Released	M	The Basement Tape, 1967
	Open The Door Homer	F	"

Too Much Of Nothing	M	"
Nothing Was Delivered	M	"
Tears Of Rage	M	"
Living The Blues	M	Johnny Cash TV Show, May 1969

Sides 2 and 4 were released as a single album under the title "Approximately" on Rocalian Records.

GREAT WHITE WONDER - Single (Blank label)

Also released under the title "Robert Zimmerman - Just As Well" with a slightly different track arrangement.

1	Baby Please Don't Go	G	Minnesota Hotel Tape, December 1961
	Dink's Song	G	"
	East Grange, N.J.	F	"
	Man Of Constant Sorrow	G	"
	If You Gotta Go, Go Now	P	"Bringing It All Back Home" out-take,. December 1964
	Only A Hobo	M	"Times ....." out-take, 1963
2	This Wheel's On Fire	M	The Basement Tape, 1967
	Mighty Quinn	M	"
	Candy Man	F	Minnesota Hotel Tape, December 1961
	Ramblin' Round	G	"
	Hezekiah Jones (Black Cross)	F	"

GREAT WHITE WONDER PART TWO - Double (Blank label). Sometimes titled "Dylan III".

The original version of this album was generally good in sound quality. However, it seems that it was copied and that these imitations were of very poor quality. A similar album of good sound quality was also released but this had some tracks missing and some tracks on twice. The usual title for the latter was "John Birch Society Blues" (Double) but it was also apparently released as "Great White Wonder Volume (or Part) 2". The tracks listed below are as they appear on the pukka "Great White Wonder Part 2".

Record 1

1	Can You Please Crawl Out Your Window	G	"Highway 61" out-take, 1965
	It Takes A Lot To Laugh, It Takes A Train To Cry	G	"
	She Belongs To Me	E	"Bringing It All Back Home" out-take December 1964
	Love Minus Zero/No Limit	E	
	It's All Over Now Baby Blue	E	"
	That's Alright Mama	E	"Another Side Of ....." out-take, June 1964
	Hard Times In New York	G	Minnesota Hotel Tape, December 1961
	Stealin'	G	"
2	I Was Young When I Left Home	G	Minnesota Hotel Tape, December 1961
	Percy's Song	G	"Times ....." out-take, 1963
	Corrina Corrina	E	The Original "Freewheelin' ", 1963
	In The Evening	G	Minnesota Hotel Tape, December 1961
	Long John	G	"
	Down In The Flood	F	The Basement Tape, 1967

Record 2

3	Million Dollar Bash	F	The Basement Tape 1967
	Yea! Heavy And A Bottle Of Bread	F	"
	Please Mrs. Henry	F	"

Lo And Behold	F	"
Tiny Montgomery	F	"
You Ain't Goin' Newhere	F	"
Mixed Up Confusion	E	The Original "Freewheelin' ", 1963
East Laredo	E	"Another Side Of ....." out-take, June 1964
4 Wade In The Water	E	Minnesota Hotel Tape, December 1961
Cocaine (Incomplete)	G	"
I'll Keep It With Mine	G	"Another Side Of ....." out-take, June 1964
Talkin' John Birch Society Blues	G	The Original "Freewheelin' ", 1963
Who Killed Davey Moore?	G	Carnegie Hall Concert, October 1963
Eternal Circle	E	"Times ....." out-take, 1963
Ramblin' Gamblin' Willie	F	The Original "Freewheelin' ", 1963

Also released as two single albums - "Dylan - Volumes 1 and 2" (C.B.M.)

If they have not already done so it might be of interest to record collectors to compare the track arrangement of this album to the single "John Birch Society Blues" and "Stealin' " albums. An album with the same track arrangement as record 1 was reputedly released under the title "Stealin' ".

GREAT WHITE WONDER REVISITED (Kornyfone - Z.A.P.) Re-release of "Best Of Great White Wonder". Generally slightly better pressed than the latter.

GREATEST SHOW ON EARTH, THE (Share Records) Same album as "George Harrison, Bob Dylan, Leon Russell, Eric Clapton"

GREEN RIVER Nothing known about this album. It may or may not exist.

GWW - BLIND BOY GRUNT - See "Blind Boy Grunt"

GWW - BBC BROADCAST - See "BBC Broadcast"

GWW - BURN SOME MORE - See "Burn Some More"

GWW - DON'T LOOK BACK - See "Don't Look Back"

GWW - ISLE OF WIGHT - See "Isle Of Wight"

GWW - JOHN BIRCH SOCIETY BLUES - See "John Birch Society Blues"

GWW - LET ME DIE IN MY FOOTSTEPS - See "Let Me Die In My Footsteps"

GWW - ROYAL ALBERT HALL - See "Royal Albert Hall"

GWW - SEEMS LIKE A FREEZE OUT - See "Seems Like A Freeze Out"

GWW - STEALIN' - See "Stealin' "

GWW - TALKIN' BEAR MOUNTAIN MASSACRE PICNIC BLUES - See "Talkin' Bear Mountain Massacre Picnic Blues"

GWW - THE DEMO TAPES - See "The Demo Tapes"

GWW - TROUBLED TROUBADOR - See "Troubled Troubador"

GWW - V.D. WALTZ - See "V.D. Waltz"

GWW - WHILE THE ESTABLISHMENT BURNS - See "While The Establishment Burns"

GWW - ST. VALENTINE'S DAY MASSACRE - See "St. Valentine's Day Massacre" (Triple)

HEAR ME HOLLER Existence of this album unconfirmed.

Cuban Blockade (World War No. 3)	Broadside Sessions, 1963
Ye Playboys And Playgirls	?(Either Broadside or Newport Folk Festival, 1963)
Paths Of Victory	?(One of the two Witmark Demo versions, 1963)

Let Me Die In My Footsteps	?(Witmark Demo, 1963, or "Bob Dylan" or "Freewheelin' " out-take, 1963)
Tomorrow Is A Long Time	?(Witmark Demo, 1963, or New York Town Hall Concert, 1963)
New Orleans Rag	?("Another Side Of ..." out-take or New York Town Hall, 1963)
Walls Of Redwing	?(Witmark Demo or New York Town Hall, 1963)
Denise Denise	"Another Side Of ..." out-take, June 1964
If You Gotta Go, Go Now	?Live
I Ain't Got No Home	Minnesota Hotel Tape, December 1961

HELP Double (Nederlandse Producite)
Record 1

1 Help	Reputedly Dylan and Beatles, 1965
Ramblin' Down Through The World	New York Town Hall Concert, April 1963
Bob Dylan's Dream	,,
Tomorrow Is A Long Time	,,
New Orleans Rag	,,
Walls Of Redwing	,,
2 Hero Blues	,,
Who Killed Davey Moore?	,,
Gates Of Eden	B.B.C. T.V. concert 1965
If You Gotts Go, Go Now (incomplete)	,,
Long John	Minnesota Hotel Tape, December 1961
Mighty Quinn	Basement Tape, 1967

Record 2

3 Ballad Of Donald White	WBAI New York, May 1962
Lay Down Your Weary Tune	"Another Side Of ..." out-take, June 1964
Percy's Song	Witmark Demo, 1963
4 I'll Keep It With Mine	,,
I Was Young When I Left Home	Minnesota Hotel Tape, December 1961
Ye Playboys And Playgirls	Broadside Sessions, 1963
Ramblin' Gamblin' Willie	Original "Freewheelin' ", 1963
Emmett Till	Gaslight Tape (1), 1962
He Was A Friend Of Mine	,,
Sound quality not known.	

HELP Single (Pirate) Poorly pressed.

Handsome Molly (I Wish I Was In London)		P	Riverside Church New York, July 1961
Doo-Wah (with Jack Elliott)		P	,,
Gypsy Lou		P	Witmark Demo, 1963
Love Minus Zero/No Limit	PA	P	Bangladesh 1st Show, August 1971
Help		P	Reputedly Dylan and Beatles, 1965
With God On Our Side (with Joan Baez)	PA	F	Newport Folk Festival, 1963
Ye Playboys And Playgirls (with Pete Seeger)	PA		,,
She's Your Lover Now		F	L.A. Band Session, 1965
Killing Me Alive		F	"Highway 61" Out-take, 1965
She Belongs To Me		F	"Bringing It All Back Home" out-take, December 1964

HELP Single Existence of this album extremely dubious.

Railroad Bill	Minnesota Party Tape, May 1961
Will The Circle Be Unbroken	,,
Man Of Constant Sorrow	,,
Railroad Boy	,,
Times Ain't What They Used To Be	,,
Why'd You Cut My Hair	,,
This Land Is Your Land	,,
Two Trains A-Runnin'	,,
It's All Over Now Baby Blue	Live?
Help	Reputedly Dylan and Beatles, 1965
Masters Of War	Live?

HERE'S ANOTHER FINE BRIDGETT YOU'VE GOTTEN ME INTO - Subtitle for "Joaquin Antique"

HIGH VOLTAGE
1 Just Like Tom Thumb's Blues
  Hollis Brown
  Mr Tambourine Man
  Forever Young
  Maggie's Farm
  Highway 61 Revisited

2 Knockin' On Heaven's Door
  Ballad Of A Thin Man
  Most Likely You Go Your Way And I'll Go Mine
  Rainy Day Women Nos. 12 & 35
  All Along The Watchtower
  Like A Rolling Stone

These are all '74 Tour tracks. Precise source is not known in most cases but "Mr Tambourine Man" is almost certainly from the 14th February Los Angeles 2nd Show. A lot of the other tracks are probably from the same concert.
Medium quality throughout, audience tape.

HIS GOTHAM INGRESS - Subtitle for "Are You Now Or Have You Ever Been?".

HOLD THE FORT FOR WHAT IT'S WORTH Double
Going Going Gone
Idiot Wind
It Ain't Me Babe
Deportees
Where Did Vincent Van Gogh? (with Bobby Neuwirth)
One Too Many Mornings
Mozambique
Isis
Memphis Blues Again
Oh Sister
You're A Big Girl Now
You're Gonna Make Me Lonesome When You Go
Lay Lady Lay
Railroad Boy (Dying Of Love)
I Pity The Poor Immigrant
Shelter From The Storm
When I Paint My Masterpiece
I Don't Believe You
Blowin' In The Wind

All tracks from the Rolling Thunder Concert at Fort Worth except "I Don't Believe You" (source unknown), "When I Paint My Masterpiece" and "Blowin' In The Wind" (last two Hartford). Audience recording, fair quality throughout.

HURRICANE CARTER BENEFIT - See "The Hurricane Carter Benefit"

I'M READY Existence of this album very uncertain.

Christmas Island	Dick Farina and Eric Von Schmidt session, 1963. See Official Discography
London	"
Glory Glory	"
You Can Always Tell	"
Mr Tambourine Man	"
Number One	L.A. Band Session, 1965
I'm Ready (not Dylan)	John Hammond?
Hattie Carroll	Live?
One Too Many Mornings	"
Like A Rolling Stone	"
Maggie's Farm	"

IN CONCERT - See "Bob Dylan In Concert"

IN CONCERT ON THE ISLAND - See "Isle Of Wight"

IN CONCERTO - See "Bob Dylan In Concerto"

IN 1966 THERE WAS A CONCERT - See "Royal Albert Hall"

IN THE WATERS OF OBLIVION Double (White Bear). Existence unconfirmed. All the Dylan performances from the January 7th '74 concert at the Spectrum, Philadelphia plus 'The Times They Are a' Changin' ' from another '74 tour concert (which one not known). Stereo, good quality. P.A. or good audience recording (reputedly).

ISLE OF WHITE (T.M.Q. 1 & 2, T.M.Q.1 full title: "G.W.W. - Isle of White")

1	She Belonge To Me (incomplete)	F
	I Threw It All Away	F
	Maggie's Farm	F
	Wild Mountain Thyme	F
	It Ain't Me Babe	F
	To Ramona	F
	Lay Lady Lay (incomplete)	F
	Highway 61 Revisited	F
2	One Too Many Mornings	F
	I Pity The Poor Immigrant (incomplete)	F
	Like A Rolling Stone	F
	I'll Be Your Baby Tonight (incomplete)	F
	Mighty Quinn	F
	Minstrel Boy (incomplete)	F
	Rainy Day Women Nos. 12 & 35 (incomplete)	F
	Mr Tambourine Man	P
	I Dreamed I Saw St Augustine	P

All tracks from the Isle of Wight Concert withTheBand, August 31st 1969. Probably all P.A. recordings except last 2 tracks which could be P.A. or audience. Also issued with "While The Establishment Burns" as a double (T.M.Q.1)

ISLE OF WIGHT (C.B.M.) See "Isle of Wight - In Concert on the Island"

ISLE OF WIGHT — IN CONCERT ON THE ISLAND (Peace Records)

1 Highway 61 Revisited
  One Too Many Mornings

I Pity The Poor Immigrant (incomplete)
Like A Rolling Stone
I'll Be Your Baby Tonight (incomplete)
Mighty Quinn
Minstrel Boy (incomplete)

2   She Belongs To Me (incomplete)
    I Threw It All Away
    Maggie's Farm
    Wild Mountain Thyme
    It Ain't Me Babe
    To Ramona
    Lay Lady Lay (incomplete)

All tracks from the Isle of Wight concert with the Band, August 31st 1969. Fair quality throughout, probably P.A. recording. Also issued as "Isle Of Wight" on C.B.M.

IT'S BEEN A LONG LONG TIME Double (White Bear). Existence unconfirmed. All the Dylan performances from the February 2nd '74 concert at Ann Arbor, Notre Dame. Stereo, good quality. P.A. or good audience recording (reputedly).

JINGLE JANGLE MORNING Double? Existence of this album very uncertain.
Boots Of Spanish Leather
She Belongs To Me
It's Alright Ma (I'm Only Bleeding)
Gates Of Eden
One Too Many Mornings
Hattie Carroll
It Ain't Me Babe
It's All Over Now Baby Blue
Mr Tambourine Man
A Hard Rain's A-Gonna Fall
Don't Think Twice, It's All Right
All tracks reputedly live acoustic. Nothing else known.

JOAQUIN ANTIQUE Subtitle: "Here's Another Fine Bridgett You've Gotten Me Into" (Kornyfone - TAKRL)

1	I Threw It All Away	G		Johnny Cash T.V. Show, May 1969
	Living The Blues			"
	Lily, Rosemary And The Jack Of Hearts	E		The Original "Blood On The Tracks", 1974
	I'll Keep It With Mine	E		"Another Side Of ....." out-take, June 1964
	Idiot Wind (with jump)	E		The Original "Blood On The Tracks", 1974
2	Except You	A	M	Chicago Concert, January 3rd 1974
	Tangled Up In Blue	E		The Original "Blood On The Tracks", 1974
	She Belongs To Me	E		"Bringing It All Back Home" out-take, December 1964
	If You See Her Say Hello	E		The Original "Blood On The Tracks", 1974
	Love Minus Zero/No Limit	E		"Bringing It All Back Home" out-take, December 1964
	Your're A Big Girl Now	E		The Original "Blood On The Tracks", 1974

It's All Over Now Baby Blue   E   "Bringing It All Back Home" out-take, December 1964

This album was deleted because of the number of complaints Kornyfone received about the record sticking on "Idiot Wind". This is nothing to do with the jump on the same track - the jump is on the tape from which the album was mastered.

JOHN BIRCH SOCIETY BLUES Single (T.M.Q.1 & 2, Blank label - Berkeley Records, various blank labels).
T.M.Q.1 Full title: "G.W.W. - John Birch Society Blues".

1	Mixed Up Confusion	E	The Original "Freewheelin' ", 1963
	East Laredo	E	"Another Side Of ....." out-take, June 1964
	I'll Keep It With Mine	E	"
	Talkin' John Birch Society Blues	G	The Original "Freewheelin' ", 1963
	Who Killed Davey Moore?	PA G	Carnegie Hall Concert, October 1963
	Eternal Circle	E	"Times ....." out-take, 1963
	Ramblin' Gamblin' Willie	F	The Original "Freewheelin' ", 1963
2	I Was Young When I Left Home	G	Minnesota Hotel Tape, December 1961
	Percy's Song	G	'Times .....' out-take, 1963
	Corrina Corrina	E	The Original 'Freewheelin' ', 1963
	In The Evening	G	Minnesota Hotel Tape, December 1961
	Long John	G	"

JOHN BIRCH SOCIETY BLUES Double
This album also seems to have been put out as "Great White Wonder Volume 2" (according to an article in Let It Rock by Tony White, alias Michael Gray). What it appears to be is a cocked-up version of "Great White Wonder Part 2".

Wade In The Water
Cocaine (incomplete)
I'll Keep It With Mine
Talkin' John Birch Society Blues
Who Killed Davey Moore?
Eternal Circle
Ramblin' Gamblin' Willie
Percy's Song
Corrina Corrina
In The Evening
Long John
The Cough Song
New Orleans Rag (fragment)
Can You Please Crawl Out Your Window
It Takes A Lot To Laugh, It Takes A Train To Cry
She Belongs To Me
Love Minus Zero/No Limit
It's All Over Now Baby Blue
That's Alright Mama
Hard Times In New York
Stealin'
I Was Young When I Left Home
Percy's Song (again)
Corrina Corrina (again)

In The Evening (again)
Long John (again)
Down In The Flood
    Source and sound quality same as corresponding tracks on copies of "Great White Wonder Part 2" except "The Cough Song" which is a "Times ....." outtake, 1963, excellent quality.

JOHN BIRCH SOCIETY BLUES/MILLION DOLLAR BASH
Supposedly a single album, no information available as to tracks or whether album actually exists.

JUST AS WELL
Full title: "Robert Zimmerman - Just As Well". Same tracks as "Great White Wonder" single album, slightly different track arrangement - "This Wheel's On Fire" and "Mighty Quinn" in reverse order.

KINDEST KUT, THE (Blank label, Blank label - Berkeley Records)
Same album as "Blind Boy Grunt"

LAST BASH, THE - Same as "Bridgett's Album" ('74 Tour version) except "Highway 61 Revisited" omitted.

LET ME DIE IN MY FOOTSTEPS (Popo, T.M.Q.1, Berkeley) T.M.Q.1 Full title: "G.W.W. - Let Me Die In My Footsteps"

1	Let Me Die In My Footsteps	M	"Bob Dylan" out-take, 1962
	San Francisco Bay Blues	M	East Orange Tape, 1961
	Jesus Met The Woman At The Well	P	"
	Gypsy Davy	P	"
	Pastures Of Plenty	P	"
	Remember Me	P	"
2	Folsom Prison Blues	P	"Self Portrait" out-takes, 1969
	Ring Of Fire	P	"
	Number One	P	L.A. Band Session, December 1965
	Walking Down The Line	P	Broadside Sessions, 1963
	Train A-Travellin'	P	"
	Cuban Blockade (World War No. 3)	M	"
	I'd Hate To Be You On That Dreadful Day	M	"
	Denise Denise	P	"Another Side Of ....." out-take, June 1964

LITTLE WHITE WONDER (Rover, Peace - both the same company)

1	Tears Of Rage	G
	Mighty Quinn	G
	Million Dollar Bash (with clunk)	F
	Yea! Heavy And A Bottle Of Bread	G
	Please Mrs Henry	G
	I Shall Be Released	F
2	Down In The Flood	F
	Lo And Behold	G
	Tiny Montgomery	G
	Open The Door Homer	G
	Nothing Was Delivered	G
	This Wheel's On Fire	F
	You Ain't Goin' Nowhere	G

LITTLE WHITE WONDER, THE - See "Bob Dylan Volumes 1, 2 and 3"

LITTLE WHITE WONDER, A RARE BATCH OF - See "Bob Dylan - A Rare

Batch of Little White Wonder Volume 1, 2 and 3"

LIVE AT THE BERKELEY COMMUNITY — ZIMMERMAN (Blank label, Blank label - Berkeley Records)
Same as "While The Establishment Burns" except "Desolation Row" omitted on some versions and quality generally slightly better. *None* of the tracks comes from the Berkeley Community Theatre.

LIVE AT L.A. FORUM 1974 - see "St Valentine's Day Massacre And More"

LIVE AT TOWN HALL - Same tracks as "While The Establishment Burns". No information available on sound quality.

LIVE IN 1974 - Dutch pressing of "Bridgett's Album" ('74 Tour version)

LIVE IN THE BIG APPLE Double (White Bear). Existence unconfirmed.
All the dylan performances from the January 28th '74 concert at the Nassau Colliseum. Stereo, good quality. P.A. or good audience recording (reputedly).

LIVE PARTS 1 & 2 (Peace)
Copied direct from "Bob Dylan In Concert Volumes 1 & 2". Considerable loss of sound quality incurred in the copying.

LONG DISTANCE INFORMATION Double (White Bear). Existence unconfirmed.
All the Dylan performances from the January 23rd '74 concert at Memphis Mid-South Colliseum except "The Times They Are A-Changin' " (source unknown). Stereo, good quality. P.A. or good audience recording (reputedly).

LONG TIME GONE 2 E.P.s
May also have been issued as one L.P. but information is scant on this.
Record 1

1	Gates Of Eden (incomplete)	P	Royal Albert Hall Concert, May 1965
	Ballad Of Donald White	F	W.B.A.I. New York May 1962
2	Nowadays (Long Ago, Far Away)	M	Witmark Demo, 1963
	Long Time Gone	M	"
	Ye Playboys And Playgirls	F	Broadside Sessions, 1963

Record 2

1	Ain't Gonna Grieve	M	Witmark Demo, 1963
	Mr Tambourine Man	P	Royal Albert Hall Concert, May 1965
2	One Too Many Mornings (with Johnny Cash)	G	Johnny Cash T.V. Documentary, Jan. 1969
	If You Gotta Go, Go Now	P	Royal Albert Hall Concert, May 1965
	Help	P	Reputedly Dylan and the Beatles, 1965

LOOKING BACK — ZIMMERMAN Double (Zerracks, Mood Music Library, Blank Label, Blank Label - Berkeley Records)
Whether the title is as above or "Zimmerman - Looking Back" depends on how you interpret the position of the words on the cover. This is a combination of two single albums equivalent to "While The Establishment Burns" and "Royal Albert Hall". Most versions good quality but some have a clunk running through one verse of "Visions Of Johanna". Also issued as two single albums, "Looking Back 1 & 2".

LOVE SONGS Double (White Bear). Existence unconfirmed.
All the Dylan performances from the January 19th '74 concert at the Hollywood Sportatorium, Miami. Stereo, good quality. P.A. or good audience tape (reputedly).

LOVE SONGS FOR AMERICA — CAST OFF LUNGS AND RETOUCHED BADLANDS (Kornyfone - TAKRL)
All the Dylan performances from the January 19th '74 concert at the Hollywood

Sportatorium, Miami, plus the following tracks from the Chicago concert of January 3rd 1974 –. "Tough Mama", "Except You", "It's Alright Ma (I'm Only Bleeding)", "Forever Young", "Something There Is About You". Stereo, medium quality throughout. Probably an audience recording.

MADISON SQUARE GARDEN AUGUST 1ST 1971 AFTERNOON CONCERT — GEORGE HARRISON, RINGO STARR, BOB DYLAN, LEON RUSSELL (Label not known - possibly B.R.K. or Carnaby Records)

That's The Way God Planned It	Billy Preston
Jumpin' Jack Flash/Youngblood	Leon Russell
It Don't Come Easy	Ringo Starr
Mr Tambourine Man	Bob Dylan
Just Like A Woman	"
My Sweet Lord	George Harrison
Introductions	"
Something	"
Bangladesh	"
Beware Of Darkness	"
While My Guitar Gently Weeps	"

This album claims to include first show performances of the Bangladesh Concert of August 1st 1971, but as "Mr Tambourine Man" was not in fact included in that show, only in the evening one, this indicates that some or possibly all of the above tracks are from the evening concert. No information available on the sound quality of the album.

MELBOURNE AUSTRALIA - See "Bob Dylan In Melbourne Australia"

MILLION DOLLAR BASH (Blank Label - Berkeley Records)

Yea! Heavy And A Bottle Of Bread	F
Please Mrs Henry	F
Down In The Flood	F
Lo And Behold	F
Tiny Montgomery	F
This Wheel's On Fire	F
Million Dollar Bash	F
Get Your Rocks Off	F
Nothing Was Delivered	F
Too Much Of Nothing	F
I Shall Be Released	F
You Ain't Goin' Nowhere	F
Mighty Quinn	F
Open The Door Homer	F
Tears Of Rage (incomplete)	F

All tracks from the Basement Tape, 1967

MOM'S APPLE PIE Double (White Bear). Existence unconfirmed.

All the Dylan performances from the January 17th '74 concert at the Charlotte Colliseum. Stereo, good quality, P.A. or good audience recording (reputedly).

MOTORCYCLE (Wheel Records)

Mighty Quinn	This Wheel's On Fire
Nothing Was Delivered	Please Mrs Henry
Million Dollar Bash	Lo And Behold
Yea! Heavy And A Bottle Of Bread	Tiny Montgomery
Nowadays (Long Ago, Far Away)	You Ain't Goin' Nowhere
Long Time Gone	Tears Of Rage
Ain't Gonna Grieve	

All tracks from the Basement Tape, 1967 except "Nowadays", "Long Time Gone" and "Ain't Gonna Grieve" which are from the Witmark Demos 1963.

Medium sound quality throughout. *N.B.* The song titles printed on the labels are confusingly abbreviated versions.

NASHVILLE SUNSET

One Too Many Mornings	I Walk The Line
Good Ol' Mountain Dew	You Are My Sunshine
I Still Miss Someone	Ring Of Fire
Careless Love	Guess Things Happen That Way
Matchbox	Just A Closer Walk With Thee
That's Alright Mama	'T' for Texas/Blue Yodell
Big River	

All tracks with Johnny Cash. Taken from the Nashville Sessions, February 1969. Stereo, excellent quality throughout.

NIGHT THE REVUE CAME TO BOSTON - See "The Night the Revue Came to Boston"

NOTHING IS REVEALED (IMP)
Also released under the title: "Tapes From Sherry's Attic" (K & S)

Sundown	Gordon Lightfoot
Coyote	Joni Mitchell
Chestnut Mare	Roger McGuinn
Muleskinner Blues	Jack Elliot
Diamonds And Rust	Joan Baez
Tonight I'll Be Staying Here With You	Dylan
Romance In Durango	Dylan
Iris	"
Oh Sister	"
Hurricane	"

All tracks from the December 1st Rolling Thunder concert at Maple Leaf Gardens, Toronto. Audience recording. Medium quality throughout.

NOW YOUR MOUTH CRIES WHOOPS - See "And Now Your Mouth Cries Whoops"

NEWHAVEN, THE ROLLING THUNDER REVUE COMES TO
Nothing known about this album. It may or may not exist.

NOW YOUR MOUTH CRIES WOLF (Kornyfone - TAKRL)

1	I Wanna Be Your Lover Baby	E	L.A. Band Session, December 1965
	Can You Please Crawl Out Your Window (fast)	E	"
	From A Buick 6	E	"Highway 61" out-take, 1965
	Visions Of Johanna	G	L.A. Band Session, December 1965
	She's Your Lover Now	G	"
2	Can You Please Crawl Out Your Window (slow)	G	"Highway 61" out-takes, 1965
	It Takes A Lot To Laugh, It Takes A Train To Cry	G	"
	Killing Me Alive (Barbed Wire Fence)	G	"
	If You Gotta Go, Go Now	E	"Bringing It All Back Home." out-take, December 1964
	She Belongs To Me	E	"
	Love Minus Zero/No Limit	E	"

These tracks are as they are listed on the album cover slip. In fact all the albums seem to have the Side 2 label on Side 1 and vice versa. The matrix numbers tally with the labels.

The album is a combination of Side 2 of "Seems Like A Freeze-Out" (TMQ) and Side 1 of "Stealin' " (TMQ). Such a combination was a very good idea on Kornyfone's part because it put most of the material available from Dylan's classic period together on one album. But having had the good idea they then made the mistake of deleting it as a single album and putting it out as a double with "Ode For Barbara Allen", an album of good, but unrelated material. They called the double "Barbed Wire Blues".

NOW YOUR MOUTH CRIES WOLF
Reputedly two hundred copies of the "Royal Albert Hall' album were issued under this title.

ODE FOR BARBARA ALLEN (Kornyfone - TAKRL)
1 A Hard Rain's A-Gonna Fall
   Don't Think Twice, It's All Right
   Hezekiah Jones
   No More Auction Block
   Rocks And Gravel

2 Barbara Allen
   Moonshiner (Moonshine Blues, The Bottle Song)
   Bob Dylan's Dream
   Boots Of Spanish Leather
   Blowin' In The Wind

All tracks from the Gaslight Tape (1) 1962, except the last three on Side 2 which are from the Studs Terkel Show, May 1963. Sound quality excellent except that later copies have a short series of clunks on the track "Barbara Allen".

ON THE ROAD AGAIN Double (White Bear). Existence unconfirmed.
All the Dylan performances from the January 3rd '74 concert at the Amphitheater, Chicago. Stereo, good quality. P.A. or good audience recording (reputedly).

ON THE ROAD 1974 - 1975 (Kornyfone - Z.A.P.)

1	I Don't Believe You	Rolling Thunder concert Bangor, Maine 1975
	She Belongs To Me	Los Angeles Forum 2nd show,
	It's All Over Now Baby Blue	Los Angeles Forum 1st show
	Except You	Chicago Amphitheater, January 3rd 1974
	Love Minus Zero/No Limit	Rolling Thunder Concert, New York 1975
	Single Twist Of Fate	"
2	A Hard Rain's A-Gonna Fall	St Louis 1st show February 4th 1974
	Desolation Row	"
	Wedding Song	Denver 1st show February 6th 1974
	Visions Of Johanna	"

Stereo, sound quality medium throughout, audience recording.

ORIGINAL GASLIGHT — WITMARK ARCHIVES - See "Dylan '62"

PASSED OVER AND ROLLING THUNDER — A COLLECTION OF PERFORMANCES FROM THEN AND NOW (Kornyfone - TAKRL, Worlds Records)
Record 1

1	Maggie's Farm (with The Butterfield Blues Band and Barry Goldberg)	PA	E	Newport Folk Festival, 1965
	Like A Rolling Stone (with The Butterfield Blues Band etc.)	PA	E	"
	It Takes A Lot To Laugh, It	PA	E	"

Takes A Train To Cry (with The Butterfield Blues Band etc.)			
It's All Over Now Baby Blue	PA	E	"
Mr Tambourine Man	PA	E	"

2
Hurricane		E	John Hammond T.V. Show 1975
Oh Sister		E	"
Simple Twist Of Fate		E	"
Tangled Up In Blue		E	"

Record 2

3
Lily, Rosemary And The Jack Of Hearts		E	The Original "Blood On The Tracks", 1974
If You See Her Say Hello		E	"
You're A Big Girl Now		E	"
Idiot Wind (with jump)		E	"

4
It Ain't Me Babe	A	F	Rolling Thunder Concert, Providence, Rhode Island 1975
I Dreamed I Saw St Augustine	A	F	"
I Shall Be Released	A	F	"
Just Like A Woman	A	F	"
Knockin' On Heaven's Door	A	F	"

Stereo throughout. Reputedly there are inferior quality pirate copies of this album around. Side 2 and side 3 issued as a single album entitled "Blood Takes".

PAST AND PRESENT Double?
An album of this title is reputedly in existence but little is known about it. It may possibly be a version of "Passed Over And Rolling Thunder" (see above).

PICNIC (V.P.R.O.)
Two Dylan tracks - "I'll Be Your Baby Tonight" (Isle of Wight) and "Ramblin' Gamblin' Willie" (Original "Freewheelin' ") plus tracks by the Mothers of Invention, Canned Heat, Steve Miller and Richie Havens. Sound quality fair.

POEMS IN NAKED WONDER (Flat Records)

1
He Was A Friend Of Mine	G
Man On The Street (Take 1 - incomplete)	E
Hard Times In New York	E
Man On The Street (Take 2)	E
Talkin' Bear Mountain Picnic Massacre Disaster Blues	E
Standing On The Highway	E
Poor Boy Blues	E
Ballad For A Friend	E
Ramblin' Gamblin' Willie	E

2
Talkin' John Birch Society Blues	G
Long Time Gone	G
Nowadays (Long Ago, Far Away)	G
Let Me Die In My Footsteps (fragment)	G
Bob Dylan's Blues	F
Masters Of War	E
Bound To Win	G
Baby Let Me Follow You Down	E
Farewell (includes small tape jump)	G

Side 1 comprises all the Leeds Music Demos 1962. Side 2 tracks are all from the Witmark Demos 1963.

PONY EXPRESS Double (White Bear). Existence unconfirmed.
All the Dylan performances from the January 25th '74 concert at Daron County Center, Fort Worth.

Stereo, good quality. P.A. or good audience recording (reputedly).

RARE SPOTS Double (White Bear). Existence unconfirmed.
All the Dylan performances from the January 16th '74 concert at the Washington Capitol Center except "One Too Many Mornings".
Stereo, good quality. P.A. or good audience tape (reputedly).

ROBERT ZIMMERMAN — JUST AS WELL
Same tracks as "Great White Wonder" single album. Different track arrangement but precise order not known.

ROLLING THUNDER ALBUMS - See under town or city where concert took place or under precise title of album.

ROYAL ALBERT HALL (T.M.Q. 1 & 2, Blank Labels, Blank Label - Berkeley Records, C.B.M., Mood Music Library, Kornyfone - TAKRL, Worlds Records. Alternate titles: "In 1966 There Was A Concert ....."; "Bob Dylan And The Band Live"; "Zimmerman - Looking Back 1"; "Zimmerman - Royal Albert Hall"; T.M.Q.1 full title: "G.W.W. - Royal Albert Hall")

1 Tell Me Mama
   I Don't Believe You
   Baby Let Me Follow You Down
   Just Like Tom Thumb's Blues
   Leopard Skin Pill Box Hat
   One Too Many Mornings
   Ballad Of A Thin Man
   Like A Rolling Stone
   All tracks from the electric half of the Royal Albert Hall Concert with the Band, May 1966. Sound quality good, probably P.A. recording.
   Also released as part of the double, "Zimmerman - Looking Back" (Zerrocks, Mood Music Library, Blank Label - Berkeley Records)

ST VALENTINE'S DAY MASSACRE Double (White Bear). Existence unconfirmed.
All the Dylan performances from the February 14th '74 1st show at the Los Angeles Forum. Stereo, good quality. P.A. or good audience recording (reputedly).

ST VALENTINE'S DAY MASSACRE Triple (T.M.Q.1 - Deluxe)
Full title: "G.W.W.: St Valentine's Day Massacre"
All the Dylan performances from the February 14th '74 2nd show at the L.A. Forum plus "It's All Over Now Baby Blue" from the 1st show of the same day. Medium quality. Audience recording.

ST VALENTINE'S DAY MASSACRE ELECTRIC Double (T.M.Q.1)
Full title: "G.W.W.: St Valentine's Day Massacre Electric"
All the remaining tracks from the February 14th '74 2nd show not included on the "St Valentine's Day Massacre - Acoustic" album. Medium quality, audience recording. This album is sides 1, 2, 5 and 6 of the "St Valentine's Day Massacre" Triple.

ST VALENTINE'S DAY MASSACRE AND MORE Double (Highway Hi-fi, T.M.Q.2, also probably Kornyfone)
All the tracks from the "St Valentine's Day Massacre" Triple (audience recording, medium quality) plus "All I Really Want To Do" from the Newport Folk Festival 1964, and "Maggie's Farm" and "Mr Tambourine Man" from the Newport Folk Festival 1965. These last three tracks good quality, P.A. recordings. Also released as "Live at L.A. Forum 1974".

SAND AND ASHES Double (White Bear). Existence unconfirmed.
All the Dylan performances from the January 14th '74 concert at Boston Gardens. Stereo, good quality. P.A. or good audience recording (reputedly).

SECOND TIME AROUND Double (White Bear). Existence unconfirmed.

All the Dylan performances from the January 4th '74 concert at the Chicago Amphitheater except "Knockin' On Heaven's Door", "Something There Is About You" and "Most Likely You Go Your Way And I'll Go Mine". It also includes a performance of "Maggie's Farm" which does not seem to have come from the same concert and the source of which, other than its being from the '74 tour is not known. Stereo, good quality. P.A. or good audience recording (reputedly).

SEEMS LIKE A FREEZE OUT (T.M.Q. 1 & 2) T.M.Q.1 full title: "G.W.W. - Seems Like A Freeze Out". Also released as "Visions Of Johanna" (Blank Label - Berkeley Records)

1	California		G	"Another Side Of ....." out-take, June 1964
	Lay Down Your Weary Tune		G	"
	Dusty Old Fairgrounds	PA	G	Carnegie Hall Concert, October 1963
	Who You Really Are		G	Banjo Tape, January 1963
	If I Could Do It All Over I'd Do It All Over You		G	"
	Whatcha Gonna Do?		G	Witmark Demos, 1963
	Farewell		G	Banjo Tape, January 1963
2	I Wanna Be Your Lover Baby		E	L.A. Band Session, December 1965
	Can You Please Crawl Out Your Window		E	"
	From A Buick 6		E	"Highway 61" out-take, 1965
	Visions Of Johanna		G	L.A. Band Session, December 1965
	She's Your Lover Now		G	"

SEVENTY DOLLAR ROBBERY (C.B.M., Blank label)

1	Jesse James	P	East Orange Tape, 1961
	Remember Me	P	"
	East Virginia Blues	G	Fanfare - Earl Scruggs T.V. documentary, 1970
	Folsom Prison Blues	P	"Self-Portrait" out-takes, june 1969
	Ring Of Fire	P	"
	It Ain't Me Babe	F	Isle of Wight Concert, August 1969
	George Jackson	G	Acoustic side of official single, Nov. 1971
2	Wild Mountain Thyme	F	Isle of Wight Concert, August 1969
	Moonshine Blues (Moonshiner, The Bottle Song)	P	Witmark Demo, 1963
	Cocaine	E	Minnesota Hotel Tape, December 1963
	Omie Wise	E	"
	John Brown	F	Witmark Demo, 1963

The sound quality ratings apply to well pressed versions of this album. There are some very badly pressed copies around.

The track list above follows the album cover slip. On the record the sides are reversed.

SKID ROW Existence of this album very uncertain.

V D Blues	Minnesota Hotel Tape, December 1961
V D Waltz	"
V D City	
I'd Hate To Be You On That Dreadful Day	? (Either Witmark Demos, 1963, or Broadside Sessions, 1963)
Walking Down The Line	"

Blowin' In The Wind	?
Trail Of the Buffalo	East Orange Tape, 1961
Girl From The North Country	Oscar Brand Show, October 1962
Only A Hobo	"

Let Me Die In My Footsteps   ? (Either from "Bob Dylan", 1962, or "Freewheelin' ", 1963, sessions or Witmark Demos, 1963)

I Shall Be Free   ? (Either Witmark Demo, 1963, or Broadside, 1963)

SNACK (HAR)
Are You Ready For The Country
Ain't That A Lot Of Love
Lookin' For A Love
Lovin' You (Is Sweeter Than Ever)
The Weight
Helpless/Knockin' At The Dragon's Door (Heaven's Door)
Will The Circle Be Unbroken
Who Killed Davy Moore?
All I Really Want To Do
   All tracks from the S.N.A.C.K. Benefit Concert of 2nd March 1975 with Neil Young and the Band (without Robbie Robertson but with Ben Keith) except the last two which are from the Halloween Concert of October 1964. Poor quality throughout.

STEALIN' - Original Version (Blank label, Har-Kub Records, Hobo Label)
1 Can You Please Crawl Out Your Window
   It Takes A Lot To Laugh, It Takes A Train To Cry
   If You Gotta Go, Go Now
   She Belongs To Me
   Love Minus Zero/No Limit

2 It's All Over Now Baby Blue
   The Cough Song
   New Orleans Rag (fragment)
   That's Alright Mama
   Hard Times In New York
   Stealin'
   Wade In The Water
   Cocaine (incomplete)
   All tracks from the same sources as the corresponding tracks on the T.M.Q. "Stealin' " (see below). Quality also similar except "Can You Please Crawl Out Your Window" which has a more natural tone balance than the T.M.Q. version which is very treble.

STEALIN' (T.M.Q. 1&2, Blank label - Berkeley Records) T.M.Q.1 Full title: "G.W.W. - Stealin' "

1 Can You Please Crawl Out Your Window	G	"Highway 61" out-take 1965
It Takes A Lot To Laugh, It Takes A Train To Cry	G	"
Killing Me Alive (Barbed Wire Fence)	G	"
If You Gotta Go, Go Now	E	"Bringing It All Back Home" out-takes, December 1964
She Belongs To Me	E	"
Love Minus Zero/No Limit	E	"
2 New Orleans Rag (fragment)	G	"Another Side of ..." out-take, June 1964

That's Alright Mama	E	"
Cocaine	G	Minnesota Hotel Tape, December 1961
Stealin'	G	"
Hard Times In New York	G	"
Wade In The Water	E	"
It's All Over Now Baby Blue	E	"Bringing It All Back Home" out-take, December 1964
The Cough Song	E	"Times ..." out-take, 1963

One version of this album (blank label - Berkeley Records) was frequently poorly pressed.

STEALIN' (2 E.P.s) (Freedom)
Record 1
Can You Please Crawl Out You Window
Killing Me Alive (Barbed Wire Fence)
Cocaine
Hard Times In New York
Wade In The Water
Love Minus Zero/No Limit

Record 2
She Belongs To Me
It's All Over Now Baby Blue
The Cough Song
It Takes A Lot To Laugh, It Takes A Train To Cry
That's Alright Mama
If You Gotta Go, Go Now
All tracks same sources as corresponding tracks on T.M.Q. "Stealin' ". Sound quality slightly inferior to the latter.

STEALIN' (label not known)
Same track arrangement as record 1 of the "Great White Wonder Part 2" double.

SUITE FOR THREE Existence unconfirmed.
Nothing known about this album.

SWANSONG Double (White Bear). Existence unconfirmed.
All the Dylan performances from the 14th January '74 2nd show at Boston Gardens except "Blowin' In The Wind". Stereo, good quality. P.A. or good audience recording (reputedly).

TALKIN' BEAR MOUNTAIN MASSACRE PICNIC BLUES (Blank label, C.B.M., T.M.Q. 1&2, Blank label - Berkeley Records) T.M.Q. 1 Full title: "G.W.W. - Talkin' Bear Mountain Massacre Picnic Blues".

1	Quit Your Lowdown Ways	E
	Worried Blues	G
	Corrina Corrina	E
	Lonesome Whistle Blues	E
	Rocks And Gravel	E
	Talkin' Hava Negilah Blues	E
	Omie Wise	G
	Wichita Blues	G
2	Talkin' Bear Mountain Picnic Massacre Disaster Blues	G
	Babe I'm In The Mood For You	E
	Emmett Till	E
	Baby Please Don't Go	E
	Going To New Orleans	G
	Milk Cow Blues	E

All tracks out-takes from the "Bob Dylan" sessions of 1962 except "Omie Wise" which is from the Minnesota Hotel Tape, December 1961.

TAPES FROM SHERRY'S ATTIC (K & S)
  Same album as "Nothing Is Revealed"

TARANTULA XI Double (White Bear). Existence unconfirmed.
  All the Dylan performances of the January 15th '74 concert at the Washington
Capitol Center. Stereo, good quality. P.A. or good audience recording (reputedly).

TASTE OF THE SPECIAL STASH - see 'A Taste Of The Special Stash'

THE ACETATE (1)
Million Dollar Bash
Yea! Heavy And A Bottle Of Bread
Please Mrs Henry
Down In The Flood
Lo And Behold
Tiny Montgomery
This Wheel's On Fire
You Ain't Goin' Nowhere
I Shall Be Released
Too Much Of Nothing
Tears Of Rage
Mighty Quinn
Nothing Was Delivered
Open The Door Homer
  The above listing is not necessarily the correct order in which the tracks appear
on the album. All tracks from the Basement Tape, 1967. Sound quality not known.

THE ACETATE (2)
All the tracks on "The Acetate" (1) plus "Apple Suckling Tree", "Clothes Line
Saga", "I'm Not There", "Odds And Ends", "Get Your Rocks Off" and the alter-
nate version of "Nothing Was Delivered", all from the Basement Tape 1967.
Precise track order and sound quality not known.

THE DEMO TAPES (T.M.Q. 1 & 2) T.M.Q.1 Full Title: "G.W.W. - The Demo
Tapes"

John Brown	M	
Nowadays	M	
Only A Hobo	F	
Long Time Gone	F	
Ain't Gonna Grieve	F	
Emmett Till	M	
I'll Keep It With Mine	M	
I'd Hate To Be You On That Dreadful Day	F	
I Shall Be Free	F	
Trail Of The Buffalo	P	East Orange Tape 1961
Jesse James	P	"
Remember Me	P	"
Cuban Blockade (World War No. 3)	P	Broadside Sessions 1963

  All tracks from the Witmark Demos, 1963 except where noted.

THE GASLIGHT TAPES — VISIONS THROUGH A WINDOW (C.B.M.,
Instant Analysis)

Blowin' In The Wind	M
Rocks And Gravel	M
Quit Your Lowdown Ways	M
Gaslight Instrumental (short doodle)	M
He Was A Friend Of Mine	M

Hiram Hubbard	M
A Hard Rain's A-Gonna Fall	T
Don't Think Twice, It's All Right	M
Hezekiah Jones	T
No More Auction Block	M
Rocks And Gravel	M
Moonshine Blues (incomplete)	M

All tracks from the Gaslight Tape (1), 1962.

THE DYLAN CASH SESSION

1 One Too Many Mornings	2 That's Alright Mama
Good Ol' Mountain Dew	I Walk The Line
I Still Miss Someone	You Are My Sunshine
Careless Love	Ring Of Fire
Matchbox	Guess Things Happen That Way
Big River	'T' for Texas/Blue Yodell

Stereo, excellent quality throughout. All tracks with Johnny Cash, from the Nashville Session, May 1969. A version of this album includes "Just A Closer Walk With Thee" instead of "Blue Yodell".

THE GREAT WHITE WONDER — A THOUSAND MILES BEHIND - See "A Thousand Miles Behind"

THE GREATEST SHOW ON EARTH (Share Records)
Same album as "George Harrison, Bob Dylan, Leon Russell, Eric Clapton".

THE HURRICANE CARTER BENEFIT (Kornyfone - S.O.D.D., Worlds Records)
1 When I Paint My Masterpiece
It Ain't Me Babe
The Lonesome Death Of Hattie Carroll
Tonight I'll Be Staying Here With You
It Takes A Lot To Laugh, It Takes A Train To Cry
The Times They Are A-Changin'
Down In The Mine (Dark As A Dungeon)
Mama You Been On My Mind
Never Let Me Go
I Dreamed I Saw St Augustine

2 Romance In Durango
Oh Sister
Hurricane
Iris
One More Cup Of Coffee
Sara
Just Like A Woman
Knockin' On Heaven's Door (with Roger McGuinn)
This Land Is Your Land (with Joan Baez, Roger McGuinn, Joni Mitchell plus unidentifiable others)

All tracks from the Hurricane Carter Benefit Concert at New York Madison Square Garden 1976 except "Knockin' On Heaven's Door", the source of which is uncertain, and "This Land Is Your Land" from Bangor Maine. Stereo, fair quality throughout, probably audience recording.

THE KINDEST KUT (Blank label, Blank label - Berkeley Records)
Same album as "Blind Boy Grunt"

THE LAST BASH
Same tracks as "Bridgett's Album" ('74 Tour version) except "Highway 61" omitted.

THE LITTLE WHITE WONDER - See "Bob Dylan - The Little White Wonder" Volumes 1, 2 & 3.

THE NIGHT THE REVIEW CAME TO BOSTON (Kornyfone - Z.A.P., Worlds Records)
It Ain't Me Babe
The Lonesome Death Of Hattie Carroll
It Takes A Lot To Laugh, It Takes A Train To Cry
Romance In Durango
Iris
Simple Twist Of Fate
Oh Sister
Hurricane
One More Cup Of Coffee
   All tracks from the Rolling Thunder concert, Boston, 1976. Stereo, medium quality. Audience recording.

THE ROLLING THUNDER REVUE COMES TO NEWHAVEN Existence uncertain.
Nothing known about this album.

THE VILLAGER Double (Kathy and Stevie Records, Blank Label - Berkeley Records)

1	Man On The Street	P	The Gaslight Tape (2), 1962
	He Was A Friend of Mine	P	"
	Talkin' Bear Mountain Picnic Massacre Disaster Blues	P	"
2	Song To Woody	P	"
	Car Car (with Dave Von Ronk)	P	"
	Pretty Polly	P	"
	California	P	"Another Side Of ....." out-take, June 1964
3	Jesus Met The Woman At The Well	P	East Orange Tape, 1961
	Gypsy Davey	P	"
	Pastures Of Plenty	P	"
4	Jesse James	P	East Orange Tape, 1961
	Remember Me	P	"
	Lay Down Your Weary Tune	F	"Another Side Of ....." out-take, June 1964
	Moonshine Blues (Moonshiner, The Battle Song)	M	Witmark Demo, 1963

   This album also lists items called "Bull Sessions 1 and 2" on the cover slip and label. These are nothing more than tune-ups. Album generally badly pressed.

TROUBLED TROUBADOR (Blank Label, T.M.Q. 1 & 2, L.M.C.)
T.M.Q. 1 Full title: "G.W.W. - Troubled Troubador"

1	2
I Shall Be Released	Million Dollar Bash
Too Much Of Nothing	Yea, Heavy And A Bottle Of Bread
Tears Of Rage	Please Mrs Henry
Mighty Quinn	Down In The Flood
Open The Door Homer	Lo And Behold
Nothing Was Delivered	Tiny Montgomery
Clothes Line Saga	This Wheel's On Fire
Midnight Train	You Ain't Goin' Nowhere
	Apple Suckling Tree
	Odds And Ends

Fair quality throughout. All tracks from the Basement Tape 1967 except "Midnight Train" which is from the L.A. Band Session, December 1965. Last two tracks on each side often not listed on cover slip.

TWENTY FOUR (Blank Label)

1	Babe I'm In The Mood For You (incomplete)	G	Witmark Demos, 1963
	Guess I'm Doin' Fine	G	,,
	Quit Your Lowdown Ways	E	,,
	Gypsy Lou (incomplete)	G	,,
	Whatcha Gonna Do	E	,,
	Percy's Song	E	,,
	Hero Blues	F	,,
2	Mama You Been On My Mind	G	
	Lay Down Your Weary Tune	G	"Another Side Of ....." out-takes, June 1964
	I'll Keep It With Mine	M	,,
	California (under title Goin' Down South)	M	,,
	Moonshine Blues (Moonshiner, The Bottle Song)	F	,,
	Only A Hobo	F	"Times ....." out-take, 1963
	Who Killed Davey Moore? PA	G	Carnegie Hall Concert, October 1963

This album also issued under the title "Dirty Drivin' Rain". There was also a Swedish version called "Bob Dylan In Concert Part 1".

VALENTINO TYPE TANGOS (E.P.) Dojo Records)

I'm Not There	G	The Basement Tape, 1967
Telephone Song	M	Dylan's Answerphone, 1975
Don't Ya Tell Henry	G	The Basement Tape, 1967
St John The Evangelist (under the title Abandoned Love)	F	The Other End Club, 1975

The recording of "St John The Evangelist" is probably from an audience tape.

V.D. WALTZ (Blank label, T.M.Q.1, Phoneygraph)
T.M.Q.1 Full title: "G'W.W. - V.D. Waltz"

1	V.D. Blues	G	Minnesota Hotel Tape, December 1961
	V.D. Waltz	G	,,
	V.D. City	G	,,
	V.D. Woman (V.D. Gunner's Blues)	G	,,
	Mama You Been On My Mind	M	Witmark Demo, 1963
	Seven Curses	M	,,
	Wild Mountain Thyme PA	F	Isle of Wight Concert, August 1969
	East Virginia Blues	G	Fanfare - Earl Scruggs T.V. Documentary 1970
2	Midnight Train (Medicine Sunday)	F	L.A. Band Session, December 1965
	Clothes Line Saga (Talkin' Clothes Line Blues)	F	The Basement Tape, 1967
	I'm Not There	F	,,
	Odds And Ends	F	,,
	Get Your Rocks Off	F	,,
	Apple Suckling Tree	F	,,
	Paths Of Victory	G	Witmark Demo, 1963

Phoneygraph versions of this album are generally poorly pressed.

VILLAGER, THE - see "The Villager"

VISIONS OF JOHANNA (Blank label - Berkeley Records) Same as "Seems Like A Freeze Out" but generally poorer pressings.

VISIONS THROUGH A WINDOW - subtitle for "The Gaslight Tapes"

VIDEO CHILE - Side 2 of "Friends Of Chile" plus Side 1 of "Bridgett's Album - A Vinyl Headstone Almost in Place". Existence unconfirmed.

WALKING DOWN THE LINE (Figa Records - Collectors label)

Emmett Till	G	"Bob Dylan" out-takes, 1962
Worried Blues (under title Worry Blues)	G	”
Corrina Corrina (under title Carena)	G	”
Let Me Die In My Footsteps (under title Die In My Footsteps)	M	”
San Francisco Bay Blues		East Orange Tape, 1961
Rocks And Gravel (under title Salad Road)	G	"Bob Dylan" out-takes, 1962
Talkin' Hava Negilah Blues (under title Chanuka)	G	”
Cuban Blockade (under title World War No. 3)	M	Broadside Sessions, 1963
Denise Denise	P	"Another Side Of ....." out-take, June 1964
Walkin' Down The Line	P	Broadside Sessions, 1963
Omie Wise (under title Naomi Wise)	G	Minnesota Hotel Tape, December 1961
Wichita Blues	F	"Bob Dylan" out-take, 1962

WATERS OF OBLIVION (Blank label)

1
Million Dollar Bash
Yea! Heavy And A Bottle Of Bread
Please Mrs Henry
Down In The Flood
Lo And Behold
Tiny Montgomery
This Wheel's On Fire

2
You Ain't Goin' Nowhere
I Shall Be Released
Too Much Of Nothing
Tears Of Rage
Mighty Quinn
Open The Door Homer
Nothing Was Delivered

All tracks from the Basement Tape, 1967. All good quality except "Too Much Of Nothing" which has a lot of hiss on it, hence fair.

This is probably the best of all the Basement Tape albums issued.

WATCHING RAINBOWS

Beatles album *some* copies of which include "Every Time Somebody Comes To Town" and "I'd Have You Any Time" with George Harrison. Rumoured to be also available as an E.P. Possibly the same as "Get Together".

WATERS OF OBLIVION, THE - See "In The Waters Of Oblivion"

WHILE THE ESTABLISHMENT BURNS (T.M.Q. 1 & 2, Winklehoffer, Blank Label) T.M.Q.1 Full title: "G.W.W. - While the Establishment Burns".

Also released as "Live At Town Hall"; "Life At The Berkeley Community Theatre" (Blank label - erroneous title - some versions omit "Desolation Row"); "Zimmerman - Looking Back 2" (Blank label, C.B.M., Mood Music Library). The original album was also copied and put out under the title "Black Nite Crash" - the last track on each side fades on the latter and the quality is inferior.

Ramblin' Down Through The World	G
Bob Dylan's Dream	G
Tomorrow Is A Long Time	G
New Orleans Rag	G
Walls Of Redwing	G
Hero Blues	G
Who Killed Davey Moore?	G
Visions Of Johanna	F
4th Time Around	F
Just Like A Woman	F
Desolation Row	F

Side 1: all tracks from the New York Town Hall concert, April 1963. Side 2: all tracks from the Dublin concert, May 1966, acoustic half.

The quality ratings given are as per good pressings. The standard of pressing of this album and its multifarious versions varies quite a lot.

ZIMMERMAN — LIVE AT THE BERKELEY COMMUNITY THEATRE (Blank Label - Berkeley Records)

Same tracks as "While The Establishment Burns" except "Desolation Row" omitted from some versions. Generally slightly better sound quality.

ZIMMERMAN — LOOKING BACK Double (Zerrocks, Mood Music Library, Blank Label, Blank Label - Berkeley)

Equivalent combination of "While The Establishment Burns" and "Royal Albert Hall". The former generally slightly better quality than the T.M.Q. and Winklehoffer versions but some copies have a clunk running through one verse of "Visions Of Johanna".

Alse released as two singles: "Zimmerman - Looking Back 1 & 2" (Mood Music Library, Blank Label, C.B.M.)

ZIMMERMAN — ROYAL ALBERT HALL (Blank Label - Berkeley Records)

Possibly a different master but still virtually identical to other versions of "Royal Albert Hall'.

Additional Note – 1978

The following tracks have now been confirmed as definitely in circulation: An additional "Freewheelin' " out-take of "Mixed Up Confusion" with slightly differing lyrics; an additional demo version of "Mama You Been On My Mind"; a piano-backed demo of "Mr Tambourine Man"; an out-take of "Hurricane" with Emmylou Harris; a 1964 Canadian radio broadcast (mentioned under "Rumours") including "The Times They Are A-Changin' ", "Talkin' World III Blues", "The Lonesome Death Of Hattie Carroll", "Girl From The North Country", "A Hard Rain's A-Gonna Fall" and "Restless Farewell".

Recently released - official 12-inch promotional E.P. containing "People Get Ready", "Never Let Me Go", "It Ain't Me Babe", and "Isis", all from the film "Renaldo And Clara" - pirate editions of this E.P. also circulating. Rumour of imminent release in Japan of official triple tour album. Tapes of U.K. and European concerts June - July 1978 starting to circulate. British and German bootlegs thereof on the way.

The song previously known by various titles, including "St. John The Evangelist" and "Abandoned Love", has now been officially published in the United States under the latter title.

Update – 1980

The following material (which includes titles cited in "Additional Note—1978" but is not indexed herein) is now available or in circulation:

Tapes

MINNEAPOLIS TAPE (ALSO KNOWN AS MINNESOTA UNIVERSITY TAPE) 1960

Red Rosy Bush; Johnny I Hardly Knew You; Jesus Christ; Streets Of Glory; KC Moan; Muleskinner Blues; I'm A Gambler; Talkin' Marine; Talkin' Hugh Brown; Talkin' Lobbyist.

"MIXED UP CONFUSION" 1963

An out-take of this song from the "Freewheelin'" sessions containing a verse omitted from the better-known version came into circulation in 1978 and subsequently appeared officially on the Japanese "Masterpieces" album (see under "Official" section below).

"MAMA YOU BEEN ON MY MIND" 1963

A previously unknown piano-backed demo.

"QUEST" CANADIAN TV REQUEST PROGRAMME 1964

The Times They Are A'Changin'; Talkin' World War III Blues; The Lonesome Death Of Hattie Carroll; Girl From The North Country; A Hard Rain's A'Gonna Fall; Restless Farewell. (Mentioned under "Rumours")

"MR. TAMBOURINE MAN" 1964

Piano-backed demo.

PHILADELPHIA TOWN HALL AUTUMN 1964

The Times They Are A'Changin'; Girl From The North Country; Who Killed Davy Moore?; Talkin' John Birch Society Blues; To Ramona; Ballad Of Hollis Brown; Chimes Of Freedom; I Don't Believe You; It's Alright Ma (I'm Only Bleeding); Mr. Tambourine Man; Talkin' World War III Blues; A Hard Rain's A'Gonna Fall; Don't Think Twice, It's All Right; Only A Pawn In Their Game; With God On Our Side; It Ain't Me Babe; The Lonesome Death of Hattie Carroll; All I Really Want To Do. (Audience recording)

"HIGHWAY 61 REVISITED" ACETATE 1965

Includes a previously unknown out-take of "Desolation Row," the lesser known of the two complete slow versions of "Can You Please Crawl Out Your Window" plus the usual cuts of the other songs from the album, though some with altered mixes. Also "Positively 4th Street."

STOCKHOLM 1966

Acoustic and with the Hawks. Same set as other '66 gigs but many of the songs incomplete. (Audience recording)

"EAT THE DOCUMENT" 1966

Direct recordings of the film soundtrack now in circulation.

"HURRICANE" 1975
Out-take with Emmylou Harris.

HELENA SPRINGS DEMOS 1978
There is a rough studio recording in existence of Dylan performing four songs written in partnership with Helena Springs. However, so far it appears that artists requesting copies of the demos have been given versions performed by session musicians. The tracks are: If I Don't Be There By Morning; Walk Out In The Rain; Coming From The Heart; Stop Now.

SANTA MONICA REHEARSAL 1978
Three tracks of studio quality recorded in a furniture warehouse in Santa Monica - *viz.* Repossession Blues; One Of Us Must Know; Girl From The North Country - plus a number of tracks recorded from the street outside, and of appalling quality, including "Absolutely Sweet Marie" and five versions of "Tomorrow Is A Long Time."

SOUNDTRACK OF FILM FOR ROME 1978
Three P.A. recorded tracks from the American leg of the '78 tour: Changing Of The Guards; Masters Of War; Mr. Tambourine Man.

'78 TOUR - AUDIENCE RECORDINGS
Audience recordings of many of the '78 tour concerts are now in circulation. Some have not become available as yet, though it is unlikely that any went unrecorded. There are also a number of sound-check recordings around, although these mostly seem to be of poor quality.

"SATURDAY NIGHT LIVE" 1979
Live performances from US TV programme: Gotta Serve Somebody; I Believe In You; When You Gonna Wake Up?

Rumours

Further to observations on a possible session having taken place with the Grateful Dead, it has been confirmed by Alan Trist, one of the Grateful Dead's Management, in conversation with Nick Ralph of Dark Star Magazine, that no such session ever took place.

It has been claimed that a P.A. recording of a 1978 Paris concert is in circulation but evidence of this has not been forthcoming. According to some sources, every '78 tour concert was recorded by the road crew, but none of these recordings has become available.

Rumours of a Bette Midler out-take of "Buckets Of Rain" with Dylan on back-up vocals have not been confirmed.

Versions of Dylan Songs
by Other Artists

SEVEN DAYS: Ron Wood on the album "Gimme Some Neck" (UK CBS 83337). (The only recordings in circulation by Dylan of this song are live audience tapes from Rolling Thunder concerts.)

IF I DON'T BE THERE BY MORNING/WALK OUT IN THE RAIN:
Eric Clapton on the album "Backless" (UK RSD 5001).

COMING FROM THE HEART: The Searchers on the album "The
Searchers" (UK Sire SRK 6082).

Official Releases

ALBUMS

BOB DYLAN AT BUDOKAN	Stereo
SLOW TRAIN COMING	Stereo

SINGLES

	Hurricane Part 1/Mozambique	Stereo (USA)
	Knockin' On Heaven's Door/A Fool Such As I	Stereo (USA)
	Forever Young/All Along The Watchtower/	
	I Want You	Stereo (USA)
	Rita May/Memphis Blues Again	Stereo (USA)
1978	Is Your Love In Vain/We Better Talk This Over	Limited number on 12″ in UK - Stereo
	Changing Of The Guards/Senor	Stereo (USA)
	Changing Of The Guards (edited)/New Pony	Stereo (Holland)
	Baby Stop Crying/We Better Talk This Over	Stereo (Holland)
	Baby Stop Crying/New Pony	Stereo (USA)
1979	Precious Angel (edited)/Trouble In Mind	Stereo (UK)
	Gotta Serve Somebody (edited)/Trouble In Mind	Stereo (USA)
	Man Gave Names To All The Animals/Trouble In Mind	Stereo (France)
	Man Gave Names To All The Animals/When He Returns	Stereo (UK)
	Man Gave Names To All The Animals/When You Gonna Wake Up?	Stereo (USA)

E.P.'s

CAN YOU PLEASE CRAWL OUT YOUR WINDOW
Can You Please Crawl Out Your Window/Maggie's Farm/On The Road
Again/Don't Think Twice.   Portugal

BOB DYLAN
Like A Rolling Stone/Positively 4th Street/Subterranean Homesick Blues.
                                                            Portugal

PROMOTIONAL
"*FOUR SONGS FROM RENALDO AND CLARA*" - 12″ E.P.   Tracks:
People Get Ready; Never Let Me Go; It Ain't Me Babe; Isis.

JAPANESE ALBUMS

There are a large number of Japanese compilation albums; one of these - "Masterpieces" (Triple, CBS Sony 57 AP 875 - 877) - should be singled out for mention because it contains several tracks not on any other album. These are: Mixed Up Confusion (out-take not previously released); Can You Please Crawl Out Your Window (fast version - deleted single); Just Like Tom Thumb's Blues (live at Liverpool 1966 - deleted single); Spanish Is The Loving Tongue (deleted single version); George Jackson (single - big band version); Rita May (single).

Samplers

HOOTENANNY SPECIAL - Various Artists
(Columbia Special Products CSP 216 S)
Don't Think Twice; House Of The Rising Sun

"MORE AMERICAN GRAFFITI" SOUNDTRACK - Various Artists
(Double, MCA MCSP 303)
Like A Rolling Stone; Just Like A Woman

STARS FOR JERUSALEM - Various Artists
(Double, CBS NU428)
Father Of Night

DISCOTHEQUE DANCE MUSIC - Various Artists
(7" LP, CBS Special Products/Wurlitzer 105018)
Outlaw Blues
Possibly a slightly unusual mix. Only a small number pressed.

THAT'S UNDERGROUND - THE ROCK MACHINE TURNS YOU ON
- Various Artists
(Germany, multicolored vinyl CBS SPR 23)
Highway 61 Revisited

Bootleg Records

All Roads Lead To Dylan (Rosephil Records) - Live in Los Angeles 1978, audience recording.
Earls Court - Live at Earls Court 20th June 1978, audience recording.

Four Songs From Renaldo And Clara (12" E.P.) - Copied from the official promotional release (see above).
Gaza Strip - Unspecified '78 concert, audience recording.

Highway 61 Revisited Again - Like A Rolling Stone; Positively 4th Street; It Takes A Lot To Laugh, It Takes A Train To Cry; Please Crawl Out Your Window (lesser known slow version); Desolation Row (out-take); Tombstone Blues. All tracks taken from the "Highway 61 Revisited" Acetate Tape (see above).

Life Sentence (Double, Audifon) - Live in Los Angeles June 2nd 1978, audience recording.

Live in Adelaide Australia 1978 (Double, TAKRL) - Audience Recording.

Live In Nuremberg 1978 (*Double*) - Reputedly audience recording but existence unconfirmed. The above may not be the correct title.

Live In Paris 1978 (*Issued both as a triple and as three separate singles*) - Audience recording.

Live '78 (*Novisad*) - Dortmund, audience recording.

Londondylan (*Disaster Limited Enterprises*) - Earls Court '78, audience recording.

Manchester Prayer (*Double, The Impossible Recordworks*) - Live in Los Angeles 15th November 1978, audience recording.

Moving Violation (*Ram's Head Records*) - The four tracks from the "Renaldo And Clara" promotional E.P. plus live material from Los Angeles 1978 (the latter are audience recordings).

No Quarter (*Double, DSI Records*) - Live in Los Angeles 1978, audience recording.

Sydney '78 - Audience recording. The above may not be the correct title.

Tangerine - One side comprises Paris live '78 and the other Los Angeles live '78, audience recordings.

The Great Summer Event (*Rosephil Records*) - Live in Los Angeles 1978, audience recording.

The Zim's Picnic - Live at Blackbush, 1978.

We Didn't Get It On Till Oakland (*Double*) - Live in Oakland with The Band in 1974. At one stage a number of albums with the above title on the cover turned out to be Rolling Stones LP's, but it has now been reasonably reliably confirmed that the pukka records do exist. Probably audience recordings.

UNTITLED BOOTLEG RECORDS
There are two untitled E.P.'s in existence. One is made up of the following copied official tracks: Can You Please Crawl Out Your Window (fast version); Highway 61 Revisited; I Want You; Just Like Tom Thumb's Blues (live at Liverpool 1966). The other comprises the following: Can You Please Crawl Out Your Window (fast official version); Just Like Tom Thumb's Blues (cut official version); Every Time Somebody Comes To Town; I'd Have You Any Time (last two from the George Harrison Session).

SINGLE
Man Of Constant Sorrow/Farewell (under title "Fare Thee Well"). Joker label, taken from the album "Bob Dylan - A Rare Batch Of Little White Wonder," Volume 1.

Index

THE TAPES

SONGS DISCUSSED AND ON TAPE